A GIFT FOR YOU FROM

KELLY

Surrender *to* Win

The Story of The Honorable Francis X. Kelly Jr.

WITH
BILL TAMULONIS
AND FRANKIE KELLY

Furniture Press Books

ISBN: 978-1-940092-18-8

My Story
gift

www.MyStoryGift.com
Bill@MyStoryGift.com
410-215-2432
Printed in the United States of America

TABLE OF CONTENTS

Afterword

DEDICATION

To God, for the way He has blessed my family and me in so many ways over the years.

To my lovely wife, Janet. I would not have a story to tell without her personal sacrifices, love, and support.

To my sons, Frank III, John, David, and Bryan, for the way they honor and serve God, have taken our family business to a level Janet and I never imagined, and allowed me the time for the public service I love most.

To my daughters-in-law, Gayle, Tee, Melissa, and Heidi, for being Godly wives to our sons and amazing mothers to our grandchildren.

To my grandchildren: David Jr., Frankie, Hannah, Patrick, Johnny, Stephen, Allie, Timmy, Jackie, Faith (deceased), Lydia, Caroline, Jacob, Daniel, Micaiah, JK, Bo, Joshua, Gibby, Eyasu, Caleb, and Eli. I pray that you will *love the Lord your God with all your heart, and with all your soul, and with all your mind, and with all your strength;* and *trust in the Lord with all your heart, do not lean on your own understanding. In all your ways acknowledge Him, and He will make your paths straight.*

IN MEMORY

My parents, Francis X. Kelly Sr. and Margaret McPartlin Kelly, who taught me when I was still in my mother's womb that human life is sacred, and that putting God first is central.

My dearest and loyal friend, Charlie Cawley, one of the most successful business people of my generation, and the most generous human being I've ever met.

ACKNOWLEDGMENTS

Like everything good that has happened in my life, this book is a product of the relationships God has gifted me. Bill Tamulonis, a friend of Frank III, approached him with the idea of publishing my life story. Frank III called to tell me, all excited, while he was still sitting across from Bill over coffee at Panera Bread. But I resisted for eight months. I didn't know Bill at all, it sounded like a lot of work, and anyway, who would want to read it? "Dad," Frank III assured me, "I know at least the family is going to want to read your book, and I think a lot of other people will too. At least I know we will have your story on record."

I eventually agreed, in part, because Frank III, knowing which of my buttons to push, brought in my grandson, Frankie, to help persuade me and to get the storytelling started. Bill, Frankie, and I first got together one evening at Vito Ristorante, where I told stories for two hours, and kept on telling more stories over the next three years.

I appreciate Bill and Frankie's vision for not only capturing the meaningful events in my life, but also for drawing out the relationships and life principles that matter most to me. Whenever possible they also double-checked my recounting of the events and conversations recorded in this book. I have done my best to be as accurate as possible, but memories fade and, in the end, all I can do is describe what happened as I remember it.

Special thanks to my family, friends, and colleagues who took the time to contribute their own personal stories to this book: my wife, Janet, and sons Frank III, John, David and Bryan, my brother, Bob Kelly, and my sister, JoAnn Burns. Also, Julie Cawley, Mike Gill, Ernie Graham, Rick Grindrod, Tim Maloney, Senate President Mike Miller, Alan

Rifkin, Cal Ripken Jr., Congressman Dutch Ruppersberger, Melody Simmons, Dr. Mohan Suntha, Walter Thompson, and Jay Wright.

I want to thank my colleagues at Kelly Associates for their help, especially Cheryl Scott, my patient assistant, for scheduling my meetings with Bill, and Jennifer Silberzahn and her team who assisted with collecting the photographs.

Without everyone's love and support, and Frank III's nudging and leadership, we'd all be reading something else right now.

A LOVE LETTER
from Janet Kelly

I've lived an amazing journey with Frank Kelly for more than 57 years. We were married in August of 1961, when I was 20 and Frank was 21. What in the world did we know other than we were in love?

We were very young and went through many ups and downs together as we walked through life. We've had many happy moments, especially the birth of our four sons, and some sad and scary ones as we started a business in the basement of our home when we had a mortgage, four sons and a foster daughter, and no savings. But one thing was for sure: Frank always made me feel safe and secure, and that things would be OK. I knew he could always make things right. This holds true for anyone who knows him—our children, grandchildren, friends, and business associates. You name it; Frank will try to help you. His greatest love is helping people. He often gets calls both day and night from people who need help—someone who needs a specialized doctor, or someone who needs advice—and he rarely says no.

I most admire his ability to be present where he is. He makes eye contact as he talks to people and gets to know them. It doesn't matter who you are. From the valets who park his car at a dinner event to sitting at dinner with the governor, he is forever present in the conversation, asking questions to get to know the people he's with and, when asked, taking the time to give advice on life's issues.

Frank's deep love for God is evident in all that he says and does. He is not afraid to give honor to God in any situation.

Frank is dearly loved by many, and especially by me.

INTRODUCTION

Visible or invisible, so much of the political and professional landscape in Maryland today bears the signature of Francis X. Kelly Jr.

The input and contributions Frank has made over decades in and around his adopted state rank large and small and number in the thousands. And true to his Irish roots, he has a story to tell about nearly all of them. That is lucky for us: This book details much of Frank's personal life as a husband, father, mentor and friend and his professional life that was dotted with risk, challenges and seat-of-the-pants years of highs and lows all strung together with a heavy dose of courage. It is a portrait of a life lived with faith, love, humor, and conviction, traits not often seen in one package, especially for a public official—no matter which side of the aisle you sit on. As a reporter at *The Evening Sun* and *The Baltimore Sun*, I covered him for two decades—he was always one of my go-to sources for context and background and, of course, great quotes.

In many ways, Frank's life story is old-fashioned and modern all at once. It shows how to take a leap, start a family business on a wing, prayer and credit card, hustle opportunities, make it happen and believe in the courage of your convictions even if it means getting bounced out of the state Senate in the primary. That makes this story one to appeal to several generations. It is both a good read and a personal and professional case study in the wireless age of the blog and social media where instant communication and tweets can build or sink a ship. Dialing it back three decades, Frank's story shows how it was done. It shows how a business grew from a basement in a Timonium split level to a corporate headquarters at 1 Kelly Way in Sparks. Today,

Kelly Associates is a multi-million dollar enterprise run by the second generation of Kellys with a third generation in training. It details Frank's life in the Maryland Senate where the willy-nilly world of state politics in Annapolis can ebb and flow in dramatic fashion each session. It details Frank's last stand on the Senate floor in an eight-day filibuster over abortion rights legislation—and his no guts, no glory finish at the ballot box six months later in the Democratic primary. He told Sandy Banisky of *The Baltimore Sun* the day after the primary on September 12, 1990: "I'm doing as well as can be expected after getting my ass kicked. I lost. It was abortion. There was no question about it...if I had it to do over again, I wouldn't do it any other way because I think abortion's the taking of innocent life. But I respect the opinion of the voters. I'm a little disappointed because people say they want politicians who'll fight for their beliefs."

This book first started as a family history project, but it quickly expanded when the scope and narrative of Frank's life took over the pages. His voice is faithful, firm and funny. The common thread is love—for his God, his wife, Janet, his sons and grandchildren, his work and his community. Looking at Frank's path today, his initials and input are engraved on places like the R Adams Cowley Shock Trauma Center, Oriole Park at Camden Yards, M&T Bank Stadium, St. Joseph Medical Center and the University of Maryland Medical System—to name a few.

The net is wide. The lessons sharp and wise. The journey so far has been, as they say, *all good.*

Melody Simmons
Journalist, Baltimore, MD

FOREWORD

When people consider the accomplishments of my father, Francis X. Kelly Jr., his contributions, business growth, success, or most importantly, his marriage, children, and grandchildren, they often marvel and ask me, *How did he do it?* They're asking about the *Win* part of the story, and that's all recorded here: the people who shaped his life, primarily his father, Francis X. Kelly Sr., and his wife, Janet; and how my father's heart for helping people, his positivity, his generosity, keen instincts, and his view that problems are opportunities to build relationships landed him in the inaugural class of *The Baltimore Sun's* Business and Civic Hall of Fame.

But to me, the *Surrender* part is the real story because my father was in bondage to fear, anxiety, and torment, and he found life, victory, and freedom. Ultimately, this story is not about my father; it's a story of God's love and grace. My father's very life was spared more than once and, similarly, our family business was on the brink of collapse more than once. My father is the first to give all the credit for his wins to God's mercy on him and our family. All my father did was hold fast to his faith and convictions, often under fierce temptation and at a high personal cost, and trust God for the outcome. That's the story he wants to share, all for the glory of God, with the hope that readers will be blessed and moved to surrender themselves in the same way.

I can't talk about my father without talking about my mother. She was the rock of our family as my father battled his demons, and she has walked alongside him every step of his recovery. If my mother had not been there those first 10 years of the family business, to help get it off the ground and to manage it when my father was in the Senate, we would not have a business today. She was really our first "Chief

Operating Officer," so while my father brought the passion and the business relationships, my mother brought the administration, the focus, and the attention to detail necessary to make it all work. Within a couple of years after she retired, we almost went under. None of the Kellys would be who we are or where we are today without my mother.

Anyone who reads this story will be challenged and encouraged, because that's my father's leadership style. He's the "Chief Encouragement Officer" of every organization he associates with. He has a unique ability to see the positive in every situation and in every person, to praise and affirm them, and to draw more positives out of them. His positive approach brings people together—even people with opposing views—to get a job done, such as building Camden Yards and reviving St. Joseph Medical Center.

This is a fun story to read because my father is fun. His adventurous and playful personality is what attracted my mother to him, even after he spilled beer on her on their first date. My father's many talents extend to jitterbugging, catching greased pigs, practical joking, and body surfing. His sense of humor is another aspect of his positivity and, after spending time with him, people almost always walk away smiling and feeling better about themselves or their situation.

My father lives in the present moment so he doesn't think about "legacy." To him, his legacy is how his four sons, daughters-in-law, and 21 living grandchildren use their God-given gifts, time, talent, treasure, and their own life stories to bless and serve others. But when I think about my father's legacy, I picture a big, beautiful lake. Many people's lives are like a pebble dropped into the lake, that creates a ripple that's pleasant to watch but doesn't go very far. My father's life is more like a cannonball fired into the lake that creates waves that are fun to ride, that roll far out in all directions, reach the shores on either side of the lake, and bless the shores.

I think about how Shock Trauma and the University of Maryland Medical System, which my father has helped to flourish, are saving lives every day, and how one of those lives might be the person who discovers the cure for cancer, ALS, or AIDS. I think about how one of the graduates from the University System of Maryland, the Community College of Baltimore County or Calvert Hall, schools that my father has helped guide, might go on to accomplish great work as a statesman or stateswoman, a business leader or a philanthropist. Maybe a child in Africa whom Kelly Associates' employees support through World Vision will develop new farming innovations or provide seed money for new businesses in their village.

I'd be remiss if I did not thank my father for helping me understand what it means to put God first in my own life. As a college student, I was looking for happiness and fulfillment on the football and lacrosse fields, in the classroom, with girlfriends, and partying. Whenever I would complain to my father about my frustrations with coaches or injuries or a class or any other situation, he would offer all the practical help he could give, and then remind me that I would never find true peace until I surrendered the things I can't control to the Lord Jesus Christ and made Him the first priority in my life. The day I reached that point of surrender, I called my father and we celebrated and prayed together over the phone. Ever since that day, he has encouraged me to daily read God's Word, and to *rejoice always; pray without ceasing; and in everything give thanks* (1 Thessalonians 5:16-18).

Though scores of family members, friends and colleagues who call my father "Big Frank," "BF" or "Pop Pop" will attest to his tireless commitment to his faith, family, and community, he will never know the full distance his waves have rolled and the complete record of people who have ridden them. But he's not concerned about that. He'll just continue to show up every day, make himself available to help people however he can, and pray as he has prayed for over 40 years, *Dear Lord, please help me not to screw things up!*

We love you, Dad.

Francis X. (Frank) Kelly III
Lutherville, Maryland

Surrender *to* Win

The Gift of the Present Moment

*Do not boast about tomorrow, for you do not know
what a day may bring forth.*
Proverbs 27:1

What could be better than working alongside my four sons? How about joining them on a retreat in the Rockies and watching them all play in the lacrosse game known as "The Miracle on the Mountain"?

In the opening round of the 1992 Vail Lacrosse Shootout, the Fellowship of Christian Athletes team (FCA) with Frank III, John, David, and Bryan Kelly, played an all-star team from North Carolina. Frank III scored a goal. *Alright!* It took me back to his days at Cornell, where he was All-Ivy League and probably the best face-off midfielder in the country. He later played professionally for the Baltimore Thunder.

And John scored a goal. *Yea baby!* I thought about his three consecutive Division III NCAA championship games at Washington College; they just couldn't get past Hobart.

Then the Kelly hat trick—*David scored!* His middle name is Eugene, but his teammates at the University of North Carolina changed it to "Eugene Automatic," because when he got the ball in the crease, he put it in the goal every time. He played on the 1986 NCAA national championship team as a freshman.

Bryan played defense—he was an honorable mention All-American defenseman at UNC and played on their undefeated 1991 national championship team—but *Unbelievable!* He scored a goal, and FCA won the game. How do you top that?

For FCA, just getting to the tournament was a minor miracle. When FCA staffer, Dan Britton, called to sign up, the tournament was already full, so they put FCA on the waitlist. Talk about a longshot. In the history of the Shootout, no team had ever dropped out. But a month before the tournament start date, the Shootout organizers called with the news that a spot had opened and gave FCA 24 hours to respond. In faith, Frank III and his wife, Gayle, ran up a $6,000 credit card bill for 20 non-refundable flights, not knowing who the players would be or if they would even have enough to field a team. "We're having a retreat in the mountains," he told the guys when he called to ask them to play, "and by the way, bring your lacrosse equipment."

The twentieth player agreed to go at the team cookout the night before their plane took off.

For Frank III, the trip was more about time for fellowship and spiritual growth than lacrosse. For me, it was an opportunity to join my sons in fellowship, prayer, and Bible study, and to watch all four of them play together on the same team for the first time. I had to go.

THE BEST TEAM EVER *VS.* THE GOD SQUAD

In the second-round, FCA faced the #1 seed and two-time defending champions, the Greene Turtle. Greene Turtle was

John, Frank III, David, and Bryan on the Miracle Mountain

stacked with professional all-stars, including Gary Gait, the "Michael Jordan of Lacrosse;" Dave Pietramala, who the game announcer called "the world's best defenseman" and is now the head coach at Johns Hopkins, and Jimmy Beardmore, the former NCAA Goalie of the Year from the University of Maryland. The newspapers called them the best team ever assembled in the 20-year history of the tournament.

FCA had a few accomplished college players besides the Kelly brothers: Dan Britton at attack, midfielders Steve Muir and Tim Spears, Steve Paletta and George Glyphis on defense, and goalie Steve Mason. But several players were fresh out of high school—that's how desperate they were to fill the roster. The newspapers called our team "The God Squad."

The game looked like the mismatch most fans expected right from the opening faceoff: Greene Turtle scores two goals in the first 45 seconds. FCA calls timeout, and as Frank III recalls, they agree not to look up at the scoreboard and vow that, no matter what happens, they will keep playing as hard as they can, as for the Lord, to the end. They promptly fall behind 5-1.

Maybe Greene Turtle is overconfident, or maybe FCA is over their jitters, but the momentum shifts in the second quarter and FCA ties the score 5-5 at the half. Frank cheats a little on the players' vow and asks Gayle to take a picture of the scoreboard.

FCA is no longer intimidated. They play even in the third quarter, which ends with the score tied 7-7. Greene Turtle goes up 8-7 in the fourth quarter, but with only a couple of minutes left in the game, FCA scores the tying goal, and sends the game into overtime. Frank III asks Gayle to take another picture of the scoreboard.

In overtime, Greene Turtle's Gary Gait has the ball up top in front of the goal, and Tucker Bailey – who is just out of high school and doesn't even have a college lacrosse scholarship – covers him on defense. Frank III turns to a teammate on the sideline and whispers, "It's over." Thousands of fans in the stadium figure the game is over, but not Tucker Bailey. The kid stick-checks Gait like I couldn't believe, and the next thing I see is Gait's stick spinning high in the air and the ball on the ground. The first overtime ends with neither team scoring.

Frank III wins the faceoff to start the second overtime and passes downfield. The defender leaves Frank III to double-team the ball. Frank III gets the ball back, wide open, dead center, ten yards from the goal. He fires a bullet toward the upper right corner of the net. Beardmore the goalie sticks out his elbow and deflects the shot back into the crease. Spears picks up the ball for FCA and hurls a shot toward the open net. Pietramala dives; the ball hits his helmet and bounces behind the goal. There's a mad scramble for the loose ball. Britton scoops it up and flips it to David Kelly.

Eugene Automatic has the ball. He's in front of the crease. He shoots—and scores! FCA wins!

Half of the crowd erupts in celebration. The other half sits quietly in stunned disbelief. Frank III calls it "the shot heard 'round the lacrosse world." The newspapers call it "The Miracle on the Mountain."

I rush out on the field with the rest of the team and smother David. Then we drop to our knees to give thanks and praise to God, who showed us how a little faith could move mountains.

'I PLANNED NONE OF THIS'

FCA beat Team Colorado, the #5 seed, in the semi-finals, and then lost to Mt. Washington Tavern, 10-7, in the championship game. But the wins and losses were not what mat-

Power of Prayer
Vail, Colorado, July 1992

tered most to me that week. My joy came as I watched my four sons play together on a team devoted to a calling higher than winning a game, and as they learned what my father had taught me: when you put God first, and persevere through difficulties, you can be a successful athlete, and you will be a winner in life.

My father modeled for me the principle that if you get up every day, praise God, seek Him first and trust in Him, work hard to achieve your goals, and approach each day with that same positive attitude, good things will happen. He also taught me that if I did it all to help other people, not for the money, I would be fine. He was right. I believe in the Golden Rule: love your neighbor as yourself, as God would love them. We are here to be givers, not takers. I have found far more joy in giving than in taking.

People who know something about the Kelly Associates business often ask me, "How did you do it?" I often wonder the same thing myself, because as I look back over the people and events that shaped me, I know that I planned none of what happened. In part that's because I wasn't astute enough to perceive where God was taking my family and me, and in part it's because when I was around 30 years old, at a retreat in Virginia, a Franciscan monk taught me a profound life lesson. I asked him what he considered to be the secret to a happy life. Without hesitation, he answered, "Son, you must learn to enjoy the gift of the present moment." I never forgot those words. Alcoholics Anonymous taught me the same principle – one step at a time, one day at a time; do not look back or too far ahead.

So, I took life one day at a time. I never sat down and said, "I'm going to marry the most beautiful, humble, wise, loving, unselfish, and godly woman in the world. Someday I will be in the Maryland Senate. Someday I will run my own business. I'll have four sons working with me, four beautiful daughters-in-law, and 22 grandchildren." All Janet and I did was get down on our knees and turn everything over to God.

Looking in the rear-view mirror, I now see the unmistakable pattern in the way God often works. He gives us a vision for the future – it could be for a lacrosse retreat, a family business, a career in politics, or anything else—but He doesn't give us a straight, smooth path to the fulfillment of the vision. There will be problems, responsibilities, and temptations along the way—more powerful opponents, an untimely death, and financial crises are some that I have suffered through—so daunting that the vision may appear to die. But if we respond with faith and trust, God will supernaturally fulfill the vision in ways we could never have imagined.

Any success I have had is the result of God making me the way I am and helping me fight my demons. I merely try to use the gifts He gave me for His glory. And I pray. I often pray for the gift of wisdom and the gift of joy, but mostly I pray as I prayed every morning when I sat in the Senate, "Dear Lord, don't let me screw things up today!"

Be present in all things and thankful for all things.
Maya Angelou

2

I've Got a Name

...the glory of the sons is their father.
Proverbs 17:6

There are many years in the early life of my father, Francis X. Kelly Sr., which I know nothing about. My knowledge of his life starts when he was 10 or 11, and his mother died of tuberculosis. He never talked about his father, and I don't think he even knew him. I don't even know what my grandfather looked like, and the only thing I know about him is that he was an alcoholic.

Francis X. Kelly Sr.

My father's aunt and uncle took him into their home, but sometime around high school age he moved into the YMCA on 9th Street and fended for himself on the streets of Brooklyn. I suspect he got some financial help from relatives, but for the most part, he paid his own way working at the Y and other odd jobs.

The YMCA on 9th Street in Brooklyn, NY

Though I only know a little about my father's childhood, I can identify with Terence in the movie *Field of
Dreams*: "The one constant through all the years has been
baseball." At 6'4", my father grew into a strapping man, and
a good enough athlete to play professional baseball in the
Wall Street league, which is equivalent to today's Double A
or Triple A minor leagues. Dad told me his baseball stories at
our own field of dreams, Ebbets Field in Brooklyn, where he
took me to watch the Dodgers. I remember and loved every
bit of those days.

I remember walking through Prospect Park on the
way to the games, stopping at a certain hot dog stand where
my dad would buy me a hot dog. To this day, I swear they
were the best hot dogs I ever tasted in my entire life.

The first thing I saw walking up to the stadium was
its 80-foot marble rotunda with that iconic EBBETS FIELD
sign. During the game, there was so much going on to create
that special aura: the organ, the fans and Sym-Phony band
taunting the umpires with *Three Blind Mice*, fans clanging
cowbells, and the enormous scoreboard were all unique to

Ebbets Field. I met many of the Dodger players and a couple of my father's friends who played in the major leagues, such as Elbie Fletcher of the Boston Braves and Max West with the Pirates.

"A phenomenal place to watch baseball."

My father had a commanding presence, and his personality was just as big. He had such charisma that when he walked into a room, everybody knew he had arrived. A natural born leader, a smart and successful salesman, everybody liked him. The quintessential self-made man, people gravitated to him. When he died, the line of people who came to pay their respects wrapped around the funeral home.

Meeting Jackie Robinson

I was proud of my father for the way he stood up for Jackie Robinson. My father believed in the sanctity of all human life, and he loved the Dodgers, so whenever he heard fans hurling slurs at Jackie, he challenged them. He was so big, they shut up fast.

One of the best memories of my childhood is the day my father took Frank and me down under the stands after a game, and we stood outside the Dodgers' locker room. Jackie Robinson walked by, still wearing his uniform, and my father introduced me to him. Star-struck, all I could manage to say was, "I love to watch you play." I reached out to shake his hand—the biggest hand I had ever seen.

-Bob Kelly

'DO YOU THINK THERE'S A CHANCE WE'RE RELATED?'

The only relatives of my father I ever knew were his two sisters, Muriel and Virginia, so, in my adult life, I visited Ireland to try to fill in some of the blanks about my family's history. My dearest friend and fellow Irishman, Charlie Cawley, arranged the trip which included my sons Frank III, John and David (they were around college age) and Dr. Seamus Flynn, an Ireland-born friend from Baltimore's Shock Trauma Center.

We tried to find my relatives, but I had little information to go on. All I knew about my ancestors was that they left Johnstown, in the center of County Kilkenny, for America around 1850 to escape the potato famine. About a million people left Ireland during the famine, and a million of those who stayed did not survive.

My favorite men's clothing store in Dublin.

We noticed that on the four Main Street corners of every village in Ireland, there always seemed to be a Catholic church on one corner, always, and sometimes a Protestant church on another; Johnstown had both. A butcher shop stood on the third corner and another shop of some kind on the fourth. A relative told us that Kellys ran the butcher shop, and there used to be a blacksmith across the street where another Kelly shoed horses.

We walked into the butcher shop and found Joe Kelly. We introduced ourselves and told him we thought we were related. He shrugged and said, "I don't know about that. I don't get into that stuff. You might want to talk to me brother Paddy, who's around the back milking the cow. He is a bit more into that." So, we walked back and found this other Kelly running a big dairy farm behind the Kelly butcher shop. It was a huge farm and, sure enough, Paddy was out there milking the cows. We tried to talk to him, but he kept his head down milking the cow.

John asked him, "Can you show me how to do that?"

"Can't you see I am busy, laddie? I will be talking to you in a minute. I've got to get this damn milk out of this cow first." He pointed the cow's teat at us and squirted us with milk.

When he finally finished, we introduced ourselves.

"We're the Kellys from Maryland. We understand we might be related."

"I would not know anything about that laddie, just wouldn't know."

"Was there a blacksmith shop across the street?" I asked.

"There was years ago."

"We've been told we are related to the guy who ran that blacksmith shop."

"Could be, laddie."

"Well, we're Kellys and you're Kellys, do you think there's a chance we're related? We came here based on information our relatives gave us."

"Yeah, laddie, could be."

Paddy had another brother who was the sexton in the Catholic church. None of them were exactly friendly. "Nice of you lads to stop by," was the extent of their enthusiasm.

Next, we searched for relatives on my mother's side. We combed the neighborhood, knocking on doors, asking if there was anyone around by the name of Powers, McPartlin, or Walsh. "Oh, yes! Mrs. Powers, she lives down on such and such street," one neighbor directed us. We found the house, knocked on the door and a woman with no teeth opened the door. Frankie jokes that I look exactly like her! She invited us in. "I am so happy you boys stopped by. Sit down. Would you be having a drink?" Above her liquor cabinet hung pictures of the Pope and President John F. Kennedy. "So, would you be having a drink?" she asked again. We told her we did not drink alcohol, so she served us warm milk. We explained who we were, and she cheered, "Yes, we are related!" She sent us Christmas cards every year until she died, and now her daughter sends us cards, and we keep in touch with her.

The Kellys and Powers we met in Ireland brought a few things into focus for me. We confirmed that our ancestors are from County Kilkenny. Also, I saw where our family's faith tradition came from. And, I saw signs that the "Irish virus"—alcoholism—has infected my family for generations. It didn't start, or end, with my grandfather.

'THE BEST ADVICE I HAVE FOR YOU'

Faith and alcohol. I watched my father wage that battle. He was always involved at church throughout his life, but alcohol became his god. He took my brother, sister and me to church on Sunday when we were kids, but there were many weeknights when he was out at the bars and did not come home. He provided all we needed financially and came to all my high school games and races, but it bothered me how he missed so many holidays and family events. When the Dodgers left Brooklyn for Los Angeles, he went on a drinking binge and we didn't see him for several days.

About the time I started at Villanova, my father started at Alcoholics Anonymous. I'm not sure what prompted him, but I thank God that he admitted his need, took the steps to recover, and won his battle. I saw changes in him right away. He started helping with the CYO and various groups at St. Denis' Catholic Church in Havertown and started a new business as a packaging manufacturer's representative.

'I would wrap my arms around his knees'

My father sometimes got mean and nasty when he was drinking, and my mother bore the brunt of his rage. Sometimes he scared me so much his six-foot four-inch frame looked like seven feet to a little kid—I would wrap my arms around his knees and fight to keep him away from her. I'm grateful that nothing terrible ever happened. Down deep he was a kind man, a good man, and finally beat the alcohol towards the end of his life. He was always a religious man, but after he got sober, he went to Mass every day, and his faith trickled down to all his children.

-Bob Kelly

Shortly after Dad started his new business, he drove me down to Jackie Gordon's Men's Store in Philadelphia on a Saturday afternoon to buy me my first suit and surprised me with words I have never forgotten. We were sitting in the car in the parking lot, and he asked me, "How would you like to go into business with me after you graduate?" I got goosebumps all over. "Oh, yes!" I said. I only wish I could have started right away.

God gave my father and me similar personalities and many similar abilities. We have many of the same weaknesses also. Alcohol dragged my father down paths he did not want to go, and would soon begin to pull at me. While he was on his sobriety journey, he wrote me a letter while he was away on a fishing trip in the Midwest. First, he told me how much he liked Janet, and that he could tell that I would marry her someday. Then he wrote, *This is the best advice I have for you: put God first in all that you do; make Him the center of your life.* I believed him then, and though my road has been bumpy and twisted, I believe him even more now, and that has made all the difference.

'Motivated and Driven'

Frank has always been motivated and driven, determined to make things happen. He was always on the move. He took after our father that way. They both held to strong principles, always had a goal they were working toward, and whatever they did, they wanted to do it well and be the best.

We all admired how our father overcame the troubles in his life and achieved such success, and I think Frank wanted to achieve what our father achieved, both in character and in business. I think he wanted to make our father proud.

-JoAnn Kelly Burns

Life Lessons in Real Time

Train up a child in the way he should go, even when he is old
he will not depart from it.
Proverbs 22:6

I would not be here today if my parents had believed in abortion.

In the fifth month of my mother, Margaret's, pregnancy, a growth developed in her womb. Her obstetrician, Dr. Murphy, said there was a 50/50 chance it was cancerous, and if it kept growing for three more months, my mother's life would be in danger. The only sure way to find out was to abort me and take out

Thank God my parents made the right choice.

the cyst. Dad told the doctor, "Save them both. We want to carry the baby to term, and then we will deal with the cyst." I was born healthy, and the cyst was not cancerous. Thank God they made the right choice. He rewarded their faith and gave me a personal lesson on the sanctity of life. I often think about other unborn babies in the same circumstances who never lived to see what I have seen, who never felt the joys and sorrows that make life worth living, because their parents did not believe that abortion is wrong.

Bobby, Frank Jr., JoAnn, Frank Sr., and Margaret Kelly

My parents were both born in Brooklyn, but that's where the similarities end. My father grew up on the streets, never graduated from high school as far as I know, and worked in the meatpacking business. My mother had a degree from Adelphi University. Her father was college-educated, worked as a stockbroker on Wall Street, and played violin in the New York Philharmonic Orchestra.

I suppose my parents met while my mother was in college. Their courtship went on for maybe a year or so, and I suspect they got married when they found out Mom was pregnant with me. They never, ever said that, but why else would they ask Father Harvey to marry them at a Franciscan monastery with no one else there?

My mother's parents did not think my father was good enough for her. Can you imagine? *This guy comes in, gets their daughter pregnant (I assume), and runs off and marries her, and they're supposed to be happy about it?* But eventually, because of my father's likable personality, charisma, work ethic, and love for my mother, they came to respect and love him.

Despite their ominous start, my parents were happily married, and soon my brother Bob and sister JoAnn came along. Like our father, we are all talkers, and all good athletes, especially JoAnn. She is definitely high energy. Bob has a great personality and was a successful salesman. Growing up, Bob and I had tremendous loyalty and love between us, always looking out for each other. My only complaint was sharing a room with a brother who had asthma. Back then, the treatment was called Asthmador, which was a powder you put in a little tin ashtray and burned like incense. The bedroom filled up with smoke, which helped him breathe but practically choked me to death!

STOOPS, PARKS, AND BEACHES

We all loved our grandparents, Omah and Pa we called them. They lived nearby, on 7th Street in Park Slope. I often begged to go play there. Their house was perfect for stoopball, so on my way over I always hoped there would not be any cars parked in front of their house. Stoopball is like baseball, but you "hit" by throwing a rubber ball against the steps. Just like real baseball, you can tell if it's a good hit by the sound. *Thud:* it's not going very far, I'm out. *Pop:* watch it fly all the

---

Like most brothers, we teased and fought a lot growing up. As the older brother, Frank tried to boss me around as much as he could. As the younger brother, sometimes I got tired of it, and since I was soon bigger than him, I'd get my revenge wrestling him down in the basement. As I recall, I won every time.

-Bob Kelly

---

way across the street and off the New York Methodist Hospital wall for a home run!

When we weren't playing stoopball, we were running around in Prospect Park, right around the corner from Omah and Pa. We could play forever in the 585 acres of playgrounds, football and baseball fields, and hiking and biking trails. It's even bigger than Central Park and completely closed to traffic.

What a blessing to have grandparents who enjoyed their grandchildren.

I loved playing stoopball at my grandparents' home in Park Slope.

The beach was the summer playground for the family. We spent most Saturday and Sunday afternoons at Breezy Point, about a half-hour from home, the ocean on one side and Jamaica Bay on the other. My parents would rent a cabana and Bobby, JoAnn and I would spend the day swimming and bodysurfing.

Our family vacations were also at the beach, usually at Avalon on the Jersey shore. We stayed there for a month, the last two weeks in August through the first two weeks in September, because school didn't start until the middle of September. One year we stayed in Atlantic City for two whole months. *This is the greatest thing that ever happened to us!* So many of the Kelly traditions and memories revolved around the beach—and still do even today.

Frank and his sons revisiting Breezy Point Beach

The only problem with the vacations was getting going. Sometimes we would be all packed and ready to go on a Friday night, waiting for Dad to come home, but he would not show up until midnight after drinking at the bars. That meant leaving Saturday morning, fighting traffic and listening to him and my mother fight the whole way. But after weeks on the beach and the boardwalk, we kids had forgotten about the rough ride, and couldn't wait to go back the next summer.

Like our vacations, holidays growing up had their

'A nervous wreck'

I was always a nervous wreck driving back and forth from visiting our aunts, uncles, and cousins back in Brooklyn, afraid that my father would pull the car over, stop at a bar and run in for a shot of whiskey.

-Bob Kelly

---

up and down moments because of Dad. On more than one Thanksgiving Day, he would leave home around noon for a bar in Havertown called The Iron Gate, on Eagle Road near the trolley station. My mother would send me down to get him for dinner around four, but when I went in he would pick me up and sit me down on the bar and introduce me to all his friends. "This is my son, Frank!" I would tell him, "Mom wants you to come home. You're missing Thanksgiving dinner." "We'll go home," he'd say. "Don't worry. I'm having one more." He would show me off for another hour; we would get home at 5:30 and ruin Thanksgiving dinner.

For the most part, he made us feel special on Christmas by going overboard with presents he knew we would love, but there were some years when he missed Christmas Eve dinner because he was out at the bars, and then wasn't in the best shape on Christmas morning.

As kids, that was the kind of sadness Bobby, JoAnn, and I felt from Dad's drinking. It was minor compared to what my mother must have endured. I'm sure she suffered much more than we did and kept it all to herself. We were blessed to have had a mother strong enough to hold the family together through such pain, and there's no way we can thank her enough for how she protected us.

DARING TO DISCIPLINE

No, our family wasn't perfect, but we never doubted that our parents loved us. They showed us how much they cared with the life lessons they taught us.

Here is an example of Dad's approach to teaching us the difference between right and wrong. When we lived on Hutchinson Court in Brooklyn, Bobby and I played a little game where we snuck behind the mailman, took the mail out of the mailboxes, read it, and threw it in the sewer. We were just little kids playing and had no idea we were committing a federal crime and throwing away the paychecks that the service men and women mailed home from the war.

One night there was a knock on the door – a policeman. "Where is Frankie Kelly?" he demanded, "We are here for Frankie Kelly." I turned white and ran up to my bedroom. My father called Bobby and me and marched us to the policeman, who teed off on us: "This is a felony, you could go to jail for this!" He scared me to death; he scared my brother to death. I found out later that the man who terrified us was really only a neighbor my father asked to dress up like a cop and scare us straight. He didn't mind making me squirm if I learned my lesson.

Sometimes Dad applied the "shock and awe" technique even to ordinary events. He woke me up about five o'clock in the morning one day and told me, "Hurry up. We are going for a ride."

"Where are we going?" I asked.

"We're going to see Dr. Eddington for your eye."

We rode three different subway lines far up the Hudson River, toward Poughkeepsie. I was only 5 or 6 years old, so it seemed like it took forever. Most people don't know this, but I was born cross-eyed, and I about peed my pants when Dr. Eddington told me he was going to operate on my eye the next day. I was even more scared when I woke up from the operation and saw nothing but black. I thought I was blind, but then the nurse unwrapped the bandages.

Looking back, I understand what a powerful lesson it was for me that my father saw more in ordinary situations than I saw, how he wanted what was best for me, and proved I could trust him.

THE MAIN LINE

I was eight years old when a company called Millprint recruited my father to open a sales office in Philadelphia. Millprint was the first company ever to print directly onto cellophane packaging—those "sell by" dates and the other information so common now on packages of bacon, Tastykakes, candy, and everything else.

We lived in a semi-attached house on Kenilworth Avenue in Merion, PA, in the suburbs known as the Main Line, perhaps the most popular section of suburban Philadelphia. Towns cropped up all around the railroad line that provides a convenient, 20- to 25-minute commute to downtown Philadelphia. Bankers would take the Main Line in the other direction all the way out to Chicago.

Families moved to suburbs like Merion in droves after World War II, looking for newer, larger homes with bigger yards, lower taxes, and distance from the growing problems of crime and blight in the central cities.

I loved the neighborhood, and I loved my grade school, St. Margaret's in Narberth. Parents sent their kids to

---

'They tied me to a tree'

We loved to play outside in the neighborhood and Narberth Park—hide and seek, handball, baserunners, riding bikes, climbing on garage roofs. We were so close in age that we had fun playing together, but sometimes my big brothers took advantage of their little sister—like the time we were playing Cowboys and Indians, they tied me to a tree and ran off. I kept waiting for the game to end and for them to come back and get me, but they left me stranded. I finally wiggled out of the ropes on my own and ran home.

-JoAnn Kelly Burns

Catholic school because they totally trusted the nuns and the priests, not only to provide quality religious education but also to reinforce the discipline and respect for authority that the parents taught at home. If a student did anything wrong, the nuns were always right—don't even try to explain yourself. Years later when I met Cardinal Keeler in Baltimore, I told him about my experiences at St. Margaret's. "I don't know about you, Your Eminence, but with my parents, if a priest or nun said I did something wrong, I did it."

After a few years on Kenilworth Avenue, Dad found a tract of new detached homes he liked in Havertown, about six miles down the Main Line on Golf Hills Road. We lived only four blocks from where Ben Hogan pulled off the "Miracle at Merion" to win the 1950 U.S. Open golf tournament at the Merion Golf Club, only sixteen months after nearly being killed when his car collided head-on with a bus. As a kid, I rode my sled down the golf course hills after snowstorms, and years later I played golf there and hit from the same spot where Hogan hit his famous 1-iron shot—the spot that's marked with a commemorative plaque.

My Havertown home on Golf Hills Road

Yes, there were families with big money along the Main Line, but we weren't one of them. My father did well in sales, and my mother took a job as a social worker in Chester after Bobby, JoAnn, and I finished high school, but we were squarely middle income and lived a middle-income lifestyle.

That middle-income lifestyle included a new technological invention, the television. We got our first TV around 1947 or 1948, with a black-and-white picture. My sister JoAnn recalls, "I think we were the first family in the neighborhood to get a big screen TV—10 inches. All the neighbors flocked to our house to watch it."

TV was a huge deal; it sure beat sitting around the radio. My favorite shows were *The Three Stooges, I Love Lucy,* and *Bonanza,* the Phillies and Eagles games, but above all, *The Untouchables.*

I often saw Bert Bell, the original owner of the Eagles

'How to stay out of trouble'

One of the main things I learned from Frank as his younger sister was how to stay out of trouble, though none of us ever got into anything serious. I never smoked because I saw what happened to Frank when he got caught. He was in eighth grade, hanging out by the pinball machines at Pop Davis', smoking a cigarette with his buddies when my father walked in. Frank told me that my father dragged Frank outside and, in front of all his friends, stuffed a couple of cigarettes down his throat and wouldn't let him open his mouth until he swallowed them. At least they weren't lit. Frank puked his guts out.

I heard my father still giving it to Frank big-time when they got home, and that was enough to keep me away from cigarettes forever.

-JoAnn Kelly Burns

and second commissioner of the NFL, at Pop Davis' drug store in Narberth. As kids, we hung out at Pop's and watched Bell go in and out with other NFL owners for meetings there: Art Rooney of the Pittsburgh Steelers, George Halas of the Chicago Bears, George Preston Marshall of the Washington Redskins, among others. At those meetings—right in my backyard—they formed the modern NFL. Did anyone know that pro football would become as popular as it is today? I witnessed with my own eyes that, yes, big businesses can grow out of humble beginnings.

TV also played a role in football's growth in popularity, as the 45 million fans who watched the 1958 NFL championship game between the Baltimore Colts and New York Giants—the first-ever nationally televised NFL game—can attest. I remember it like yesterday—Frank Gifford getting nailed, Raymond Berry making those clutch catches as the clock wound down, and Alan Ameche's touchdown to win the game in overtime. Johnny Unitas was Mr. Cool in those two-minute drills. To the delight of Bert Bell, *Sports Illustrated* called it "the greatest game ever played."

'FINISH WHAT YOU START'

As the oldest child, my parents expected the most from me. I could sense that, and I had to set the standard for my brother and sister. On Friday nights and Saturday mornings Mom had a list of chores, and NOBODY left the house until they were all finished: mow the lawn, clean the garage, whatever. I would wake up at 7 a.m. and be busy with chores until ten o'clock. "Can I go out now, Mom?" "Sure." Then my brother would come rolling down the steps, "OK, what do you want me to do?" knowing I had already finished all the work. His little sham really ticked me off, but it paid off for him at the time.

My father wanted me to get a job as soon as I could. "I want you to go to work to learn the value of a dollar and learn that you need to work for whatever you get in life," he told me. "I want to teach you the importance of being responsible and fulfilling your commitments. If you start something, you should finish it." My first job was delivering newspapers when I was 9 or 10 years old. I liked working and earning my own keep. I could never sit around and waste time doing nothing.

Here's another way Dad taught me to finish what I started: I'm pitching in a little league game, throwing a no-hitter into the sixth inning. Dad's the coach, puffing his chest out a little farther with each batter I send back to the bench. But suddenly, my arm goes dead, and I cannot get the ball over the plate to save my life, but Dad keeps me hanging out there and I walk 14 batters in a row. That's eleven runs, all by walks. At least I had my no-hitter!

After the game, I asked him, "Dad, why didn't you take me out? We could have won the game." "Because I wanted you to finish what you started," he said. He learned

---

'Get the ball over the plate!'

Frank and I played a lot of baseball in the backyard. He was the pitcher, I was the catcher. All that practice made us strong battery-mates on our Narberth Youth League teams, all the way up until we were high school age. Frank's best pitch was his fastball. He usually had good control, but when he lost it I'd have to go out to the mound to tell him to "Quit fooling around and get the ball over the plate!"

-Bob Kelly

Monsignor Bonner High School

his lessons that way growing up on the streets – struggling in the middle of tough situations where he had to make his way out – and that's how he taught me.

Some lessons took me a while to learn. I started high school at Archbishop Prendergast. We called it "Prendie," for short. My neighbor Allen Murphy and I hitchhiked a mile-and-a-half to school every day. Well, just about every day. Occasionally we couldn't hitch a ride in time, so we played hooky—we just went home and goofed off. We could have walked and shown up late to school, but we got so much grief for being late it was easier to stay home and forge our parents' signatures on sick notes. We got away with it a few times, but my father eventually found out and grounded me for a month.

I continued playing sports in high school. Now, hardly anyone from Philadelphia believes me, but I actually have a football letter from an all-girls high school! During my first year at Prendie, the Archdiocese built a new school next door, Monsignor Bonner. Bonner became the boys school and Prendie switched to all girls. So, I lettered in football for Prendie before transferring to Bonner. I played both ways, linebacker on defense and tight end on offense. After two years of football, I traded in my helmet for an oar on the crew team and learned a tough lesson about team building.

Every day some of us on the crew team hitchhiked ten miles from Bonner to Boathouse Row on the Schuylkill River.

I still don't know how we pulled that off, but somehow, we always made it. I rowed in a quad, which is four people in the boat with two oars. I was the Stroke; I sat up front and set the pace. If the Stroke loses power, the whole boat slows down, so I had to be in good shape. Our team made it to the National Championships in Poughkeepsie, NY on the Hudson River: me,

Bonner senior yearbook portrait

Paul O'Rourke, a third Irish guy named Ted Hendricks, and Dick Seracini, who we affectionately called "the guinea."

In the championship race, we were at the 3/4 mark and ahead by four lengths. *We are going to win the National Championship!* But O'Rourke got excited and started celebrating too soon and caught a crab, which means his oar got stuck in the water. The boat nearly capsized, we almost flipped overboard, and we ground to a dead stop. We finished third in a race we totally had won. *Note to self: miracle finishes can go both ways; build a competent team that can perform under pressure.*

I made the swim team one year, but waking up at five in the morning to train? No thanks. I finished the season but had enough of swimming.

Of all the sports I played, I liked baseball the most. I played American Legion ball, and the best part of my game was my strong arm. I think I could have become a respectable pitcher if I could have spent more time playing and less time working part-time jobs. I bagged groceries and ran the cash register at the Penn Fruit store, and when I turned 16, I started a second job at a drug store, driving around in an old Volkswagen delivering prescriptions to customers. Every week I handed over my paycheck to my father, and he handed me twenty bucks back. *The value of a dollar!*

Throughout my high school years, my father was my biggest fan. He came in the afternoons to watch my practices, came to all my games and all my races. He showed me what it looks like to be present in the moments of your child's life.

SPARED AGAIN

As usual, my friends and I were hanging out at Pop Davis' drug store one night. I was 15 years old. Tommy Hilberts had his car; he was 17. Joe Chambers had his car also, and a bunch of us decided to go for a ride. I sat in the back of Tommy's car with Joe Winters and my brother Bobby. Emmett O'Connell, one of my best friends, sat up front with Tommy. Emmett was a good-looking kid, with big pompadour hair, and the girls loved him, even the older ones (he was 15 like me). I was just getting interested in girls at the time, and I must admit I was a little jealous of him.

There were also five guys in Joe's car when we took off, but Joe dropped three of them off at their homes. Tommy turned around to us in the back and said—I will never forget it, I can still see him—"Listen, we have five guys in my car, and Joe only has two. Why don't a couple of you get out and ride with Joe?" I said, "Yeah, I'll switch," and hopped into Joe's car. Bobby came with me. We were out past Villanova on a new road that wound and twisted through the woods.

Tommy stepped on the gas and started flying ahead of us, and Joe put his pedal down to keep up with him. I leaned forward and screamed into Joe's ear from the back seat, "Joe, don't follow that crazy guy! He's going too fast! Slow down!" Joe slowed down, and we lost sight of Tommy's car. I exhaled and sat back…until we came around the next curve and saw Tommy's car flipped upside down. They had hit a tree.

The crash threw Tommy out of the car, and the car rolled over on his neck. We ran and pulled Joe Winters out, but Emmett was stuck in the front seat shouting, "Help me, help me!" I reached in, couldn't get the car open, blood all over me, I will never forget it. I held Emmett's hand for what seemed like hours, but actually, the fire department arrived fairly quickly and pried Emmett out. I heard them say he was bleeding profusely and it did not look good.

One of the policemen screamed at us, "What is it with you f—— kids? This is so useless!" I suppose he was a father of a teenager and imagined this could have been his child. He took us to the police station and called our parents. There was no alcohol, we were not drinking, but the scene was every father's nightmare. And there I stood, covered with blood.

Joe Winters was not hurt badly, but Tommy Hilberts died instantly under the car, and Emmett O'Connell bled to death. Just seeing my friends' dead bodies…I can still picture the accident scene now, over 60 years later.

This was the first time I really had to come to grips with death, and I couldn't understand it all. In one sense, when your day is up, it's up. But at the same time, choices matter. In my case, my decision that night to switch from Tommy's car to Joe's, and all the way back to my parents' choice to let me be born. All I could do was thank God for sparing me, again, and tell Him I would do my best to honor Him with the gifts He gave me.

HAIL, BLUE AND WHITE

Nobody on the Kelly side of the family had a college degree, and my father wanted me to be the first. The idea sounded good to me, and I knew I could make more money with a degree than without one. I did not know what field I wanted to get into, and I didn't have straight As, but I applied to Penn State,

The Villanova years

Villanova, and St. Joseph's, and made it into all three. My parents and I agreed on Villanova.

My father also wanted me to appreciate how much an education costs, so he required me to work and pay my own

---

'Driven'

"Driven" is how I would describe Frank as a teenager. He was never around the house, but always on the go—working, playing sports, and going out with his friends. I'm amazed how he paid his own way through college.

-Bob Kelly

---

tuition. I think it cost me $1,500 a semester, hard to imagine it was ever that low, but it sounded like a fortune to me at the time.

From sophomore year until I graduated, my schedule kept me going until late at night. My daily routine consisted of taking three or four classes between 8:30 in the morning and 3 in the afternoon, hopping on the Philadelphia and Western trolley—the P & W, or the Piss and Whistle, as we called it—to the subway, and riding into downtown Philly to the First Pennsylvania Bank at 15th and Chestnut Streets. I worked in a group of five college students collecting delinquent accounts on the telephone. We covered the Big Five: myself from Villanova, and one each from Temple, LaSalle, Penn, and St. Joe's, and oh my, the fights we got into! Our shift ended at 9:30, and I didn't get home until eleven o'clock.

My work schedule left me no time to study, but I was not there to earn a 3.5 GPA or to make the Dean's List. My whole attitude was simply to get the degree, period. I felt just having the degree would open doors for me. And this was college, so I had to find some time for partying also. This was the 1950s, the rock and roll era: Elvis Presley, Johnny Cash, Bill Haley and the Comets. I still think '50s music is the best music for parties and dancing. You can't even understand what they are saying in the songs nowadays.

'Always on a path'

Frank always set his mind on something. It might have been something simple, like getting his chores done early so he could go out and play with his friends or making arrangements to go out on a date; or bigger things like making the baseball team or working his way through college. He was always on a path.

-JoAnn Kelly Burns

In Philly, the dancing craze started with the television show *American Bandstand*. Bob Horn was the original host, and later Dick Clark took over. Teenagers stood in line to get in the studio, dance to the records and the studio singers, and hoped the TV cameras would

Practice wins dance contests!

point their way. Some of the kids danced on the show every day and became stars. They came right off the streets, but everybody in Philly knew them.

I could cut a pretty good rug. I took a date to *American Bandstand* once and we made it on TV! My date was with the girl I had met at another dance at Gwynedd Mercy College. She was a better dancer than I was, and during college, we won several dance contests doing the jitterbug. Over the next couple of years, my date that night, Janet, and I danced into each other's hearts and got married!

Most college students look forward to more parties and dancing, and some rest and relaxation over the Christmas break. But my father knew someone at the post office and got me a job delivering mail from early December until Christmas Day in my junior and senior years. Of course, they gave temporary guys like me the worst routes, but they paid big money. In those three-week periods, I made $3,000 and gave every penny to my father for tuition. All totaled, working during the school semesters, Christmas breaks, and summers, I earned enough to pay my way for all four years.

THE EAGLES, FRANKLIN FIELD, AND THE PALESTRA

I never missed an Eagles game. I saw them win the championship in 1960 at Franklin Field. Norm Van Brocklin was the quarterback; Pistol Pete Pihos, the tight end, had the rare combination of size and speed, and led the team in touchdowns. Chuck Bednarik played both ways - center on offense and linebacker on defense. Players did that in those days—they never came off the field.

You drive by Franklin Field today, and it looks the same as it did in 1960. I remember going to college football games there, and the Penn Relays. Villanova always had a winning track team and did extremely well there. In the 1980s I watched Frank III play football and lacrosse there for Cornell.

The college basketball games next door at the Palestra—"The Cathedral of College Basketball"—were the best games I ever saw in my life. Former University of Maryland coach Gary Williams played there, and if you say "Palestra" to him or any of those old-timers, and anybody who grew up in that era, they will tell you that you did not want to be on the opposing team playing there. It holds about 9,000 people, all right on top of the court, and the noise can be deafening.

SINK OR SWIM

I worked as the Waterfront Director at a Catholic youth camp in the Catskills during my summers in college. The boys camp was on one side of a lake, and the girls camp sat across on the other side. My job was to teach kids how to swim. The lake was enormous and deep. A 60-foot boardwalk surrounded it, so I could walk beside the kids and quickly jump in and grab them if they got into trouble.

Pedro, a Puerto Rican camper from Brooklyn, was afraid of water. His parents were pleasant but determined; they brought Pedro to camp for only one reason: "Mr. Kelly, you must teach Pedro how to swim. We will not take him home until he knows how to swim."

Pedro's parents visited every weekend to check on him. "Pedro still can't swim? We want to see Pedro swim." Every other kid at the camp learned to swim, but Pedro would only go in the water if I held him. We were in week seven of an eight-week camp.

I told Pedro's parents, "I have an idea, but I need your permission."

"What are you going to do?" they asked.

I explained my plan and assured them, "I guarantee you he is going to learn how to swim."

"If you think that will work, do it."

I felt so terrible. Pedro trusted me and, boom, I push him off the boardwalk into the deep part of the lake that is over his head. He goes under, he comes up, he has this look,

---

'Pushing the limits'

Frank has always liked to try new things and push the limits. He helps others push their own limits also. He has been that way for as long as I can remember. When we were all very little—Frank was maybe five years old—my parents gave us a little, black cocker spaniel puppy for an Easter present. It could barely stand up, but Frank wanted to train it to walk down steps. He carried the cute little thing to the top of the steps and gave it a nudge. I cried as the poor pup rolled all the way down. Leave it to my brother to come up with a sink-or-swim method of dog training.

-JoAnn Kelly Burns

---

like, *How could you do this to me?* Down he goes again. "Pedro," I bark, "move your arms! Kick your feet!" He starts moving his arms and gets his head above the water shouting, "I can swim!" His parents are watching it all and they are thrilled! I cheer him on, "Keep moving, Pedro, you are not going to drown. Doggie-paddle, tread water. You are going to do it for ten minutes!" Just in case, I had three other lifeguards standing by, and had promised Pedro's parents that if he went under three times, we would pull him out. Pedro learned to swim.

I survived enough of my father's "sink or swim" lessons to know that there are some situations where nothing else works. If I put someone in the position where they have no choice but to do or die, they will do it. My management style is to find the right people and let them do their jobs.

Just ask my sons about my "management training" program when they came into the company. It consisted of my telling them, "I am here. If you get in trouble, I can help you and give you advice, but otherwise, go to it guys!" I want them to keep me informed, but I do not micromanage. I'll step in if they ask me; I won't let them drown.

I also emphasized to my sons that people have to know that when they ask you to do something, they can trust you to get it done. A person can have the greatest education in the world and exceptional talent, but if they're not reliable, nobody will want them. You can't let people down. These valuable lessons have helped me my entire life. People have complimented me for finishing tasks and honoring my commitments.

"To keep something, you have to give it away," I learned in AA, and I believe that applies to the mind, gifts, and experiences God has given me, so I want to continue helping others for as long as I can. God did not put me in this world to sit on my rear end! The last thing I want to do is stop working and do nothing. A week of that is fine, but after that, I'm crawling up the walls. I hope I can keep solving problems until I'm 90.

LAST GAME

On the Friday of Memorial Day weekend my junior year, 1960, my father was on his way home from a business trip in New York and stopped to see his sister, my Aunt Muriel, in New Jersey. While he was visiting with her and my Uncle Frank, he started feeling stomach pains. The pain got so intense that Aunt Muriel called her doctor, who came to the house to look at my father. He was having a diverticulitis attack. Aunt Muriel's doctor wanted to take him to the emergency room in New Jersey, but my father insisted on going to his own doctor in Havertown, Dr. Scotty Boyle, so Uncle Frank drove him home.

Dr. Boyle referred Dad to one of the leading GI surgeons in town, who performed emergency surgery on Dad that night. The surgeon came out afterward and assured us the operation was a success and that Dad should be OK within a week. When the surgeon left us, my mother turned to me and whispered, "I smelled alcohol on his breath. I don't believe him. I don't trust him." I asked, "What do you want to do, Mom?" "I don't know, Frank," she said, "I just don't trust him."

Dad and I watched the Phillies game in his hospital room on Saturday. He didn't get out of bed at all, but he could watch the game and hold a conversation. That turned out to be our last ballgame together.

JoAnn: When my mother saw Dad on Saturday, she didn't think he was responding as well as he should have been. She tried to call the surgeon, but he was away for the holiday weekend and never returned her calls. On Sunday he started having some kind of seizures—jumping out of his bed and disconnecting the IV tubes in his arms. I ran to get a nurse, and they finally restrained him in the bed.

Bob: The pump that was supposed to be removing fluids from his body wasn't working right. It was pumping the infectious fluids right back into him.

JoAnn: Mom called her distant cousin Peggy, who worked at the hospital, and told her the surgeon wasn't returning her calls. Peggy called the head of the hospital and asked her to do something.

Bob: Finally, on Monday, the hospital doctor on call corrected the pump problem.

JoAnn: The on-call doctor said Dad would need another surgery, which he scheduled for Tuesday when the surgeon would be back from his holiday weekend. Mom asked me to go to the chapel and pray. But when the surgeon arrived on Tuesday, Dad was too sick for surgery.

When I got to the hospital on Wednesday morning, I took a couple of steps into my father's room and froze. He was lying unconscious on the bed with all kinds of tubes hooked up to his arms, burning up with peritonitis and a 108-degree fever. Doctors did not have the antibiotics then that we have now, and his brain fried. By one in the afternoon the fever had killed him. My heart broke. I felt sick. He was gone, and it happened so fast. *How?* He was only 47; he was finally sober. He had plans for our future in business together, but we never got the chance. *Why?*

As Mom and I were leaving the hospital, two interns came up to my mother and told her, "Mrs. Kelly, we know what happened around here this weekend, and we don't think your husband should have died. Some things went on here that were not right, and if you want to do something about it, we will support you. We are willing to testify about what we witnessed if you need us."

It was final exam week at Villanova. I called my professors and begged, "Can I take the tests in a couple of weeks? My dad died." They cut me no slack. "No, you need to take the exams, or you'll get an incomplete," which meant I would have wasted the whole semester. I was so busy and so torn, but now, I had to be the strong one.

The line to get into the viewings at the funeral home wound around the block, and I'll never forget how packed the church was for his funeral. We could see and feel how much Dad was loved by so many people. The tribute comforted us and lifted our spirits, but nothing could fill the hole in our hearts and our lives.

Finish what you started, Dad always told me. The day after we buried Dad, I took my two exams and passed both. Now, what would Dad want me to do about the doctor? Mom and I talked to a lawyer. Dad certainly suffered unjustly, and we might have won our case, but it would have been a long fight, we had no money, and I didn't think Dad would want to drag Mom through a grueling legal process, so I told her I did not think we should pursue it, and she agreed. The wisdom of that decision was further confirmed for us two months later when my mother was diagnosed with breast cancer.

As hard as it was to work those evening shifts after class every day, and to give up my Christmas breaks to deliver mail, I was thankful that my father had me take those jobs. With him gone, there would have been no way Mom could afford for me to finish at Villanova.

I feel sad for my father when I think about how alcohol and his untimely death kept him from becoming all he could have been, and from achieving so much more in his life. I believe that I have been driven by a desire to complete the journey that my father began, but never fulfilled for himself, and God has graciously given me the opportunity to live the dream that Dad could not. God conveyed that grace primarily by bringing another person into my life: my wife, Janet.

4

The Godly Woman

A woman who fears the LORD is to be praised.
Honor her for all that her hands have done
and let her works bring her praise at the city gate.
Proverbs 31:30-31

JANET: It was false advertising, no question about it, but he sold me. I was cleaning up after a jazz concert at Gwynedd Mercy College, when Frank approached me and offered, "I'll help—what do you want me to do?"

"Do you mind sweeping?" I asked as I handed him a broom. He swept the floor for me, which was sweet of him, and that was the last time he ever held a broom. He only asked because he was stuck there waiting for a ride back to Villanova with his friend Jack, who cheerfully helped his girlfriend Joan clean up.

FRANK: Jack had invited me to the concert. "Why don't you come up with us, and who knows, you might meet somebody?" The first thing I noticed was they served no booze. I was not even thinking about trying to meet anyone, but then Joan introduced me to Janet, and as soon as I met her, I thought, *Wow, I really want to get to know this girl!* I could tell immediately that she ran the whole show, and found out she was the president of the student body. I just watched her for a while, and then I asked her to dance. We danced a couple of times, and I liked her right away.

JANET: I was attracted to Frank because he was in the "fun" crowd and I was in the "holy and serious" crowd.

FRANK: So, I helped her clean up, and we talked, and I asked, "Can I call you sometime?"

Janet ready for a dance at Gwynedd Mercy

JANET: That would be a fun time, I thought, so I said, "Sure."

FRANK: Villanova had no fraternities, so twelve of us—we called ourselves "The Twelve Apostles"—started our own and named it Mu Lambda Chi (translation: The Main Line Club). One of our traditions was huddling up every Thursday morning at the Pie Shoppe at school for coffee and doughnuts, and letting each other know who we planned to ask for a date that weekend. We did not want two of us calling the same girl.

I told them I was going for broke—I was going to ask Janet DeMaine for a date. I called her on Thursday night. "Hi, how are you doing? I really enjoyed sweeping the floor with you."

JANET: I said, "I bet that was a first."

FRANK: I asked, "What are you doing this weekend? My fraternity is having a big party on Saturday night. How would you like to come?"

JANET: I told him I already had plans for the weekend. "You're going to have to give me a lot more notice than two days, Frank."

He asked me if I had a boyfriend. I told him I was dating someone steadily, but there was no commitment.

FRANK: Joe Finnegan; he was in love with her.

JANET: Frank called again on another Thursday. He intrigued me, but again I already had a date. *What is the thing with those guys, waiting until Thursday to ask for a date?*

FRANK: We did not think about what day it was when we called the girls. We hosted terrific parties most weekends, and whoever wanted to come, great! If not, there was always next weekend.

I called Janet again around Easter. The club wasn't going to plan a party on Easter weekend, but Easter Monday was a holiday, so why not have a party that day?

I wised up and called her about ten days in advance. There is no way she has a date on Easter Monday, and if she does, then *three strikes and you're out,* it was not meant to be.

"We are having a party on Easter Monday," I said. "You can't tell me you have a date on Easter Monday!"

"No, I don't, and I would like to come, but I need to check with my parents," she said.

"What?"

44

"I didn't even drink beer!"

"Well, it's not a Saturday night, and I usually study on Monday," she said.

"I will hold," I said.

JANET: I want to be clear—I wanted to go on that first date, but I had to say no because I had a commitment and I do not believe in canceling on someone because something better comes along. I wanted to go on all three occasions, so I was thrilled when he asked me for Monday, and I was open.

My parents were very strict when it came to dating. They wanted to know how I was getting there, how I was getting home, and who I was going with. I could not just flip around. I needed to be back in the house no later than midnight.

FRANK: It was 11—she had to be home by 11.

"I knew she was the one for me."

JANET: Frank always says that, but I think it was midnight, maybe quarter of, but my parents definitely ran a tight ship. I would always warn Frank, "I can't be late," and he would say, "Don't worry about it." When we came home late, my parents let him know they were not pleased.

FRANK: The party was hopping. We laughed and danced for about an hour when I went to pour her a beer. Somebody bumped into me, and I dumped the whole pitcher of beer in her lap.

JANET: And so began our relationship. I did not even drink beer, only soda.

Frank was fun, he always had me laughing and enjoying myself, and that is what attracted me at first. Fraternity parties were much different from my normally strict settings, and I was not accustomed to it, but I liked it. We both enjoyed movies and dancing, we danced and danced and danced, and we won several jitterbug contests over the years. Sometimes we would just talk; he loved to talk. We held similar values and the same faith. He had a kind nature, always welcoming to everyone.

FRANK: From the first moment I met her, I knew she was

the one for me. She was intelligent, a leader with strong character and morals, and she was beautiful. I was not looking for a party girl.

Our second date was a double date with John and Cathy Baird, at a party in North Philly. After the party, we stopped on the way home for burgers at Howard Johnson's. I ordered the biggest orange freeze they made. Janet wore a cute pirouette skirt, and I did it again—knocked the orange freeze off the table and into her lap. The skirt turned stiff as cardboard.

Despite my klutziness, Janet went out with me again. Standing on her porch, I gave her a quick kiss goodnight and noticed a car down the street with its parking lights on.

"Janet, who is that?"

"It's Joe Finnegan."

"What the hell is he doing?"

"I don't know, but I don't like it."

"Well, I am going to go take care of him!"

"No Frank! Don't start any problems."

Janet's parents, Marguerite and John DeMaine

23 Congress Avenue in Springfield, PA

JANET: I called Joe later and let him know I did not like him following me, acting like he owned me, and it was over between us.

MEET THE PARENTS

JANET: We continued dating, and he eventually met my parents.

They were not in love with Frank at first. He was a party boy, and they worried I was getting into a situation that would not be good for me. But Frank respected them and worked hard to obey the rules. He treated me so well and was so friendly that they grew to like him, but they still worried.

I grew up in a very simple, semi-detached home at 23 Congress Avenue in Springfield, about four miles from where Frank grew up. My father was a pipefitter for Philadelphia Electric. He met my mom there, who had started working when she was 16. He was 25, and she was 20 when they married.

My father was Episcopalian. My mother's parents were immigrants from Italy, and devout Roman Catholics, which was not a big hit with my father's parents. In those days, couples could not get married in the Catholic Church if both spouses were not Catholic, so they held their wedding ceremony in the parish rectory. My mother's parents held a small reception for them afterward.

Janet playing in the backyard

They led a simple life. My father saved his money; his main form of entertainment was listening to the Phillies games in the evening. If he wanted to buy a new radio, or anything, he paid cash. Mom stayed home with me and my sister Joan, who was nine years older than I was. Joan and I did some things together, but there were so many years between us, we were like two only children in many ways.

Our home was well organized, thanks to my mother. She was in charge, and was the disciplinarian. When I was little, I took my bath at 4 PM every day and put on a clean dress to be ready for Dad when he came home from work. Mom—she really did dress up like Mrs. Cleaver on *Leave It to Beaver.* We ate dinner at the same time every day, and you could not be late. I thought every household worked that way until I started going to Frank's house for dinner, where it was hit-or-miss. "I forgot to put the potatoes in the oven," his mother would say, "so it's going to be another hour until dinner is ready," and we would end up eating at eight o'clock.

I am like my mother in many ways. I was a very pious girl, well behaved, and I obeyed all the rules—the kind of girl who is picked to be the May Queen and place the crown on the Blessed Mary statue in the church. Frank still teases me about obeying all the rules—if the sign says, "front-end parking only," I would never even think of backing in, whereas Frank would say, "That doesn't mean anything."

My father was the hugger, the cheek pincher, the piano player, banjo player, and singer. He loved Jesus. I also played the piano, and the two of us loved to play and sing duets of the old hymns—*The Old Rugged Cross, In the Garden,* and all the classic Christmas songs. He read Scripture to me and taught me to love the Bible. It always bothered me that he could not go to church with us, and I could not go to his church with him, but he never complained. He signed an agreement when he married Mom that the children would go to the Catholic church and Catholic schools. That's how it worked in those days.

Years later, when I visited home with my own kiddos one weekend, I decided, *this church business is foolish*, so I declared, "Pops, we are going to church with you today!" We all sat down in the pew at the Episcopal Church of the Redeemer. It was the first time he ever sat with his family next to him in church, and it brought tears to his eyes.

Through going to church faithfully and watching Billy Graham with my father, my mother's love for Jesus became more real and personal over the years. She always took meals to people, and our home was always open. She loved when I had friends over—not only because of her gift of hospitality but also so she knew who my friends were.

Mom was especially generous at Christmas. She always invited the down-and-out people, like Uncle George, a stumbling alcoholic with no family, and Mrs. Seaman from up the street, who had dementia. (My mother would sometimes see her walking around the neighborhood with no clothes on, and go wrap her up in a blanket and bring her home.)

When I was little, Santa not only brought the gifts, he also put up the tree. When I went to bed on Christmas Eve, the house was empty. I woke up to a bright, beautiful tree, with presents stacked underneath. My parents were generous when it came to gifts, and they wanted to give me and Joan what we wanted. I was a doll girl. I let Santa know which doll I wanted, and he always came through. I loved Christmas as a little girl, and I still do.

SCHOOL DAYS

JANET: I went to St. Francis of Assisi Elementary School. I was a good student, and took piano lessons and sewing lessons after school and on weekends. I was not much of an athlete, but I loved to square dance and roller skate.

I went on to high school at Notre Dame, an all-girls Catholic school. My parents paid something around $100 a year, and the archdiocese paid the rest. Things don't work that way anymore!

I had the "first child syndrome:" you work hard, and you do well. I don't think I ever saw a C on a report card. I was elected to student government, played in the orchestra, and sang in the chorus.

Frank's sister, JoAnn, and her best friend, Mary Ellen, also went to Notre Dame, so Frank and I knew of each other, but did not really know each other. Frank's father bet Mary Ellen that Frank would not go to the senior prom with her, but she asked him, and he said yes! As it turned out,

Mary Ellen ended up marrying Frank's brother, Bob!

Dances at the Catholic schools were the center of social life for teenagers in those years. Holy Cross held a dance every Sunday night. Groups of girls and groups of guys from all the Catholic schools in the area piled into the gym. We took our shoes off and jitterbugged in our white socks to Chubby Checker and all the classic '50s music.

Not as many women attended college in the 1950s as today, but I won several academic awards in high school, and college seemed like the right next step for me. I was the first in our entire family to go to college, and still the only one to this day, as far as I know. My parents probably remortgaged their house to send me.

Gwynedd Mercy is a university now, but it was a two-year college then. I commuted every day—an hour and ten minutes up and an hour and ten minutes home, back and forth on Route 320; the Blue Route didn't exist then (that's Interstate 476, which runs between I-95 and the Pennsylvania Turnpike). Three friends from the neighborhood also went to Gwynedd Mercy, so we carpooled and took turns driving.

I did not have grandiose aspirations. I took classes in medical technology, which is preparation for becoming a medical secretary. Some of my friends went to Immaculata for a four-year degree, and it would be nice to have a bachelor's degree, but nobody ever asks me what kind of degree I have. In fact, in Baltimore, if someone asks, "Where did you go to school?" they mean high school.

FRANK: Her peers at Gwynedd Mercy recognized that she was a natural leader and elected her president of her class and then president of the entire student body her senior year. She knows how to get things done. I think she's a visionary who knows how to implement her vision.

JANET: I see the big picture, and I often know how to get there. I'm not afraid to speak my mind and make recommendations.

'A MOMENT OF GLORY'

FRANK: We continued dating steadily— going out to movies,

Queen's Court Reigns At Senior Gala

Prom Queen Janet DeMaine (middle photo) featured in The Villanovan

our parties at Villanova, her dances at Gwynedd Mercy. The Gwynedd Mercy dances, with no alcohol and a record player, seemed like an afternoon tea compared to our parties, with drinking and live bands.

I took Janet as my date to Villanova's junior and senior proms. The senior prom was a major event on campus. Tickets cost $5 per couple, and it always sold out. The highlight was the crowning of the Prom Queen. I nominated Janet, and 1,500 other Villanova men nominated 99 other women, not only from Villanova, but also from the surrounding women's schools— Gwynedd Mercy, Immaculata, Rosemont, and Cabrini.

The Villanova Queen Contest judges narrowed the field down to ten, with Janet included. The Philadelphia Modeling and Charm School selected five semifinalists, and Janet made the cut. Then, at the prom, Arlen Saylor, the leader of

Photo by Andy DaPuzza

A moment of glory . . . just after the presentation of the queen of the Senior Prom, Janet DeMaine. Her escort, Frank Kelly, and Gary Susnjara, Prom m.c., look on.

the band that played at the prom, had the honor of selecting the winner. He invited the five finalists up on stage for short interviews.

JANET: The amazing thing was that Frank and I had gone out dancing up in Willow Grove a few weeks before, and the band was none other than Arlen Saylor's Orchestra! When he came to talk to me, I went on about how I had heard him play before and how much I enjoyed dancing to his music. I think that gave me an advantage.

FRANK: Everyone could see that Janet was head-and-shoulders above the others—and Saylor crowned Janet the Queen!

JANET: My "moment of glory," as the *Villanovan* described it in the next week's edition. That is what I mean when I say Frank was fun to be with. His adventurous spirit was something new and refreshing for me, and I enjoyed being with him.

We would go to the beach sometimes—I would go to Ocean City, NJ with a bunch of girls, he would go with a bunch of guys, and like magic, we would catch up with each other. Funny how that happened!

Once I was with some girls at the beach, met up with Frank, and he offered to take me home. That was not exactly the plan my parents had agreed with, so I had to call them.

"Frank Kelly is here, and he said he could bring me home."

"That will be fine," Mom said, "but I want you in the house no later than 9."

Frank thought that was ridiculous, "We'll run into all the traffic! We would be better off waiting and leaving later."

"I am going to be in trouble," I told him.

"Don't worry about it," he assured me, "we'll call."

My parents met us at the front door when we walked up around eleven o'clock, and boy, did they ever read him the riot act.

'WE WERE SO YOUNG'

FRANK: We dated for about a year, and got engaged in September of my senior year—1960. I never had any doubt about marrying her. To this day, I never had a doubt.

JANET: I remember we talked about getting married, and that we had no money; we were so young.

FRANK: I borrowed $500 from Janet to buy the engagement ring. She had finished her degree and was working as a medical secretary in Downtown Philly, while I still had another year of college, so she was the one with money in the bank.

JANET: One night, we ate dinner at Frank's house, and then went for a lovely, quiet walk. He gave me the ring and asked me to marry him, and I said yes. He did not get down on his knee or anything dramatic like that. We came back and told his family, and that was it.

There must be something about cleaning up dance halls together, because Jack and Joan, who had invited Frank to that first jazz concert at Gwynedd Mercy, also got married.

Our wedding was at St. Francis of Assisi Church, in Springfield, PA, at noon on August 19, 1961. August can be brutally hot, but we had a beautiful, beautiful day—sunny, cool and breezy. My parents did not have much money, so the wedding was simple. The bridesmaids were my sister Joan, Frank's sister JoAnn, and my friends Mary Scott and Cathy Baird. Frank's brother Bob was the best man, and Frank's friends Harry Arnold, Paul O'Rourke and Al Murphy were groomsmen. After the wedding, we had a reception at the Treadway Inn.

FRANK: That was in St. Davids, about a half-mile west of Villanova on Route 30. It's now the Radnor Inn.

JANET: There was no alcohol. The reason was not that my parents were teetotalers, it was the cost, so we

served punch. We had a little band playing, and we danced, of course. We ate chicken for dinner. Believe me, it was not fancy.

Some of the guys left the reception to sit at the bar of the Inn, and I think Frank's mother would have enjoyed a cocktail. In retrospect, it would have been nice to offer a little toast, but that's how it was, and I sure did not argue about it. We drove to Pocono Gardens for our honeymoon.

FRANK: I had to borrow my brother's car because I did not have my company car yet.

JANET: We were driving up the turnpike, and someone started beeping their horn at us. We looked over and saw the Conroys—a couple we knew who were married on the same

day and headed to the same place for their honeymoon! Some of our mutual friends had flitted back and forth between our two weddings and receptions. We met up with the Conroys in the Poconos and had some fun together.

FRANK: Everybody staying there was on their honeymoon, so the lodge director planned games and activities for the couples to do together. He picked Janet and me for a game of hide-and-seek.

"Early tomorrow morning, I want the two of you to come with me out in the woods, dress up in these Indian costumes, and hide," he told us. "I'm going to tell the others that there is an Indian couple out in the woods and their job is to find you. Got it?"

He took us out to the woods and dropped us off by a big tree. We sat there wearing huge Indian headdresses, looking silly as can be, and waited; and waited. We saw nobody. We heard nothing. I said to Janet, "This is a prank, we have to go back."

JANET: I didn't believe him; I did not believe they would do a thing like that to us.

'He totally outkicked his coverage'

My dad wouldn't be writing this autobiography if he hadn't married my mom. She kept it all together—managed the business operations, got four boys and a foster daughter where they needed to go, and organized the political campaigns. He's the man he is today in large part because of her. He married up, I'd say; totally outkicked his coverage.

- Bryan Kelly

FRANK: Another hour passed. "Janet, this is a joke," I said. "They're playing a big joke on us."

JANET: If I was told to do something, that's what I did. I told Frank, "We can't go back and ruin the game. We can't have all of those poor people come out all this way looking for us and not find us."

Our first home in Havertown

FRANK: After nearly three hours, I finally convinced her to go back. Everyone split their sides laughing at us as we walked up to the lodge. "You almost broke the record," the director told us, "most people are back in an hour or two!"

A FULL PLATE

JANET: About a year later, when Armour and Company promoted Frank to manage their field office in Johnstown, I moved away from my family for the first time. Both of our families were sad that we were leaving, but I was OK with moving—it was one of my adventures with Frank. We did not know a soul, but we made friends quickly.

When we returned to Havertown for Frank's new job with Eugene Dietzgen the next year, we lived in an apartment for a while, then bought a beautiful, little two-story red brick house. At the neighborhood newcomers tea, I struck up a conversation with the woman in line behind me, Julie Cawley. She and her husband, Charlie had recently moved in from Massachusetts. We both had a child about the same age and started getting together, usually with the kids, but we also

Julie and Charlie Cawley became our special, dear friends.

got away for bridge lessons and other fun things by ourselves. Eventually, we got our husbands together to play cards as a foursome, and Julie and Charlie became our special, dear friends.

FRANK: What a small world it is. I almost fell over when I found out that Julie grew up in Park Slope in Brooklyn,

---

'They bring out the best'

Getting in line behind Janet at that newcomers night seemed like a chance meeting, but it was meant to be. Our friendship over all these years is very rare, special, and precious.

They both bring out the best in people. Janet's love, care, and support for her family and friends are incredible. Frank is the most positive person I know. He boosts the spirits of everyone around him.

They were there for Charlie and me during Charlie's illness; praying, calling, and visiting. They came to Maine to be with me at the end, and have cared for me since Charlie's death. I appreciate how they include me in everything they possibly can.

-Julie Cawley

right around the corner from my grandparents. I must have walked past her house a thousand times. Her maiden name was Murphy, and her father was Dr. Murphy, an obstetrician. The doctor's name on my birth certificate is Dr. Murphy. We figure he probably delivered me! Then we move into the same neighborhood in Havertown, and years later, we all end up in Baltimore. Amazing.

When I met Charlie, he was making $90 a week running a Beneficial Finance office in Manoa. I was making $95, and he was all ticked off because I made more than him. Not only did I make $5 more a week, I rubbed it in. "And I have a car, and you don't." He was bent on making more money than I made. He would come to me and say, "I just got a raise, what are you making now?"

Charlie went on to be one of the most successful business people of our generation, particularly as the founder and first CEO of the MBNA credit card company, and he was one of the most generous human beings I have ever known.

JANET: I'll tell you what close friends we became. When I was pregnant again after John, only a couple of months along, and Frank was away, I started bleeding. Charlie rushed over and took me to the hospital. Frank was somewhere up in the mountains of Virginia, and I was admitted to the hospital. Charlie finally reached Frank, explained what happened, and Frank drove straight back to Pennsylvania. But there was no Interstate 95 to speed home on so Charlie checked in on me at the hospital while we waited for Frank. When Frank arrived, he told the nurse "I am here to see Janet Kelly, I'm her husband," but she did not believe him. "I have seen her husband—he has red hair," she said, describing Charlie!

My miscarriage was a sad and scary experience, but we made it through, and did not have to wait long until David came along.

Our home in Timonium,
124 Tregarone Road

When we moved to Baltimore for Frank's new job assignment, the boys were two and three, and we had no family around. Frank's parents were deceased. My parents lived back in Springfield, but they were wonderful and came down to help as much as they could. They would stay for a few days at a time, and they were worker bees—bringing care packages of food, doing laundry, and whatever else it took to get me over the hump. They were in their sixties, which seemed so old to me back then, and I always told my mother, "Mom, you're doing too much. You shouldn't be working so hard."

She would say, "I can go home and sleep, but you can't." I always looked forward to them coming, and they helped us acclimate to Baltimore.

They would stay with the kids while Frank and I looked at houses. I wanted a neighborhood where other young families were buying, and we found a new community being built in the Baltimore County suburb of Timonium. The

split-level house Frank wanted cost much more than I would ever have considered—$29,000. Frank is the accelerator, and I am the brake. But he insisted that the larger space would be perfect for kids and their activities, and he was right. We enjoyed that home for 20 years.

After David and Bryan were born, we had four boys under age five running around the house. The commotion felt like Grand Central Station, but we did not cower in the house and feel sorry for ourselves. We kept busy

and established roots quickly. I was involved mostly with school. I was president of the PTA, hosted spaghetti dinner fundraisers, and made the costumes for the school plays. I was active in my kids' lives, and I loved it. I did not want to do anything else—that was my salvation. The biggest blessing for me was being home when the children came home from school.

The kids often brought their friends over to play. I

'A good spirit in my heart'

Growing up I remember feeling a good spirit in my heart and soul. Every morning Dad would be sitting in the living room with his cup of coffee and his Bible, reading the Scriptures. Seeing him reading and praying brought me into a close relationship with the Lord. I love you Dad.

-Sharon's letter to Frank on his 70th birthday

like a neat house, so I would pick up and try to clean, but it was hopeless—kids running in and out, boots and dirty clothes and junk and bags everywhere. I could not keep up with the mess, so I decided cleaning would not be part of my life at that stage; *It can wait for another day.* If I needed to escape for a while, I would slip into the living room—my separate little refuge.

Our foster daughter, Sharon, joined our family a few months before Bryan was born. She came to us when she was six years old, through St. Vincent's Center, where we volunteered. She stayed with us for a weekend, then another, five or six weekends altogether, and then the nuns told us she was available for foster care. Her mother was in a mental health institution, and her father had abandoned her.

Sharon often challenged us, such as the time she ran away from us on a Saturday night while we were on vacation in Sea Isle, NJ. St. Vincent's told us it was common for foster children to run away, and she would most likely come back, and sure enough, she did.

There were times when I thought I could not take it anymore, but Frank would say, "Let's keep trying a little harder."

FRANK: And there were times when I was ready to give up, but Janet wanted to hang in a little longer.

JANET: She tried a few times to move back with her father, but it never worked out for long, and she stayed with us until she turned 18. We love her, and she loves us and considers us her family. We gave her away at her wedding. I talk to her a couple of times a week, and we keep in touch with her three sons.

SOME ASSEMBLY REQUIRED

JANET: Christmas Day could be a little crazy in the Kelly home. It helped that we nixed the tradition of Santa putting up the tree and delivering the presents the night of Christmas Eve. We put the tree up well before then, and let the kids open a present on Christmas Eve—usually pajamas or something else new to wear for the pictures.

On Christmas morning, the kids would wake up early and sit in a line on the steps leading down from the bedrooms, watching me make the coffee and waiting for Frank to come down. Until then, they could not move off the steps.

"Mom, where's Dad?" they would whine.

Frank would tease them, "I'm just going to sleep for another hour or so!"

"Assembly Required" was a warning label as far as Frank was concerned. One year, he started putting a bike together, realized he didn't have all the tools he needed and took it across the street to borrow tools from a neighbor. Apparently, our neighbor did not

"I would love a monogrammed sweater."

have the right tools either because when Frank tried to ride the bike back home, *crunch!* It smashed to smithereens!

Frank's Christmas shopping consisted of running to the store on December 24th to find something for me. His nickname isn't "Big Frank" for nothing—he does everything big. One year he asked me what I wanted. "I would love a monogrammed sweater," I told him. On Christmas morning, he hands me five boxes, all the same size. I open the first box, and it's a red sweater, with a monogram the size of Superman's emblem. The next one is blue, and the next one is yellow—all with the same huge monogram of my initials, "JKD." Frank was all excited, "Aren't they great?"

"Yes, they are very nice," I said, but thought, *When will I ever wear them?*

'DROP 'EM, BOYS!'

JANET: As the boys got older they got in little jackpots from time to time. At Pot Spring Elementary one winter, an announcement came over the loudspeaker, "Will the boys from Tregarone Road please report to the principal's office." The police waited for them—they had been throwing snowballs at cars.

The snowball incident was not the only time the police called or paid a visit. There was the time the police found them swimming in Loch Raven Reservoir—skinny dipping I should say—and the time we came home to flashing patrol car lights because Frankie and his friend Tommy from next door thought it would be funny to moon a car full of girls out on York Road.

FRANK: I must confess that they might have learned the mooning thing from me, and here's why. One night, the boys, Janet, and I are driving up I-83 on the way home from dinner in Little Italy, and a car full of teenage boys pulls up next to us. I guess they saw my Senate license plate and figured they would mess with the old fart. They toot the horn, the driver looks at me and points to the back seat of his car, where three big, bare butts are pressed up against the window. I just laughed and gave them a thumbs-up.

They drive away, but I can't let it end there. I look back at the kids and give the charge, "Drop 'em, boys!"

JANET: I screamed, "Don't you dare. Don't you dare!"

FRANK: I caught up to the other car, honked my horn, glanced back and admired my sons' four full moons. The guys in the car laughed and gave us a return thumbs-up. Hilarious.

JANET: It's much funnier now than it was then. Nobody robbed a bank, but they were rascals sometimes.

We're beach people!

MUST LOVE DOGS, AND SAND

FRANK: I remember when my father would take us to Avalon, there was a house with a white picket fence around it near the one we rented. There were always a lot of kids playing in their yard, and I could see the parents and the grandparents all together with them. To me, the ocean and the beach always said, "family." I loved summers at the beach as a kid and as a father, but I lost my grandparents and parents at such an early age that I never enjoyed a scene like the one at the house with the white picket fence. The thought of recreating that scene with my own children and grandchildren always lurked in the back of my mind, so our family continued the Kelly tradition of summer vacations at the beach.

We would go to the New Jersey beaches—Avalon, Sea Isle, or Stone Harbor. We always took a week. I don't know how we pulled it off because half the time I didn't have the money to do it.

Vacations often brought out the difference between Janet the planner and me the improviser. I always had her on edge.

JANET: Someone said to me, and I believe this is true, "The thing that attracts you most to your spouse is the thing that can drive you crazy after you're married."

FRANK: One year Janet asked me where we were going for vacation. I said, "Let's go to Stone Harbor for a week!"
"But we don't have a place yet," she pointed out.

I called a motel that had two nights available, so I booked it. "We're all set to go!" I announced.

We piled the kids and the dog into the Country Squire and rode off to Stone Harbor. The kids loved the motel and the pool. Janet was worried sick we would be homeless on the third day, but I found a house to rent right on the ocean in Sea Isle, and that week turned out to be one of our best vacations. We rode the waves and played on the beach all day, ate out every night, and turned the kids loose in the amusement parks. "See, Janet," I crowed, "you don't need to plan. You just go with the flow and see what happens."

JANET: "Whose flow?" I would ask, "yours or mine?" Though I did not want to admit it, I had fun.

FRANK: By 1984, the business was

Maddie

doing well, and we bought a condominium in Ocean City, MD. When you have a place at the beach, the kids and grandkids will come. Ten years later, we built the house in Bethany.

FRANK: Dogs have always been a part of our family as well. Each one lived 15 years. Schnopsy, a Schnauzer, was our first, then came Brandy, a Golden Retriever, then Tibers, a Yorkie. We were empty nesters by the time our Yellow Lab Merks died, and we did not get another because we traveled so much.

JANET: But the boys kept telling me, "We have to get Dad another dog." I said, "No. No, no, no, our dog days are over." But my daughters-in-law, Melissa and Gayle, both had Malteses that Frank thought were really cute. "Why don't you just look at them?" the boys asked me. Well, you know what happens when you look. Melissa and I went to a breeder she knew. I saw Maddie, who was the runt of the litter and about the size of a teacup, but she was gentle, and since we were older, I didn't want a high-strung dog. Melissa noticed that Maddie's mother had a mellow temperament also, so I chose Maddie and gave her to Frank for his 70th birthday. Our dog days are back, and I love her!

JUGGLING ACT

JANET: Before we started Kelly Associates, when Frank was between jobs and not sure what he wanted to do, I suggested, "I will get a job in the meantime." I interviewed at McCormick for an administrative assistant position, and they called me the next day with an offer. I immediately felt sick to my stomach. *My gosh, I can't leave these kids, I can't do this.* It was a good job, and we could have used the steady income, but I called back and told them, "I can't take this job; I really can't."

I put my organizational and administrative skills into high gear when we started Kelly Associates. I took care of all four boys and Sharon. I handwrote all the invoices on a carbon copy ledger, paid all the carriers, and balanced all the books.

We moved the office from the spare bedroom to the basement, so I would work down there, answer the phones, do the laundry, sort the mail, and run upstairs to cook dinner. If the kids were off from school for a snow day or summer vacation, there were many times when the phone would ring and the kids would be running around throwing balls, so I would answer, "Good morning, Kelly Associates," and put the caller on hold while I scolded the boys.

'The backbone of the family'

Don't discount Janet! Like Frank, Janet is extremely smart and compassionate. Theirs is a great American story of hard work and determination, and it would never have happened without Janet. She is the force behind many of Frank's activities in the community and their family's tradition of philanthropy. She is the backbone of the family.

-Congressman C. A. Dutch Ruppersberger

There were days when I would put the kids to bed, then go down to the basement and finish working because there was so much confusion in the daytime that I could not get everything done. Still, the best part was being at home with the kids. I had a personal phone and a business phone, and I could juggle all the balls.

I'm thankful that all the boys did well in school; I couldn't have handled any more juggling.

FRANK: Academically, they took after their mother.

JANET: I helped them with their homework and projects— thinking through with them how to get it done and taking them to buy the supplies and materials.

FRANK: But they got their competitiveness and athleticism from the Kelly side. I coached their baseball teams and helped with their football teams. John was the first to pick up a lacrosse stick. They all played football and lacrosse at Calvert Hall and played lacrosse in college. They pounded each other in the backyard, so when they took the field for a game, they were ready.

Each one graduated from college on time, which I was thankful for because even at that rate we had to take a second mortgage to cover all the tuition.

PASSING THE BATON

JANET: When I say I am proud of my family, I include my daughters-in-law, Gayle, Tee, Melissa, and Heidi, who are very special in my life. People have asked me, "How in the world do you manage four daughters-in-law? I don't even talk to mine. I don't like the way she does this, that, or the other."

I ask them, "Do you talk to your daughter-in-law on the phone every week?"

Melissa, Gayle, Janet, Tee, Heidi
"I love them and treat them like my daughters."

"No, I call my son," they all say.

"No, no—do you call your daughter-in-law?"

They'll say, "I talk to my son, so I know what is going on in the family."

I tell them, "Call or text her every week, even if it is only a five-minute conversation to say, 'I'm thinking of you,' or 'I just called to say hello.' Better yet, get together with her for lunch."

One of my friends actually took my advice, and a couple of months later told me, "Now I talk with her about everything—calling her is a highlight of my week!"

On their birthdays, I do not feel comfortable buying a card that says, "Happy birthday, daughter," since they have their own parents. I always buy a card for daughter-in-law and cross out the "in-law" part. I am not their mother, but I love them and treat them as if I were.

FRANK: All the qualities I love in Janet I see in my daughters-in-law. If I had to choose wives for my sons, I could not have ever chosen four more beautiful—inside and out—God-loving women than my sons married. They're all different, but they're all perfect. I consider them my own daughters.

JANET: They are responsible for the next generation. If we ever get into discussions about problems with the kids, I never dictate, "This is what you should do." I will just let them know, "I went through something similar, and this is what I did." I don't expect them to follow my family traditions; I want them to establish traditions of their own.

I have watched them raise beautiful children. All four of them love the Lord, and they have passed that on to their children. I have watched them give to the community. It is almost a handing over of the baton.

These days, I still find myself at a lot of the grandkids' lacrosse games. I laugh and smile at the younger ones, but at the high school and college games, I bite my fingernails the whole time.

FRANK: After my sons were grown and married, I was sad to think, *It's all over*—no more plays to go to, no more ballgames, no more of those activities and experiences Janet and I enjoyed so much. But I never dreamed what grandchildren could do. They give us life.

JANET: They keep us beyond busy. The boys have their sports. Some of the girls also play—soccer, field hockey, and lacrosse. We also enjoy the choir performances, eating at their restaurant fundraisers, and everything else they're into. Some of my favorite memories with the girls are the days I take them shopping. "Lunch and shop," we call it.

We never, ever missed a graduation at any level, and that wasn't always easy. One year two of them graduated from college on the same weekend, in different states. We watched Hannah walk across the stage at Penn State on a Saturday, then got up at 5 AM on Sunday and flew to North Carolina for Stephen.

FRANK: As part of our succession planning for Kelly Associates, a consultant interviewed all the grandchildren. He asked each one, separately, to talk about their favorite Kelly family memory. Every single one of them, without exception, said the same thing: "Christmas at Grandmom's." Not "Pop Pop's," but "Christmas at Grandmom's." The consultant said he had never before heard any response that was so universal.

JANET: They only get one gift, but I spend months finding that one special gift that is personal to each grandchild. It might cost $25, or it might cost $250, but they love it.
Without a doubt, my family is what I am most proud of in my life.

LEARN, DO, TEACH

JANET: Bible study has always been number one on my list of activities. In the 1980s, I started in Bible Study Fellowship, and later joined Community Bible Study, where I served as the assistant teaching director in Baltimore for several years.

When we began spending our winters in Vero Beach, I found a small group of eight women who were praying for a Community Bible Study to start there, but most of us were snowbirds who could not meet the year-round requirements, so we adopted a similar format: homework-study-teach-share in a circle, and called it the Discipler's Bible Study. Recently we changed the name to "Engage." I lead a group of 45 women who meet at our house. I love to have people in my home. I never want to say, "Sorry, I have no room." I can always squeeze in more chairs.

The "Engage" Bible study group in Vero Beach

FRANK: She doesn't have to call and invite people...they just come to be there with her.

JANET: I don't consider myself a visionary, but I can see how to get something done. I might have an idea in mind, but I want to hear what everyone else has to say first, and often someone will improve on my idea, and to me it is more fun to let someone else come up with the plan. Then what I like to do is figure out who should be in charge of what to get the job done.

FRANK: In the Senate, I helped Carolyn Manuszak, president of Villa Julie College, obtain more funding for the college, so she asked me to join their board. I told her I couldn't but suggested she ask Janet because I knew how capable Janet was and how much she could help the school.

The Kelly family portrait, commissioned for Janet and Frank's 50th anniversary, highlights the importance of family and faith.

JANET: When Frank told me about it, I said, "No, if she wanted me on the board, she would have asked me first." In truth, I did not want to be on the board in any case.

Four or five years passed by, and Carolyn called me. "I am calling you directly—I don't want him—I want you." This time, I accepted, and served on the board for 15 years.

I loved the people I met and the challenge of growing the school. Villa Julie began as a small junior college and transformed into Stevenson University, a large university with several schools, master's and doctorate programs, and even a new stadium. Some of my contributions included finding property, inviting the governor for tours, and introducing Carolyn to people who might be influential in obtaining funding.

I was also on the board of Stella Maris. Both of my parents died in hospice there, and I was grateful for the qual-

ity of care Stella Maris provided and the compassion of the staff. In the mid-1990s the board asked Frank and me to co-chair a capital campaign to renovate the hospice wing. We ran the campaign, and then they invited me to join the board. I took Sister Karen to Annapolis to introduce her to legislators and worked on the community relations committee.

We have dyslexia in the Kelly family, so I know how important it is for dyslexic students to have tutors who understand their unique learning needs. I also know how difficult it is to find and afford those tutors, so I was happy to help the Dyslexia Tutoring Program raise scholarship money to send children to summer reading camps.

I've helped with fundraising events and mail campaigns for other nonprofits that different friends in Vero Beach have introduced me to. Around 2009 I began helping Habitat for Humanity raise money to build two homes every year in the nearby Gifford and Fellsmere neighborhoods. At different times over the years I've helped at SafeSpace, which provides housing and legal, educational, and employment resources for abused women, and I've put my background in health care to work for the Indian River Medical Center.

FRANK: I am often recognized as the leader of the family in politics and business, but Janet is also a natural leader, and a rock. I don't know where I would be without Janet. All my success followed after I married her. Every step of the way, she stood with me.

She has a tremendous gift of humility, which is not one of my strengths. She never looks for credit. In all our years together, I don't think I have ever seen her put herself ahead of anybody else, ever.

In Proverbs, Chapter 31, where it describes the excellent wife, it is describing Janet.

JANET: To stay together over 55 years takes, above all else, faith. When things are not going well, our love for God keeps us on solid ground. When one of us is struggling, the other walks alongside. It takes love and forgiveness.

FRANK: I've learned the importance of resolving conflicts right away. *Do not let the sun go down on your anger, and do not give the devil a foothold,* Ephesians 4:26 says. Unresolved con-

---

'A living symphony'

Frank and Janet are a living symphony. Unless people know Janet, and I say this with much love and a bit of humor, they give Frank too much of the credit for what he has accomplished. He's the happy Irishman—gregarious, engaging, story-telling. She's the Italian mother—comforting, by the book and to the point.

I see in their sons that Frank and Janet's DNA has passed right down the line. The legacy of who they are and what they have achieved will live on for generations to follow, to the benefit of us all.

-Mike Gill, Secretary of Commerce, State of Maryland

---

flicts cause nothing but pain; they build up over time and blow up when the trials come. Janet and I have not had many fights, and I can't even remember what most of them were about. I was wrong most of the time, and I felt disturbed in my spirit. I felt no peace until I resolved everything with her.

JANET: Frank and I give each other the freedom to do what God calls us to do. We are not clingy; we are not jealous of each other's time and community service. We celebrate each other's success.

On top of all that, it certainly helps to make it fun along the way!

The Godly Woman

PROVERBS 31:10-31

A wife of noble character who can find?
She is worth far more than rubies.
Her husband has full confidence in her
and lacks nothing of value.
She brings him good, not harm,
all the days of her life.
She gets up while it is still night;
she provides food for her family
and portions for her female servants.
She considers a field and buys it;
out of her earnings she plants a vineyard.
She sets about her work vigorously;
her arms are strong for her tasks.
She sees that her trading is profitable,
and her lamp does not go out at night.
She opens her arms to the poor
and extends her hands to the needy.
Her husband is respected at the city gate,
where he takes his seat among the elders of the land.
She is clothed with strength and dignity;
she can laugh at the days to come.
She speaks with wisdom,
and faithful instruction is on her tongue.
She watches over the affairs of her household
and does not eat the bread of idleness.
Her children arise and call her blessed;
her husband also, and he praises her:
"Many women do noble things,
but you surpass them all."
Charm is deceptive, and beauty is fleeting;
*but a woman who fears the L*ORD *is to be praised.*
Honor her for all that her hands have done,
and let her works bring her praise at the city gate.

5

Money, Sex, and Power

*Do not worry then, saying, 'What will we eat?' or 'What
will we drink?' or 'What will we wear for clothing?' for your
heavenly Father knows that you need all these things. But seek
first His kingdom and His righteousness, and all these things will
be added to you. So do not worry about tomorrow; for tomorrow
will care for itself. Each day has enough trouble of its own.*

Matthew 6:31-34

My boss, J.P., was a party guy, and I was a drinker
when I started working for him in 1967, so I thought
we would get along just fine. I had opened the Baltimore
sales office for an engineering and drafting supply company
called Eugene Dietzgen, and a year or so into the job, J.P.
invited me to a convention of government agency prospects
in Washington, D.C. I will never forget it. He wanted me to
"work the floor," as he called it, and get to know how the
government types operated.

On a Friday afternoon, at about four o'clock, I was on
the convention floor working our display booth when some
guy came up to me with a note instructing me to come up to
room 604. I walked in the room and froze when I saw two
women sitting on the bed in bathrobes.

"Let me introduce you to 'Mary' and 'Jane,'" J.P. said.

"They're here to service our clients."

"What do you mean?" I asked.

"You know what I mean. When guys come to the booth, give them your card with this room number on it and send them up. Why don't you take a turn with them?" he offered.

That was not the first day, nor the last day that I faced a day with "trouble of its own" as I moved out into my professional life, and as Janet and I started our married life. The question was always, would we let the troubles and temptations derail us? Or would we *seek first God's kingdom and His righteousness,* as Jesus taught in His sermon on the Mount?

WORKING SMART

When I graduated from Villanova in 1961 with a B.S. in Economics, and a major in marketing, my father had advised me that if I wanted to learn how to market, merchandise, and sell a product, I would learn best in the retail grocery business. So, when Armour and Company came recruiting on campus, I interviewed for a sales position in their grocery products division.

Armour offered me $95 a week, a company car, and the possibility of a bonus. The car clinched it because I could not afford to buy one on my own, and they allowed me to use it for personal driving. I started out selling Dial soap, Dash dog food, canned meats and various other products to supermarkets, out of our offices on Vine Street in Philadelphia, near the Ben Franklin Bridge.

My father taught me to work hard, and I've worked hard all my life. But my job at Armour taught me that you could work hard and fill up a lot of hours but end up like the mouse on the running wheel and not get anywhere. To truly succeed, it's just as important to work smart. I made my first ever sales call to an Acme in West Philadelphia; I can still see the store. I was selling Dial soap, which ranked number two in sales at the time, behind Ivory. My goal was to convince the grocery manager, Ernie Greco, to put Dial soap on the store shelves at eye level next to the Ivory, where more shoppers would see it and buy it. Of course, every other soap salesperson was trying to convince Greco to do the same thing, and it took me a while to get smart about how to win him over.

I walked into the Acme and asked for Ernie Greco.

"He's in the back room," a clerk told me.

I found the back room, the warehouse, and asked the guys working there, "Is Ernie Greco here?"

"Yeah, that's me, what the f*** do you want?"

"I'm Frank Kelly from Armour and Company."

"So what?"

"Could I have a couple of minutes?" I asked.

"What do you got for me?"

I was a proud rookie and boasted, "I don't have anything for you, just a good product. Can we talk about it?"

"I don't talk to the company kiddies," he scoffed, "come back to me when you have some experience and you know what to tell me."

I walked out of there thinking, *Oh my God, is this what merchandising is all about? I worked my way through college for this?*

I knew what they wanted, but Armour policy forbade giving cash to customers. Maybe if I had a good enough giveaway—lunch, tickets to ballgames, coolers—I could nab the prime spots on the shelves. I gave it a shot. I started bringing Ernie and the warehouse guys hoagies and shooting the breeze with them over lunch. When we got to know and respect each other, I could make my pitch. "Ernie, do me a favor," I would say, "I need a display on the corner of an aisle for my Chiffon liquid detergent. Can you give it to me?"

"Yeah, OK Kells, you got it."

With Acme, I learned the importance of building relationships. With my next customer, A&P, I learned the power that comes from joining separate entities together into one large pool. I asked Janet to introduce me to the father of her best friend Sally, who oversaw a dozen A&P stores.

"So, you're with Armour," he said to me when we met. "I tell you what, let me know when you are calling on one of my stores with a new promotion, and I will call the manager to tee it up for you."

When I introduced myself to the A&P store managers, they would say, "Yes, my supervisor told me you were coming." Working through the supervisor was huge because I got my displays into twelve stores at a time. My boss was ecstatic. "Nobody has ever done that before! How did you do it?" Sometimes, it's all about who you know.

Through trial and error with countless stores and managers, I learned that working smart also means following the "three strikes" rule: if someone tells you "no," go to someone else higher up the organization chart to try to get a "yes." Keep trying until you hear "no" three times, and only then move on to another prospect. And working smart means doing your homework on your prospects before you meet with them. With the proper due diligence, you won't get to strike three very often.

'WHAT DO YOU MEAN YOU CAUGHT THE PIG?'

By working hard and working smart, I earned a promotion about a year later to run the field office in Johnstown, PA. We moved away from home for the first time and bought a nice little house on the top of a hill in the Westmont neighborhood. Johnstown is just a big hole in the ground, which is why it always floods, but the folks were friendly. My next-door neighbor, Jimmy, managed the local grocery store, and within six months, I had Dial soap at eye level.

Jimmy invited me to the annual Grocery Managers' Picnic, where managers from all over western Pennsylvania came to a local farm for a barbecue, and a greased pig contest. They would coat a pig in grease, and a hundred or so grocery managers in teams of two chased after it. The team that holds onto the pig wins and has bragging rights for the year, which Jimmy explained was a big deal; the winners made the front page of the newspaper.

Jimmy tells me, "Look, Kells, watch your drinking because we can snag this freaking pig if we work together. The other guys are all going to be sloshed out of their minds, so we'll let them fall over themselves. The pig will come squiggling out, you chase it towards me, and I'll catch it. I know how to do it."

They let the pig go and sure enough, all the other guys are crocked, chasing the pig around and puking their guts out. They dive on top of the pig and it squirts right out of their hands. Jimmy and I hung back, and everyone else is pooped out after about fifteen minutes. Then I steer the pig towards Jimmy. *What's his secret method?* He squats low to the ground, waits until the pig is a step past him, then snags its hind legs. Got him! *Now that's working smart!*

After dark, we hit the road for the traditional barhop

with the pig—ten bars in all. We crated the pig and sat him right up on the bars with us. Free drinks for the house! People came up to pet the pig and congratulate us. We were the toast of the town, and you can imagine what kind of shape we were in leaving the tenth bar.

We're driving home at three in the morning, the pig is oinking and grunting in the back seat, and it dawns on me, "Jimmy, what are we going to do with this pig?"

"I have an idea," he said. "My wife's family has a farm up in Dubois. She and Janet can take it up there tomorrow, and we can roast it for Thanksgiving dinner."

"Sounds delicious!" I agreed.

When I got home, I was still so excited, I could not help myself. I lugged the pig into the bedroom. I don't know whether it was the oinking or the smell that woke Janet up, but I boasted, "Janet, we caught the pig!"

"What do you mean you caught the pig?"

"We caught the pig, the greased pig—we're heroes."

"You are not a hero with me, waking me up at three in the morning. You are no hero."

The next morning, after some coffee and hearing the whole story, she calmed down and thought the whole thing was funny.

We loaded the crate into the trunk of the car, and the wives drove off to Dubois, along with the neighbor's four kids in the back seat. About an hour up the road, the kids started screaming. Janet turned around to see a big snout coming through the trunk. The pig had chewed his way out of the crate and right through to the back seat of the car. They made a U-turn, found Jimmy at the store, re-packed the pig in a stronger crate, and delivered it to the farm. We never did eat him for dinner.

That's how I built my network in Johnstown—I made

friends with one person, Jimmy, and after living there for only a year, almost everybody knew us. That proved to me how important it is to get to know people and blend in with them, even if their claim to fame is catching greased pigs.

Knowing the right person led me to my next job. In 1963, after working two years at Armour, I got a call from Al Wankmiller, a neighbor from Havertown, who worked for a family-owned engineering supply company named Eugene Dietzgen. "Look," he said, "you are getting good experience with Armour, but you don't want to get bogged down in that grocery business." I made about $6,500 a year with Armour at that point, but *five* figures, $10,000—that was big bucks. "You can come into this business," my neighbor promised, "and make some real money." Dietzgen offered me a $10,000 salary, and we packed up and moved back to Havertown.

'ALWAYS READY, ALWAYS THERE'

The same year I started with Dietzgen, the United States had expanded its involvement in the Vietnam War. With my college degree, I automatically qualified for officer's candidate school, but that required a commitment of full-time service for four years. I was married and building a career in sales, so I did not want to commit to full time. But I did not want to be drafted either, so I joined the Army National Guard. That meant a six-year commitment, but only part-time, and it gave me some choice in where I would go. I chose the Nike Missile Division.

Nike missiles were outmoded anti-aircraft defense missiles, and I figured that if the Army never used them in the war, they would never use me in the war either. Most people serving in the National Guard were like me, building careers in business, not trying to climb the ranks of the military.

I completed my basic training in Fort Jackson, South Carolina, and then served six months of active duty at Fort Bliss in El Paso, Texas. Janet came with me to El Paso. We shared an apartment with another couple, which was quite awkward at times, but saved us money. After those six months, I returned to my job at Dietzgen and served two weeks every summer in the Army Reserve.

'A TIME TO GIVE BIRTH AND A TIME TO DIE'

I was happy with my new job at Dietzgen, but that was not the most important thing to Janet or me. We wanted to start a family in the worst way. But after three years of praying for children, we began to worry that we were not able to have any. We saw a doctor about it; he gave us all the fertility tests available and assured us that nothing was medically wrong. His advice was, "Relax; it will happen." That sounded trite, but he was right, and the children started coming, one right after the other.

Frank III was born at Bryn Mawr Hospital. In those days, hospitals did not allow fathers in the delivery room. The father's job was to rush the mother to the hospital, and

Welcome, Francis X. Kelly III

then get out of the way; to sit in the waiting room or out at a bar.

I took Janet to the hospital early in the afternoon. I stayed in the waiting room for a while, did not hear anything, then found the doctor and told him I was going across the street to Paolini's for a meatball sandwich. He promised they would call me when something happened. Ten o'clock came; I had not heard anything, so I plopped down again in the waiting room. A few hours later, I had the thrill of my life when I first laid eyes on Frankie.

We left the hospital three days later—in the middle of a blizzard. I drove a 1953 stick shift Chevy that I paid $150 for, through ten inches of snow, while Janet held the baby in the front seat—no car seat, no seat belt, and no airbag. A drive that normally took 25 minutes took an hour and a half, and by the time we made it home, Frankie needed a diaper change.

"I want to help you," I offered, "let me do it."

Janet laid him down, and he kicked his little feet.

"How do you do it?"

"Undo the pin and take the diaper off."

I managed to get the diaper off, held his feet, and put my hand under his little bum. "Come on Janet, give me the diaper!" But it was too late. It felt like warm toothpaste oozing through my fingers. The first thing my precious son did to me was poop all over me. I told Janet, "I'm not cut out for this!" I'm driven to succeed—just not with this. I never changed another diaper.

Within a few months, Janet was pregnant with John. We doubly thanked the Lord for him because his birth confirmed for us that God was allowing us to have a growing family.

But in the midst of the joy of the babies, my mother died of breast cancer, which she had battled for four years. She was only 53. I remember the ambulance taking her to Bryn Mawr Hospital and thinking, *She'll never come back home.* She died in the hospital a few days later. I'm grateful that my brother Bobby, my sister JoAnn and I were there to pray with her at the end, and I'm grateful that, in the months before she died, she was well enough to hold her grandson, Frankie.

A few months after my mother died, Janet and I made our next trip to Bryn Mawr Hospital; to the maternity ward this time, where we rejoiced at the birth of our second son, John.

Making them proud

After Mom died, all Frank, Bobby and I had were each other. I think that's why we've remained so close. Frank walked me down the aisle at my wedding. Our parents instilled certain traits in us—faith, love of family, and doing the right thing, and since they weren't with us, I think that motivated us to live our lives in a way that would have made them proud if they were here.

-JoAnn Kelly Burns

'PUT BALTIMORE ON THE MAP'

I sold mountains of engineering paper and supplies for Dietzgen, and in 1967, my boss, Al Wankmiller, came to me with a proposal.

"Our company has been in business for 85 years. We are very strong in the big cities—New York, Philadelphia, and L.A.—but the one city we can't crack is Baltimore, Maryland."

Baltimore had a reputation for not accepting outsiders, which made me hesitate, but Al knew which of my buttons to push. "Why don't you go down there and be the first guy to put Baltimore on the map for us?" When he put it that way, my ego said, *I'll show them!* Al also offered me a raise to $18,000.

For a few months, I lived and worked during the week at a Holiday Inn in Baltimore while the family stayed in Havertown. My business development strategy was simple: build a network of prospects who liked to go out for dinner and drinks. That's how I got to know the manager at Westinghouse who purchased all the blueprint paper, and I convinced him to give us a trial order for our Diazo blueprint paper. That meant reams and reams because the Westinghouse engineers went through it like toilet paper. I sped home and celebrated with Janet, "This is it! We're in the money! We're going to kick butt!"

I started looking for a house in Baltimore. We wanted something in a neighborhood with plenty of young families with children and found the one we liked for $29,000 way out in the sticks—on Tregarone Road in Lutherville-Timonium. We packed up the '53 Chevy, which was falling apart by this time, drove down Route 1, and began our new life in Baltimore.

Janet and I made new friends quickly in Timonium

the same way we made friends in Havertown—through a newcomers social group. Several couples took turns hosting bridge games and dinner parties, and I fit right in—most of the men were drinkers; heavy drinkers. Our next-door neighbor, I'll call him B., relaxed with martinis every night. Our friend D. was drunk every time I saw him. Another neighbor, J. would drink an entire half-gallon of rye at every party. "How come they can drink like that and I can't?" I protested to Janet, "it's not fair!"

Not only did Janet and I get to know new people in Baltimore, but we also got to know a new maternity ward. David's birth at GBMC was quick and easy, and Bryan followed two years later, with a scare. We arrived at the GBMC delivery room around three in the afternoon. They wheeled Janet away and left me in the waiting room. Five o'clock came, eight o'clock, nine o'clock, ten, and finally, I could not stand it any longer and asked the nurse, "What is going on? How is my wife doing?"

"Wait a minute, let me check," she said, and came back a half hour later and asked me, "Have they told you yet?" I shot to my feet. "Told me what? Is everything OK?"

"Oh yes, you're the father of a baby boy!"

"That's wonderful, but when can I see him? Why didn't somebody tell me?"

She said, "Well, the doctor was supposed to tell you. Let me see if I can find the doctor."

Fifteen minutes later the doctor came in, rubbing his eyes. "Mr. Kelly," he said, "first of all, you have a beautiful, healthy son. Everything is fine. I am sorry I did not tell you sooner, but he came out feet first, and I struggled to keep him alive. We were scared to death that we would lose him altogether or damage his brain. I was exhausted and went to my office to take a nap, and the nurse just woke me up. I didn't intentionally ignore you—I was just relieved that your child did not die."

You're relieved? Once my heart started beating again, I was also relieved, and grateful that God had spared Bryan's life, and spared Janet and me from the pain of losing another child.

'This is it!'

Day after day through the mid-1960s, the newspapers reported how the Vietnam War continued to escalate, and in 1968 the Army began alerting the National Guard for active duty. With three young children, I was scared to death that I would wake up one morning and find out I was going to Vietnam.

I did not like the war, or Lyndon Johnson, and did not buy the domino theory on communist takeovers, but if they called me, I would have gone. Other kids were dying for our country.

In my mailbox one day I found a letter from the U.S. Army National Guard, and I thought, This is it. I held my breath and read, "This is to certify that you have been granted an honorable discharge for service rendered to the United States Army."

I learned later that the Army could not call me up because in those days if you had two or more children, the Army considered you a hardship case and would not activate you. Raising three young boys was not always easy, but they kept me out of Vietnam and possibly spared my life yet again.

When I am at events and they ask veterans to stand up, I stay seated. Yes, I served six years and earned an honorable discharge from the United States Army National Guard, but I think the honor should go to those who fought in Vietnam or had their lives on the line.

'IT'S NOT THE WAY I DO BUSINESS'

Al Wankmiller was my boss, but he worked out of the New York office, so I reported locally to J.P.—the one who liked to party with clients and prostitutes. When J.P. asked me in that Washington convention hotel room, "Why don't you take a turn with 'Mary' and 'Jane?'" my gut immediately told me to run out of that room as quickly as possible. *Put God first*, my father had written to me before he died. The thought of being unfaithful to Janet made me want to vomit.

"I don't want any part of this," I told him, then I bolted out of the room. J.P. chased after me hollering, "What's the matter with you? This is how we do business in Washington. This is what these guys expect. If I didn't give them what they want, I wouldn't get any business."

"It's not the way I do business," I said, and headed straight home. I called Al Wankmiller in Havertown. "Is this what you promote?" I screamed, "Is this the way you want to do business? If you want me to run Baltimore, let me run Baltimore my way." I wanted to follow the good conscience that my parents had built into me. I wanted to win business based on the quality of my product and my God-given talent, not bribes and illicit favors.

Al called J.P. and me together to his home to negotiate a compromise. I would still report to J.P., but I would be allowed to do business my way. Al told J.P. that he owed me an apology, and he did apologize, but I knew he would never change, and it didn't take long for him to prove me right.

A few days later, my phone rang, and my customer at Westinghouse gave me an earful. "What kind of crap did you send me?"

"What's wrong with it?"

"It's old paper, and I can't copy on it. Take it back."

Diazo paper has to be fresh to make proper copies; it is worthless if it is not shipped from the warehouse and used within 90 days. The shipments came from the Washington office. I called Washington and spoke with the supervisor of the warehouse. "What are you doing to me? Westinghouse has lost confidence in us."

"If you can talk them into taking one more shipment, I guarantee it will be fresh," he promised.

I persuaded Westinghouse to give me another chance, and everything ran smoothly for a couple of months, but then I received another irate call about more stale paper. "I am not doing business with you anymore!" the manager barked at me, "I can't trust your product."

J.P. was jealous that I won the Westinghouse account that he was never able to land, and afraid that I was after his job, and he sabotaged me.

I could not take it anymore. I wanted to quit and leave on my terms, rather than have J.P. eventually fire me. I drove to Washington on a Friday—I did not tell Janet what I planned to do—I marched into J.P.'s office and announced, "I quit. Here is my paper, and here is my key. I cannot work for you and I am not going to spend another day here. I can't even thank you because you did nothing to help me; I am out of here."

"Good," he said, and I stomped out.

I walked in the front door at home, and Janet asked me right away, "What's the matter? You have that look on your face."

"I just quit my job."

"Did you get severance? Did they fire you?"

"No, I was too stupid to let them fire me. I just quit."

"What will you do?" Janet asked.

I had been thinking about that on the way home.

"Well, I like this town, and I want to sink my roots here in Baltimore. I can get into real estate, or maybe insurance."

Al Wankmiller called me from Havertown and tried to talk me into staying, but it was too late; I had made up my mind.

GENESIS

Janet and I had four sons and a foster daughter, and five months of savings to last us while I searched for a new career. I took a job in direct sales for Aetna insurance during the day and took community college courses at Dundalk and Essex at night to earn my insurance and real estate licenses. I quickly realized that it was impractical to work in both fields and decided on insurance.

During the 1972 election, I had volunteered with Democrats for Nixon, where I met Harry Rodgers, the owner of Tidewater Insurance, a small brokerage firm near the airport. He offered me a job. I liked the idea of a smaller company, so I made the switch. Working at Tidewater, I realized that I preferred to be a broker who represented the client over being an agent who represented the insurance company. That realization, and two more people God put in my path, set the course for my future.

The first of those people was Jim Dunbar, who owned Federal Armored Express. Jim told me that he had a nice business going, but his top competitor, Purolator, had protection from the state Public Service Commission that gave Purolator a monopoly on serving the banks in Baltimore City and a 35-mile radius around the city. That protection made it difficult for Dunbar to grow his business.

Jim and I got to know each other well, and as we talked more about his business predicament, I suggested to him,

"Maybe I can help you. I know some legislators in Annapolis." Jim offered me a $30,000 salary for the job of breaking the armored car monopoly in Maryland. I accepted his offer and left my job at Tidewater. Jim gave me an office on Grundy Street in Highlandtown, and other than getting together for lunch, he left me alone to work on changing the law.

I approached John Coolahan, known as "The Lion of Halethorpe" and an honest State Senator. "John, how would

The Sixties

The sixties was a turbulent decade, but I was too busy raising our kids, establishing my career, traveling, and concentrating on surviving to think too much about hippies and social revolution. I was happy drinking Manhattans and Martinis, but I was afraid of smoking pot, popping LSD, or taking other drugs, and I did not hang out with people who did. I knew what alcohol would do to me, but I was afraid of the harder drugs. They are more dangerous, and illegal.

The Women's Liberation Movement grew in the sixties also. Janet has always been conservative and did not get involved. Me? I guess they would have called me a male chauvinist.

I did not personally witness racial prejudice, but I was aware of how unjustly we treated blacks in our country and admired Martin Luther King Jr.'s nonviolent approach to addressing the problem. I was not involved in politics in the sixties, but I supported civil rights.

Looking back, I see how the Vietnam War festered revolutionary responses to the government when in the past, very few people questioned their government. Our morals started breaking down, definitions of right and wrong became looser and looser, and our national character eroded to the point of devaluing life itself, which culminated within the next ten years with Roe v. Wade. Many insidious attitudes and behaviors rose up in the sixties, and we are paying the consequences even today.

you like to introduce a bill to break up a monopoly?" I asked. He liked the idea because even the Maryland Constitution calls monopolies "odious." He introduced a bill that terminated the state's treatment of Purolator as the sole carrier for Baltimore area banks, and it passed. From then on, Jim Dunbar wrote business like crazy, changed the company name to Dunbar Armored, and grew into the fourth largest armored carrier in the country.

The second person God sent across my path in this transition time was Jim Gede, a lawyer for the Licensed Beverage Association of Baltimore County who I met at a Democrats for Nixon function. He told me that none of the taverns or restaurants could obtain health insurance for their employees because they were too small, and the employee turnover was too high, and asked for my advice. I only worked on property and casualty insurance in my days at Tidewater, but I told Jim I would think about his problem.

I talked to my former Tidewater colleague, Gary Chick, about Jim's question. Gary had been in the insurance business for 25 years and understood the technical aspects of insurance better than anyone I knew. He said, "You know, Frank, if you can get that association to endorse us, I know someone at BlueCross, Sam Costa, and they might be willing to write a health insurance plan for all of their members combined. I will set up a luncheon."

Gary called Sam and me to schedule our meeting. At that luncheon, the three of us planted the seed that would become Francis X. Kelly Associates, Inc. I was ready to step out and seek the kind of work environment where I could maximize my talents and operate by God's kingdom values. It was a step that changed the trajectory of my career, but my next twelve steps changed my entire life.

6

Worries into Prayers

"I say to you, do not be worried about your life, as to what you will eat or what you will drink; nor for your body, as to what you will put on. Is not life more than food, and the body more than clothing? Look at the birds of the air, that they do not sow, nor reap nor gather into barns, and yet your heavenly Father feeds them. Are you not worth much more than they? And who of you by being worried can add a single hour to his life?"
Matthew 6:25-27

GOD GRANT ME THE SERENITY TO ACCEPT
THE THINGS I CANNOT CHANGE

I had my first drink when I was 16 years old—a 7 & 7. *Wow, what a nice buzz,* and soothing sense of well-being. I did not drink much more until my college years. My schedule of classes all day and working all evening made for long, hard weeks, so I partied on Friday and Saturday nights to reward myself with some fun and relieve the stress and strain. Alcohol seemed to make me feel better and enhance my already happy nature.

When I started working in sales, I did what my dad did. My clients who drank, I took out to lunch so I could drink with them at lunch, or met them after work at a bar so I could tell Janet I would be out late doing business. Clients who did not drink, I met them at their office.

For years, I left home most weeks on Monday and returned on Friday. I was out on the road alone, which made drinking more tempting and easier to hide. I hated staring at hotel room walls, so I sat in the bars and restaurants and made friends with fellow travelers over drinks.

Yes, I had heard that "the sins of the fathers are visited on the children," but I swore to myself that I would never let it happen to me, that I would never let alcohol rob me the way it robbed my father. I kept it in check when I had to. I did not ruin holidays and vacations the way my father did. None of my friends or co-workers thought I had an alcohol problem. My brother and sister did not think I had an alcohol problem.

But I knew something was wrong with me. I did not like who I was, and I felt a fear of the future that had never haunted me before, which drove me to drink even more to get relief from reality.

I would tell my doctors what I was feeling, and they would say, "Oh, you have four kids, you're in sales, you're under a lot of pressure, take some Valium like everybody else." But something inside of me warned, *Don't do it!* I was scared, and I begged God to show me what was wrong with me. Finally, another doctor told me the hard truth, "I think you might have an alcohol problem. Go to Alcoholics Anonymous and deal with it."

THE COURAGE TO CHANGE THE THINGS I CAN

I was open; I was looking for the truth about myself. I read everything I could about alcoholism to find out how bad my problem was.

Counting my drinks each day, 1970

The most helpful book for me was Marty Mann's *A New Primer on Alcoholism.* Mann recommends keeping track of the number of drinks you take for 90 consecutive days. According to Mann, you must have at least one drink a day, but not more than three on any given day, for 90 consecutive days. The principle is, if a person can't stop at three drinks every day for 90 days in a row, they're most likely an alcoholic.

I failed miserably. I started counting in April of 1970 and kept track in a little notepad. There were many days that I drank nothing at all, and there were many days I had just a couple of beers. But there were weddings, dinner parties, golf outings, Thanksgiving Days and New Year's Eves when I had 6, 8, 10, up to 15 drinks in a single day.

That convinced me to take the first step of Alcoholics Anonymous: to admit that I was powerless over alcohol and that my life had become unmanageable.

I walked into my first AA meeting, a dark and smoky basement of an old house in Towson that has since been torn down. It was suffocating. I asked Janet to come with me, and she came along to support me. The group consisted mostly of 50- to 60-year-old men, most of whom were in hardcore, desperate situations: some suicidal, some falling-down drunks, some who had lost their jobs or had DWIs. I had trouble identifying with them, and wondered, *could I help any of them? Could any of them help somebody like me?*

One of the AA meeting rules is that no one is forced to say anything if they do not want to. The Chairman will go around the room and ask if you want to share anything, but he will not embarrass you, and you can pass. For once in my life, I sat in a group and did not say a word. After about three meetings like that, I thought, *this is not for me*, and quit going. I tried to dry out on my own, but after beating the air for about a year, I was exhausted from trying and failing, and sick and tired of being sick and tired. I might have given up if not for a friend's wise encouragement, "Why don't you go back to AA? That's where you belong."

I returned with my mind more open to listening to the others in the group and believing we could help each other. AA tells members: if you don't like what you hear one night, keep coming back, and sooner or later, you will hear your story, connect with someone, and help each other get sober.

Eventually, I met Bob C., who was a successful lawyer, had a family, and suffered no overwhelming issues other than not liking the way he felt. He shared openly about his problems and mistakes, what he was doing to overcome them, and the failures and successes he was experiencing along the way. I talked with him after meetings, and we became friends. We would go to Howard Johnson after meetings to talk more about how we were feeling and how we were dealing with our problems. We always picked Howard Johnsons or another diner for our sugar fix! I had never realized how much sugar is in alcohol, and, therefore, how much sugar we craved to replace. We loaded up on ice cream sundaes and milkshakes and chased them down with coffee.

IF I SURRENDER TO YOUR WILL

The second step of AA is to believe that a power greater than yourself can restore you to sanity, and the third is to turn your will and your life over to God. I felt God's gentle hand on my shoulder. I realized that whatever was wrong, I had to empty the alcohol out of my system. I could not rely on crutches that were not of God. The answer would come in seeking God, and He would reveal Himself to me somehow.

The fourth step is to take "a searching and fearless moral inventory" of yourself. I felt like I was going to confession. The process is to write down your inventory, share it with someone else, then rip it up and throw it away. You discard the negative memories and start replacing them with positive memories. Then you go to the people you have hurt and offended to ask forgiveness and make amends.

Janet never gave me an ultimatum but supported me every step of the way. My AA friend introduced Janet and me to other couples like us who had little homes in the suburbs and were not in grave trouble, but just needed help fighting their alcoholism. I started spending more evenings with them than with my drinking clients and drinking buddies.

'Everybody's situation is different'

When I met Frank in college, I did not think too much about him drinking beer. But when he started working and coming home at three in the morning from Washington after a night at the bars, I worried. He played the game of, "I just could not leave, I could not leave," and I would say, "Frank, if someone ties you up on a bar stool and won't let you leave, you should call the police."

Frank's friend, Terry Flynn, was also a salesman covering Washington, DC, and they would meet down there and introduce each other to their clients. Then Terry would follow Frank back to Baltimore, spend the night, and leave the next morning to go home to Philadelphia.

One night they stumbled in at 3 AM. I had all these kids and Frank didn't come home, and I scolded him. "Where have you been? You made me a wreck; I was so scared!"

Terry mumbled, "Excuse me, but I will just go down to my bedroom."

I swung around, pointed my finger and ordered him, "Don't you move an inch!"

Frank was always remorseful: "I'm sorry. I didn't know what time it was. It got away from us."

I knew that Frank should stop drinking, but I did not badger him. I encouraged him, "You will be fine," because he began feeling nervous and anxious, trying to decide what he should do about his drinking. He quit smoking to prove he had discipline. I felt that he would figure it out. I am not saying this is the right approach in every case, because everybody's situation is different, but it was right for me. Frank was not a boastful or an abusive drunk, he was a frightened drunk, which is something completely different. He needed to come to grips with his fears, and that took time. If I had been in an abusive situation, there would have been ultimatums, and I might have had to leave.

-Janet Kelly

LIVING ONE DAY AT A TIME

One night a big, older steelworker from Dundalk stood and spoke. What I remember most about him was that he was full of joy. He said, "All you people out there, I can promise you, that if you stay away from alcohol one day at a time, one drink at a time, and work the twelve steps, I can promise that you will feel peace and joy, you will no longer be afraid, you will no longer have anxiety or depression..." He went on quoting all the promises from *The Big Book of Alcoholics Anonymous.*

It hit me, "That's what I want." I went home and re-read the promises.

AA promises that if you thoroughly follow their path, stay away from alcohol one day at a time, turn your life over to God—a higher power—and keep coming back to meetings, you will find the peace and joy you are seeking without alcohol.

Those promises are absolute truth. AA kept its promises to me.

I have not had a drink since January 10, 1971.

I believe AA is the finest program of our time. So many people are plagued by addictions they cannot control—it can be sex, it can be gambling, it can be alcohol or drugs. Anyone who works the twelve steps can find hope and release. The principles of AA are all biblical principles, they are the principles I have lived my life by, and they work.

If someone had told me when I was drinking that I would feel better if I stopped drinking, I would have told them they were out of their mind. Now, I am the one telling other people they will feel better not drinking. The twelfth step is to carry the message to other alcoholics. If someone calls me or comes up to me and asks for help, I simply tell them my story. I tell them about the problems I have had, what I did to get out from under them, and what my life is like now. If they can relate to what happened to me, then we can help each other.

Churches have invited me to come and speak. *The Baltimore Sun* interviewed me for articles on alcoholism. I had people in the Senate come to me. You never know who is watching. I once met a man at a social function who opened up to me about his addiction. I offered to meet with him to talk about it, but he surprised me with, "You have already helped me; you don't even know."

I wrote this addendum of praise to Jesus and Janet in my drink-count notepad 33 years after taking my last drink.

"What do you mean?" I asked.

"I have admired you from afar," he said.

I had no idea that he even knew who I was.

I have to help others if I can, because their lives could be at stake. Five of my drinking buddies from the Timonium newcomers group were all dead within six years after I took my last drink, all from alcohol-related causes. As I got the news about each one, I reflected on my parents' decision not to abort me, and how I switched into Joe's car before Tommy crashed into the tree back when I was a teenager. Had God spared my life again, three times now within three decades?

How could I not let Him use me as He saw fit?

I pray that God has used me to break the cycle of alcoholism in the Kelly family. I love my sons, and I thank God that I was able to quit drinking before any of them understood what I was doing or actually saw me take a drink. The boys had their drinking sprees when they were young—wild fraternities, parties, and some stupid antics—but as adults, they all watch themselves closely and have never had problems with alcohol. For my sons and grandchildren, I pray that they will keep God first in their lives, and recognize that alcohol is a potential killer, always lurking, especially for the Kellys.

The Promises of AA

If we are painstaking about this phase of our development, we will be amazed before we are half way through. We are going to know a new freedom and a new happiness. We will not regret the past nor wish to shut the door on it. We will comprehend the word serenity and we will know peace. No matter how far down the scale we have gone, we will see how our experience can benefit others. That feeling of uselessness and self-pity will disappear. We will lose interest in selfish things and gain interest in our fellows. Self-seeking will slip away. Our whole attitude and outlook upon life will change. Fear of people and economic insecurity will leave us. We will intuitively know how to handle situations which used to baffle us. We will suddenly realize that God is doing for us what we could not do for ourselves. Are these extravagant promises? We think not. They are being fulfilled among us—sometimes quickly, sometimes slowly. They will always materialize if we work for them.

-The Big Book of Alcoholics Anonymous, Chapter 6

ACCEPTING HARDSHIP AS A PATHWAY TO PEACE

Years of dependence on alcohol took a physical, emotional and spiritual toll on me, and I did not recover overnight. Getting sober solved one problem, but exposed the deeper, root cause of the panic and fear that, without the numbing of alcohol, bore down on me like a Mack truck. I drew closer to God through AA, but after so many years of living under the lie of alcohol, I struggled to walk by faith every day. But God had a plan to help me with my spiritual recovery also.

The Catholic charismatic renewal was spreading in the mid-1970s, and a friend invited me to a prayer meeting at St. Joseph's Church in Cockeysville. I mentioned it to Janet. "There's a prayer meeting up at church and I heard it is really good, do you want to go?" Always there to support me, she went with me.

It was standing room only in a meeting room overflowing with a spirit of joy we had never witnessed before. The music was beautiful. Everyone was singing and raising their hands in praise and worship. *What is going on in here?*

Janet saw a woman she knew who had just lost a child, but there she stood, praising God and rejoicing in Him. Those people had something we didn't have, and we wanted it.

We kept going back and signed up for a course on life in the Holy Spirit at St. Thomas More Church. The class introduced me to the Scriptures, and the baptism, filling, and the gifts of the Holy Spirit. I learned that God so loved the world that he sent his son, who lived in our world, was crucified, died, was buried, and rose from the dead, and that I could have a personal relationship with Jesus Christ.

After the class on the baptism of the Holy Spirit, Janet and I walked up to the teachers, dropped to our knees and accepted Jesus Christ as our personal Lord and Savior. The teachers prayed over us, we asked God to fill us with the Holy Spirit, and immediately felt God's hand upon us. That was the most important decision of our lives; everything else is immaterial by comparison.

And to think, we almost didn't go to class that night. We couldn't find a babysitter, and Janet was nervous about leaving the boys home alone with Frankie in charge, but I told her, "They'll be fine. Let's go."

When we got home, the boys were in bed and the house was calm, dark, and quiet.

"See, Janet? I told you everything would be all right."

But we noticed that the kitchen was really warm. Then I walked down into the family room and, *What the?* I blurted as my hand sprang to my head to wipe off a drop of water—a drop of the brown, stinky water that was streaming down from the ceiling. I ran up to the bathroom, which looked like a bombed-out sewer: a puddle of poop on the floor and chunks of it on the walls, wads of wet toilet paper stuck to the ceiling, the towel rack lying on the floor in a pile of broken plaster, and two holes where the rack had been ripped off the wall.

"See Frank," Janet yelled, "I told you we can't leave them alone!"

I was fuming, but I cleaned up and we went to bed. But when I rolled over in the middle of the night, *BOOM!!* the bed collapsed.

"BOOOYYYYS!!!" I screamed.

They had made pizza for dinner but never turned the oven off, leaving a sweltering kitchen and an oven full of ashes. They had seen a spider on the bathroom ceiling and bombarded it with wads of wet toilet paper, which stuck on the ceiling. When they climbed up on the towel rack to reach the ceiling and pull off the wads of toilet paper, the rack and the plaster tore off the wall.

It got worse. They flushed an apple core down the toilet, then when they used the toilet for what it's really made for, it overflowed, and a poop-flinging fight broke out. They picked up chunks of it with their bare hands and threw it at each other, but most of it stuck to the walls and ceiling. The fight moved into our bedroom where they jumped on the bed and busted one of the bed legs. They propped up the bed with a few volumes of the World Book Encyclopedia, covered it over with the bedspread, and hoped we wouldn't notice.

Patience is a fruit of the Spirit, and here was our first test, but we lost our cool—not the kind of response to trials that we had learned about in class a few hours earlier. Our heated response confirmed that we had a lot to learn about walking in the Spirit day by day. Looking back, I see the incident as a symbolic confirmation that our renewed faith was real—the devil didn't like that we asked Christ and the Holy Spirit to come into our lives, so he threw all his crap at us when we got home.

TRUSTING THAT YOU WILL MAKE ALL THINGS RIGHT

Janet and I continued in Bible study at St. Thomas More, where one of our favorite teachers was Stelman Smith, a Baltimore City policeman, ordained minister, and Chaplain of the Fraternal Order of Police. Stelman helped me deal with the waves of fear, depression and panic attacks that were stronger than I had ever experienced before. Anxiety seemed to be tightening its grip on me. I no longer escaped with alcohol, and I was scared.

One morning, I woke up so fearful and depressed, I

Stelman saw that sobriety was not the whole solution to my problem.

couldn't go to work. I never missed work, so this was hitting bottom for me. Janet called Stelman, who came to the house right away. Stelman had the insight to see that sobriety alone was not the sole solution to my problems, because my problems were not solely physical, but also spiritual—*For our struggle is not against flesh and blood, but against the rulers, against the powers, against the world forces of this darkness, against the spiritual forces of wickedness in the heavenly places* (Ephesians 6:12).

Stelman explained that when Jesus rose from the dead, he defeated the world, the flesh, and the devil, and not only in the universal sense but also for me, personally. Since God already defeated Satan, I could have victory through Jesus Christ. That was a revelation to me; it boggled my mind to realize I could be free of these demons through Jesus Christ when I submit my will to His, trust and rely on Him, and pray for wisdom. Stelman talked with me and prayed that God would deliver me from the forces attacking me. As I prayed with him, I felt the spirits of fear and depression leave me.

The answer to fear is faith, prayer, submission to God, and accountability. These are the daily requirements for a victorious life. Stelman and I prayed together for nearly 30 years, through all my ups and downs at home, in the business, and through all the Senate debates and votes. Few people knew Stelman, who was such a humble man, but he had more influence on my spiritual life than anybody besides Janet. Through prayer with Stelman, God set me free from fear and anxiety, and I believe God broke the bondage or curse of alcohol that had plagued generations of Kellys.

AND BE SUPREMELY HAPPY WITH YOU FOREVER

Janet and I continued to grow in our faith through wonderful fellowship in a variety of churches and groups through the 1970s. One of the first was the Lamb of God community, a large fellowship that met for prayer, teaching, and community service. We attended their retreats in Atlantic City with thousands of others who were on the same journey, grew close to a small group of couples at St. Joseph's Church—the Donohues, the Lynches, and the Ibellos—and set out to strengthen each other's faith and ignite our church with the Spirit.

Our kids were wondering, *what is going on with Mom and Dad, going off to prayer meetings?* We always went to church as a family, and the kids continued to go as teenagers, but Janet and I started sharing the Scriptures with them and praying with them. I specifically prayed with each one as they went off to college, and we prayed with them over the phone while they were away at college. In some way, it made a difference. Yes, they sowed their wild oats and they did their things. But they learned through various trials and experiences that they could not cut it on their own, and one by one, they came to the Lord. Their faith has strengthened, and now I see them sharing their faith, giving back to the community, loving their wives, and loving their children. If there is one message I have for my grandchildren, it is to put your faith in God through his Son, Jesus Christ.

In the 1980s, Janet and I attended Grace Fellowship. I loved the teaching there, and we were involved in their small group house churches. A business friend, Jim Morgan, who also attended Grace Fellowship and was seeking something more in his life, asked me to start a Bible study. "I think that's a good idea, Jim, but I need to pray about it."

That caught Jim by surprise. "I never heard of doing something like that," he said. "Pray about it? Why would you pray about it? Either you do it or you don't." He laughs about it now, but he came to faith through that Bible study.

Nick Tsakalos, of H&S Bakery, was in the same group. When he died, his three sons came up to Janet and me at the viewing and told us, "That little circle was so wonderful for our father. He found Jesus in your group." Nick never said much in our Bible studies, so we had no idea.

Now, I feel that the Spirit is alive at the Church of the Nativity, led by Father Michael White. Their fresh approach to worship, teaching, and fellowship appeals to people like me who always considered themselves Catholics but grew a little tired of the Catholic Church and had not always been fed there in the past. Nativity is the kind of church Janet and I have been looking for since back in the 1970s.

I look back at my parents, Janet, AA, and the churches, prayer groups, and mentors that have helped me. They are all gifts from God that I did not earn or deserve. He took me through a great deal of pain so that I can use the gifts He has given me and the lessons He has taught me to help others. I am far from perfect, but I believe that my role is to set the best example I can with the way I live my life.

I might still get anxious about certain things, but they do not consume me anymore. That is what happens when you truly surrender—when you say, "OK God, this is in your hands, and I am not going to worry about the outcome."

The Serenity Prayer
Karl Paul Reinhold Niebuhr

GOD, grant me the serenity to accept the things
I cannot change, courage to change the
things I can, and the wisdom to know the difference.

Living one day at a time; enjoying one moment at a time;
Accepting hardship as the pathway to peace.

Taking, as He did, this sinful world as it is,
not as I would have it.

Trusting that He will make all things right if I
surrender to His Will;

That I may be reasonably happy in this life, and supremely
happy with Him forever in the next.

Amen

THE TWELVE STEPS OF ALCOHOLICS ANONYMOUS

1. We admitted we were powerless over alcohol—that our lives had become unmanageable.

2. Came to believe that a Power greater than ourselves could restore us to sanity.

3. Made a decision to turn our will and our lives over to the care of God as we understood Him.

4. Made a searching and fearless moral inventory of ourselves.

5. Admitted to God, to ourselves, and to another human being the exact nature of our wrongs.

6. Were entirely ready to have God remove all these defects of character.

7. Humbly asked Him to remove our shortcomings.

8. Made a list of all persons we had harmed, and became willing to make amends to them all.

9. Made direct amends to such people wherever possible, except when to do so would injure them or others.

10. Continued to take personal inventory and when we were wrong promptly admitted it.

11. Sought through prayer and meditation to improve our conscious contact with God, as we understood Him, praying only for knowledge of His will for us and the power to carry that out.

12. Having had a spiritual awakening as the result of these Steps, we tried to carry this message to alcoholics, and to practice these principles in all our affairs.

7

Secret Sauce

*Trust in the Lord with all your heart and do not lean on
your own understanding. In all your ways acknowledge
Him, and He will make your paths straight.*
Proverbs 3:5-6

The business model was very simple. Gary Chick, my colleague from Tidewater Insurance, and I pitched our idea for writing one group insurance policy for all the restaurants

My partner, Gary Chick, in 1976

and taverns in the Licensed Beverage Association over lunch to Sam Costa from BlueCross. Sam paused, thought about it, and then proposed, "If you can get 100 people in a group and the association endorses you to run the insurance through them, BlueCross can write a group policy and save everyone a lot of money."

Most small businesses, including local restaurants

and taverns, faced the same problem: not many brokers sold health insurance, and none wrote health insurance policies for them. But if Gary and I could combine dozens of small businesses through their trade association, each individual business could get the same health insurance benefits as a larger company. This was a way we could create a business by helping existing businesses, and how I could sink roots into the community and earn a living at the same time.

I was still employed at Federal Armored Express while Gary and I worked on the Licensed Beverage Association deal. I had more than earned my $35,000 salary by opening the Baltimore market for Jim Dunbar, and though my lobbying work was winding down, I could have moved into the Sales Manager position. But Jim and I had different ways of doing business, and I thought I could do better following my own vision. Should I stay, or should I go? Two big questions remained: would the Association buy into the group insurance policy concept, and was there enough money in it for me to make the break from Federal Armored Express? While I waited for the final answers, I prepared for "go" by officially incorporating Francis X. Kelly Associates, Inc.

When I approached the Licensed Beverage Association with the group policy idea, they agreed to endorse me to negotiate a deal for them. What a sense of humor God has! Here I was, a recovering alcoholic who quit drinking six years before, knocking on every tavern door in the county. I pooled together 150 people from 50 taverns and restaurants, negotiated rates for a group health insurance plan, and added 10 percent to cover our fees and administrative expenses. The tavern and restaurant employees had access to affordable health care coverage never before available to them, and Janet, Gary and I had revenue of $2,200 a month coming in. That was hardly enough to support two families, and 1975 was not exactly a boom time for business startups in Maryland. This was 20 years before the dot-com explosion, the rate of new business startups was on a downward trend, and the unemployment rate was close to 7%, but we believed we had found a niche with lucrative upside potential. Gary kept his full-time job for the time being, but I resigned from Federal Armored Express, and Janet and I set up an office in the spare bedroom and started building a business.

TURNING IT OVER TO GOD

The crucial question was, how do we pay the bills until the business gets off the ground? God often provides in ways we cannot even imagine. I told my AA friend, Bob C. the lawyer, about my new venture and cash flow problem over milkshakes at Howard Johnson after an AA meeting one night. "If you need money," he said, "I'll invest in your business. How much do you need?"

"I don't know," I said, "I have nothing right now."

"How about $100,000?" he offered.

"Wow, that's a lot of money," I said.

"You can find a nice office in Towson. If people see that you look successful, you'll be successful. I would be happy to invest in you."

"This is amazing Bob, I really appreciate it!"

I hurried home to tell Janet. She had some reservations about Bob and was not completely in favor, but we were desperate; *What other choice do we have?*

I called Bob. "I'd like to take you up on your offer. How about we meet tomorrow morning for breakfast at Howard Johnson's?"

I left the house the next morning, excited about picking up a check for $100,000. But as I sat there with Bob, an alarm sounded in my gut; a wave of doubt came over me, and I could not shake it off. I felt it was the Lord telling me, *No. I don't want you to do this. I don't want you to start your business beholden to somebody else. Once Bob puts the money in, he is going to own you. You can't serve Me if you're serving him.*

I started to panic. *Bob's sitting right in front of me, ready to give me the money; how do I handle this?*

I took a deep breath. "Bob, I think I'm going to delay taking your investment. I'm going to try to start this on my own."

He seemed confused because he knew how desperately I needed the money. "I guess I understand…you're an Irishman like me, and we always like to try things on our own."

"I'm grateful you're willing to do this, but I want to take a run at it myself."

"Well, you've made your decision," he said.

I had to go home and explain to Janet.

"Janet, you won't believe this."

"What happened?" she asked.

I explained how I felt about this pang in my gut, and I felt it was the Lord telling me not to take the money, not to become unequally yoked. She understood completely; it was the right decision. But we were both thinking the same thing: *What are we going to do now? We only have a little money in the bank, so how are we going to fund the business and feed the kids for the next two weeks?*

That is when we knelt down at the foot of our bed and surrendered our business to God in prayer. *Lord, we know You want us to start this business, so we are going to trust in You. We commit to turn the business over to You every day, and then give it our best effort. We ask for Your protection, Your wisdom, and Your help.*

Next, I had to call Gary and tell him we still had no money.

We watched $100,000 come and go in a flash, but Janet and I both knew in our hearts that we had made the right choice. It was a tempting but worldly solution. We felt that God was telling us to follow His leading, not the world's. We decided we would eat hot dogs and take a second mortgage on the house. Gary negotiated $10,000 in advance commissions from a life insurance company. My good friend, Charlie Cawley, then running the credit card division at Maryland National Bank, gave me a $10,000 line of credit on my MasterCard, and Gary's mother-in-law, Mrs. Khlor, lent us $10,000. How's that for a capitalization plan?

'GOD WILL TAKE CARE OF THE KELLYS'

God was indeed faithful. We signed up the Greater Washington Service Station and Automotive Repair Association, which brought our revenue up to $7,000 a month. My job was to collect all the applications and premium payments from the gas stations, and BlueCross sent one large invoice to us each month.

We moved the office to the basement, where Janet managed installations, enrollment, and billing, plus ran the "service center." A customer would call, and she would answer the phone, "Good morning, Kelly Associates, how can I help you?"

"I have a question about our bill."

"I'll transfer you to the billing department. Please hold."

Janet would put the call on hold, take some laundry out of the washing machine and put it in the dryer, walk over to the other desk where she kept the bills, and pick up the extension.

"Billing department. How can I help you?"

It wasn't like we had regular callers who recognized her voice, so nobody ever caught on.

I made what seemed like a million sales calls, and we gained momentum, one group at a time. We still ate plenty of hot dog casseroles but made enough to cover expenses. For me, who didn't know any association people in Maryland before I started calling them, it was a miracle. Pooling was our secret sauce. We could put together insurance plans that nobody else could match. Within another year, enough revenue was coming in for Gary to quit his job and for him and his wife, Betty to join us officially as partners. We then traded as Kelly-Chick & Associates, Inc.

I felt God's hand on Janet and me. I believed He gave us the business to glorify Him. He blessed me as I conducted business the way I had always wanted: building relationships, dealing honestly with people, and not going for the quick buck or taking shortcuts.

Mrs. Khlor was such a sweet lady that she would only let us pay her back $100 a month. We could have repaid the entire loan much quicker, but she liked having $100 a month coming in.

Charlie Cawley was a different story. He kept a close eye on our cash flow and our payments. He was pleased as he watched our revenues grow so rapidly and wanted to help us with more loans. One day he called me into the bank to meet with him and Raymond Nichols, a VP in consumer lending with a reputation as a marketing guru.

"OK, Frank, explain to Ray what you're doing."

I explained the concept of pooling small businesses through endorsements from their trade associations so they could get health insurance and we could earn administrative fees.

"Why are you operating out of your house?" Nichols asked.

"Because I can't afford to operate anywhere else."

"You should have a nice office in Towson, with wood paneling and gold letters on the door. To be successful, you have to look successful."

It was the same line I heard from Bob C. "Raymond, I don't have the money to do that," I told him.

"We'll figure out how to lend it to you."

"No," I said, "I don't want to go into any more debt. I want to grow my way into a Towson office…if I decide that's what I want."

Nichols kept trying to convince me, and I kept turning him down. He turned to Charlie and said, "This stubborn SOB isn't listening to me. I'm not going to bother trying to help him anymore."

Charlie growled at me. "I brought you in here so Raymond could give you advice. You've got to listen to him."

"Listen, Charlie and Raymond," I said, "I appreciate the line of credit—I couldn't run the business without it—and I appreciate your advice. I understand what you're telling me, but it's not your money, and I don't want to go deeper in debt. Don't worry about me, OK? God will take care of the Kellys." That ended the meeting.

Later that night, Charlie called me at home around 8 PM. "Don't you ever, ever mention God in a business meeting again, or you will be doomed to failure."

I was silent as I gathered my thoughts, then I answered, "Don't you ever, ever, ever tell me when or where I can mention God. My relationship with God is important to me, and I trust in Him."

Click. I hung up. I was a little worried since he was my friend and the one who approved my line of credit.

Around 11:30, the phone rang again. "That's Charlie," Janet said, "I knew he would call you back."

I picked up the phone, and sure enough, it was him. "All right," he said. "I get it. God will take care of the Kellys. I'm fine."

As the months passed, the business continued to grow, and Charlie watched our cash flows and profits increase. He would call me to say, "I guess God takes care of the Kellys!" After three more years of growth, Charlie told me he showed my numbers to Raymond Nichols. "All I can say," Nichols told Charlie, "is that God takes care of the Kellys."

God takes care of the Cawleys too. After Charlie helped found MBNA, he went down to the alumni association at his alma mater, Georgetown University, and pitched them the idea of sponsoring a credit card branded specially for their members. What I called "pooling" became known as "affinity marketing" and helped MBNA grow into a $120 billion credit card company.

From Havertown to the Adriatic Sea

From the Havertown days when we'd pool our money for a meatball hoagie or a pizza, to an elegant dinner while cruising the Adriatic Sea, we've loved your enthusiasm, energy, optimism, loyalty, faith, and love for your friends and family. "God takes care of the Kellys," and all of us who love them.

-Julie and Charlie Cawley
From their letter commemorating Frank's 70th birthday

MOVIN' ON UP

We continued to expand our markets and add clients. We worked with Von Paris Moving and Storage, which had nearly a hundred employees covered on their plan at the time. That gave us a track record of success with a

Out of the basement and into the attic at 10635 York Road

larger employer and gave us credibility with other large organizations, such as The Maryland Motor Truck Association. When they endorsed us to renegotiate and market their existing plans they had about 350 members, then grew to over 1,100. That account put us over the top financially.

In 1979, we moved our headquarters out of the Kelly family basement up to the attic of 10635 York Road in Hunt Valley. Soon after, the Maryland Veterinary Medical Association signed on with us, and we could afford to upgrade Janet's typewriter and carbon paper with our first computer, a Wang mini-mainframe.

We made a bold move in 1981 when we purchased our first office building—really a small house at 1 Shawan Road. Suddenly we had higher overhead but could work more efficiently in the larger space.

Our first building at 1 Shawan Road

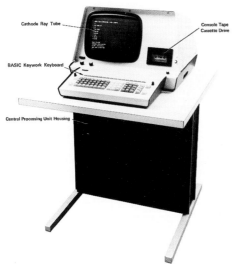

Cathode Ray Tube

Console Tape Cassette Drive

BASIC Keywork Keyboard

Central Processing Unit Housing

Our first computer

We added another product line, Kelly-Chick Property & Casualty, which helped us diversify and cross-sell to our existing clients. Best of all, Frank III, John, David, and Bryan, while still in high school and college, passed their insurance licensing exams and began working part-time as telemarketers.

All this while Gary and Janet managed the day-to-day operations and I split my time between Baltimore and Annapolis because, in 1978, two years after launching the business, I made my second run for a seat in the Maryland State Senate.

'Shine those shoes!'

I might be the only business associate around today that remembers Janet working out of the basement office, answering the phones in between loads of laundry. I met Frank in 1979 in the kitchen of a mutual friend's house in Annapolis. Our camaraderie was instantaneous when we discovered that at one time we lived about six miles apart on the Main Line, and that my closest friend had worked with Janet's father at Philadelphia Electric.

"What do you do?" he asked me. I told him I was the newly appointed president of the Maryland Motor Truck Association, trying to grow membership. Then he told me about his insurance business which sold to associations. When I told him that our association's insurance wasn't working very well, Frank, always confident and aggressive, told me he could come up with something better, and indeed he did. Our members got broader health insurance coverage at a lower rate than they were paying before. Our membership tripled, and one of the major reasons people joined was to gain access to Kelly-Chick's excellent insurance program.

After young Frankie joined the business, Big Frank wanted me to start dealing with Frankie on the day-to-day matters of our account. At first, I resisted. I had built a good relationship with Frank, and besides, it bothered me—a stickler for a neat appearance—that Frankie always came into my office with scuffed-up shoes. "Shine those shoes, you look terrible," I would bark at him. But Frankie did such a great job for us that I reached the point of telling Big Frank that since he was always in Annapolis and getting out of date with the products, I did not want to deal with him anymore, only Frankie. Oh, he got so insulted and so mad. He hooted and hollered, and turned red-faced as only he can!

I dealt with Frank in his role as a legislator also. He was a tremendous legislator, dedicated to the job and very effective for his constituents. He knew the State budget inside and out. He worked hard for the citizens of Maryland, and the crowds that turned out for his rallies, functions, and fundraisers were unbelievable.

Frank sponsored an awful lot of legislation. He had a unique personality and ability to forge relationships with everyone on both sides of the aisle—the dyed-in-the-wool hardliners, the moderates and the conservatives—gain their support and pass legislation because he looked at all sides of an issue. And though Frank was involved in so many political issues while also building a business, he would never do anything that even hinted at a conflict of interest.

Frank and I were good for each other, and it does my heart good to see his success and know that I had a part in it. And over the years, whenever any of the Kelly sons came to my office, the first thing they did was point to their shoes to show me how shiny they were.

-Walter Thompson

8

For the People

*Unless the Lord builds the house, its builders labor
in vain. Unless the Lord watches over the city,
the watchmen stand guard in vain.*
Psalm 127:1

Entering politics was the last thing on my mind when it happened. I had never been active in politics my entire life, and I didn't know a single elected official. It probably wouldn't have happened if I had not stopped drinking, but because I wasn't out at bars every night, I had time for more meaningful and productive endeavors.

'He used the time well'

When Frank stopped drinking, he gained a tremendous amount of extra time that otherwise would have been spent sitting at a bar. He used the time well—to start a business and a career in politics, for charity work, and to be at all his kids' and grandkids' games. Does he ever miss a game? He would not have accomplished all that he did if he had not stopped drinking.

-Bob Kelly

TAXES ON PROPERTY

THE HOMEOWNERS VOICE • P. O. BOX 10012 • TOWSON 21204 MARYLAND

    The Executive Committee would like to take this opportunity to express our sincere appreciation for your support of Operation STOP. This communication is long overdue but we are sure you understand the reasons why. We have been very busy studying budgets, preparing and presenting testimony before State and County legislators and considering legal action to relieve the property owner of excessive, inequitable and regressive taxation.

    As you know, Operation STOP is a group of concerned citizens who organized about the first of this year after many property owners received unbelievable reassessments. The movement originated in Baltimore County when the leaders of several community organizations joined forces to lobby for legislative action from the Maryland General Assembly to freeze property assessments at the level of June, 1971 in line with Federal wage freezes. Our lobbying efforts culminated when over 1500 homeowners "marched" on Annapolis on March 6th. Although our legislation was killed in the final minutes of the session, the support of Operation STOP was recognized throughout the State. The Baltimore News American editorially supported STOP on six separate occasions. The Sun supported us twice and the County papers have given us wide coverage. Our views were also expressed on the "Man to Man" and "Point Blank" television shows. We have earned recognition from the Governor, the State legislators and the County Council.

    Our testimony at the Baltimore County Council budget hearing, when we questioned the "waste" in the education budget and made solid recommendations, was heralded by interested citizens throughout the state. In April, the proposed Baltimore County budget would have required a tax increase of $1.38; the actual increase announced in June was ten cents. We strongly feel that the efforts of Operation STOP was largely responsible for the reduction.

    The question now is "Where do we go from here"? Our goal is two-fold. First, we pledge to work for permanent tax relief for the overtaxed homeowner. We will work for the elimination of the property tax as we know it today. We feel property taxes should only be used to pay for services directly related to property. Secondly, we pledge to work for fiscal responsibility in government. We intend to review and carefully scrutinize the budgets of any agency financed by our tax dollar. We feel that reform tax legislation is not the only answer. We must STOP excessive, irresponsible and unnecessary government spending.

An Operation STOP letter to supporters

My political career began innocently enough when, after our neighborhood association elected me president in 1972, the state happened to raise everyone's property tax assessment—in many cases, they doubled. Lower taxes were a major reason people moved to the suburbs, so my boiling mad neighbors in the association called me and demanded, "What are you going to do about it?"

Do about it? Until that moment, I hadn't given a thought about doing anything about it, but the neighborhood was ready to revolt, so I had to do something. I called for an emergency association meeting.

The newspapers reported the same outrage across all of Baltimore County. We didn't know it then, but we were on the leading edge of an advancing property tax revolt that was brewing across the country. I opened my directory of neighborhood association presidents and wrote a letter inviting them to a taxpayer meeting at Loch Raven Senior High School. I had no idea what to expect, and no plan when I walked into a mob of 500 angry taxpayers.

"We're all upset," I said to the group, "but does anybody have any ideas for what we can do about it?"

A guy in the back lit the fuse when he stood and shouted, "Abolish the property tax!" Ten more people sprang up, "Yeah, abolish the property tax! It's not fair!"

We discussed the idea for about an hour; then somebody suggested that we form a taxpayer association and introduce a bill in the state legislature. "Let's call it STOP—for stop taxes on property."

"Do we have any lawyers in the house?" I asked. A lawyer stood and volunteered to draft the papers.

"I'm a CPA," said another, "I can manage the finances."

"We need someone to lead the association," I said, "who's going to lead it?"

"You!" they cried, "you're our leader!"

The Operation STOP rally got Governor Schaefer's attention.

"But I don't know any of you, or anybody in politics," I said.

"You had the guts to call this meeting; we're following you," they answered.

As the new leader of Operation STOP, I started calling state legislators to tell them how upset the voters were, and that we wanted them to abolish the property tax. Most of them just laughed, and when I reported that at the next Operation STOP meeting, the group wanted to push back at the politicians even harder. Someone urged, "Let's rent buses and get everybody we can to go down to Annapolis and demonstrate at the Capitol!"

Angry taxpayers filled the buses in droves. We took 5,000 demonstrators to Annapolis, marched around the state house, and caught the attention of the legislators. We convinced some of them to introduce a bill and could hardly believe that it actually passed! Maryland became the first state in the country to abolish the property tax. But the idea shook up the governor so much, he vetoed it.

GO FOR IT!

After such an exhilarating exposure to the workings of state government, in my heart I felt, *maybe this is something I ought to give a shot at doing.* I was not the only one with thinking along those lines. In 1974, several people asked me to run for the State Senate.

I asked Janet what she thought about the idea. She hesitated. "I'm not sure; we have five young children, and so much to juggle already." We prayed about it for months.

The 1970s was an era of corruption in Maryland politics. Spiro Agnew, the former Baltimore County Executive and governor who became vice president under Richard Nixon, was investigated for accepting kickbacks, pleaded no contest to tax evasion, and resigned from the vice presidency. Dale Anderson, who succeeded Agnew as Baltimore County Executive, was forced out of office when he was sentenced to prison in 1974 for tax crimes, extortion, and conspiracy. I could go on listing Maryland politicians who were convicted of various crimes throughout the decade.

Democrats far outnumbered Republicans in Maryland and had controlled the Maryland state legislature since 1900. It was machine politics—small groups of politicians met in back rooms and decided how everyone would vote. But I had no political contacts, let alone a machine. Yes, I was a registered Democrat, but Timonium was in a rare Republican district where no Democrat had ever won, so there was no democratic machine for me to join even if I wanted to.

Should I change parties? I did not agree with every principle of the Democratic Party—I was conservative—but because the Republicans held power in my district and were well entrenched, and it was nearly impossible for a relative newcomer to make it onto the ticket, I remained a Democrat. Besides, I am quick to accept a challenge, especially trying something nobody had ever accomplished before. If I was going to make it, I would have to make it as an independent-minded Democrat.

I felt that the Lord was saying, "Go for it." Janet was still hesitant but sensed Him telling her, "If you say 'yes,' then I'll change your heart about it." I took that as another "Yes."

We had no money, but I felt strongly that God did not want me to go into debt for this. We ran the campaign as a family affair. Janet organized garage sales and sent the kids door-to-door selling pumpkins and cookies, and we raised about $15,000.

In the general election, I ran against the Republican incumbent, Porter Hopkins. Without Porter's knowledge, his campaign put out a letter mentioning that I had previously worked at Tidewater Insurance, trying to implicate me with the Tidewater executives who were indicted along with Governor Marvin Mandel in the racetrack racketeering scandal. I had left Tidewater before that even started and was not involved at all. Between the dirty tactics, my relative inexperience, a shoestring campaign budget and lower name recognition, I lost, though not by much, and we shook up the establishment. Porter later apologized to me for the Tidewater letter.

Four years later, Porter called to tell me he was not running for re-election, and told me, "I think you ought to run. Even though you're a Democrat, I can convince the Republicans to endorse you and support you in the general election." I was still making up my mind when Charles A. Ruppersberger III came by my office to let me know he planned to run and asked me about my intentions.

Ruppersberger, who went by his childhood nickname, "Dutch," was an assistant state's attorney. He decided to run for office after nearly dying in a car accident while investigating a drug trafficking case. The Shock Trauma Center saved his life, and he wanted to go into the Senate to help advance Shock Trauma's cause. I liked Dutch. He was trustworthy, outgoing and friendly, and he was running for a good reason. I said I wasn't sure what I would do but would tell him when I decided.

In May, I let Dutch know that I was going to run also. That summer, we began campaigning against each other in the Democratic primary. At the time, the district encompassed the northern parts of Baltimore, Harford, and Carroll

Meet Frank Kelly...
- 34 years old
- Married (to the former Janet DeMaine), father of four sons (Frank, Jr., 10; John, 9; David, 6, and Brian, 5) and one foster daughter (Sharon, 12)
- Graduate of Villanova University (B.S., Economics; major, Marketing)
- Honorable Discharge, U.S. Army National Guard (NIKE missile btn, 1962-67)

ACTIVITIES...
- Operation STOP, co-founder, first Chairman (1971-72), volunteer lobbyist (1972-present)
- Maryland Foster Parent Association, organizer, first President (present)
- Greater Timonium Community Council, Vice-President (1972-1974)
- Coachford Community Improvement Association, President (1971-72), Board of Directors (1971-73)
- St. Joseph's Parish Council, Texas, Md. (elected 1972-74), Vice-President (1972)
- Maryland State Advisory Board on Foster Care
- Board of Catholic Social Services
- "Maryland Action for Foster Children" Committee
- Pot Spring Elementary School PTA

ACTIONS SPEAK LOUDER THAN WORDS...
ELECT FRANCIS X. KELLY

(By authority of Simon P. Jarosinski, Jr., Treasurer)

★★★★★★★★★★★★★★★★★★★★★★★★★

ELECT FRANCIS X. KELLY
MARYLAND STATE SENATE
DEMOCRAT
NEW 5TH LEGIS. DIST.
★★★★★★★★★★★★★★★★★★★★★★★
★★★★★★★★★★★★★★★★★★★★★★★

Our campaign flyer

Counties, from Conowingo to Westminster, so we logged a lot of miles appearing at the same functions and forums, often debating each other. At all our campaign appearances, Dutch constantly talked about Shock Trauma.

Even though we opposed each other for the same office, we liked each other, and there was no animosity between us. Many nights, after a debate, we stopped at Pizza Hut on the way home and built a strong friendship. One night I promised him, "Dutch, I don't know who is going to

On the campaign trail

win this race, but I give you my word, if I win, I will look after Shock Trauma."

I knocked on a lot of doors. The garage sales, pumpkin sales, and other fundraisers brought in about $50,000 this time. I also got a major assist in Carroll County, where I didn't know a soul, from Senator Charles Smelser, a banker, a tough World War II hero who survived a glider plane crash in Normandy, and a nuts-and-bolts fiscal conservative Democrat who represented a different district of the county. He called me and grilled me about my background and my views on different issues, then said, "I like you, and I want you to win. Can you give me a day to take you around Carroll County? We'll start at 6 in the morning and go until 6 at night. I'll introduce you to the key people up here, and if you do as well as I think you will with them, you'll win the county."

"All you need is one day?" I asked. "That's all I need," he said.

Now that's working smart!

Our first stop was a drug store luncheonette. "Just be yourself," Smelser told me before we went inside, "don't try to impress them, and don't speak unless you have something worthwhile to say. Answer their questions as best you can." We entered the drug store, and he introduced me to the breakfast crowd at the counter, about a dozen farmers dressed in their denim overalls and checkered flannel shirts. "Kelly's the one who took those 5,000 people to Annapolis to rally for lower taxes. He's our kind of guy, and we need him in the

The Kelly campaign team selling pumpkins to raise money

Senate," he told the farmers. I sat with them for three hours, listening to their stories and answering their questions. I knew I had connected with them.

Our next stop was Miller & Maurer Meats in Manchester. Smelser took me to the butcher shop in the back of the store, where two brothers were slicing up a cow's carcass hanging on a hook. Smelser introduced me. "Kelly's the one who took those 5,000 people to Annapolis to rally for lower taxes." "Oh yeah," the brothers cheered, "way to go buddy! That's what we like! Tell us how you organized all that." After about an hour and a half, they advised me that if I really wanted to get some votes, I should go into the front of the store and talk to their mother, Mary. "She knows everybody," they said.

We went to the front of the store and met Mary, and chatted in between her serving customers. I told her about my days selling to grocery stores for Armour, and we hit it off.

After Miller & Maurer's, Smelser drove me to a farm. "We're going to have tea with this next lady," he told me. "She's over 80 years old. Just sit and visit and be yourself. If she likes you, that's worth 2,500 votes, easy," he said. I

Dutch and Frank

sat down and asked her about her family history, and the history of Carroll County. I asked her opinion about what was important to the people in the district. We visited for three hours, and I think she would have talked with me all day, but Smelser gave me the eye, and we said goodbye.

'A Best Friend'

It's hard to put into words the impact our decades-long friendship has had on my life. It was hard to dislike Frank—he was smart, honest and it was clear that his passion for helping people was genuine. I was impressed by his straight-up style. In the end, Frank beat me. It was the first (and last) election I ever lost, but I gained so much more. I had gained a best friend.

I still talk to Frank a couple of times a week. He's smart and experienced, and I like to get his opinion on all the issues—insurance, health care, anything really—he has strong and informed opinions on everything. We're both very competitive, we disagree, and we fight. I remind him that he used to be a Democrat! We fought over the Affordable Care Act in 2010 and Janet had to mediate. I often ask Janet for her opinions as well. I want to hear all sides of the issue, and just because we disagree doesn't mean we can't have our debates and remain friends.

Frank is always there for me, in good times and in bad. I wish more people in Congress had a friend like Frank. We would all be better off.

-Congressman C. A. Dutch Ruppersberger

When we got to the car, Smelser said, "We don't even have to see anybody else. You're going to win. I could tell that she loves you, and she's going to spend all day tomorrow calling her friends and telling them to vote for you." We did keep our next three appointments, which took us up to six o'clock, and then called it a day.

I beat Dutch by about 3-1 in Carroll County. He didn't know what hit him, and when he saw me after the election, he shook his head and asked me, "How did you do that?" In Baltimore and Harford Counties, I beat Dutch in every precinct and faced George Price in the general election.

Most people assumed that I had little chance against Price, who had served in the House of Delegates for sixteen years and came from a highly respected Angus Beef cattle farming family that had lived in Baltimore County for over 100 years. But I pulled off the upset and became the first Democrat ever elected to the Maryland State Senate from northern Baltimore County.

Dutch and I remain close friends to this day. His race against me was the first and last election he ever lost. After I won the seat, Dutch became my campaign finance chairman, and I worked on his campaigns for County Council, County Executive, and the United States House of Representatives. My biggest contribution was telling Dutch, "Listen, Charles A. Rupperberger III is hard to say, hard to spell, and can barely fit on a car bumper. Go down to the courthouse and officially change your name to C. A. Dutch Ruppersberger. No one will forget that name!"

CHALLENGING THE MACHINE

Senator Malkus swears me in.

Now I had to learn the ropes of Senate politics. My first test came when Senator Charles Smelser called me. He said, "one of the first things we have to do is elect a President of the Senate. Have you made any commitments yet?"

"No," I said.

"Let me tell you about Jim Clark. He's a farmer from Howard County, a fiscal conservative like you." He went on about his record, and I liked what I heard. "Can I count on your support for Jim Clark?" he asked.

"Charlie, you helped me so much, and you say he's the right guy, so I'll support him."

A week later, the day before Thanksgiving, I was called to a meeting at the Holiday Inn on Cromwell Bridge Road with the seven other Democrats in the Senate delegation from Baltimore County. They welcomed me, the newcomer, and then revved up the machine. The purpose of the meeting was to get all eight of us to agree to support the person that Norman Stone, the chairman of the delegation, wanted for President of the Senate: Ed Conroy from Prince Georges County. "We all have to be together on this," said Norm. He went around the room one by one, and everyone agreed to vote for Conroy. Then he looked at me. "What do you think, Frank?"

"Guys, I'm sorry," I said, "but I don't know Conroy,

and I've already made a commitment to Senator Smelser to support Jim Clark."

"What? What do you mean?" they shrieked at me with eyes bulging. "You're in Baltimore County, and you made a promise to Smelser from Carroll County?"

"First of all, I represent part of Carroll County," I said. "Second of all, Smelser is my friend, and he helped me get elected—you guys didn't. And I've researched Clark, and he's my type of guy. I'm voting for Clark."

Senator Stone said, "I think it will help Conroy's chances of winning if the entire Baltimore County delegation supports him. Frank, I'll give you the weekend to think it over, and call you on Monday."

"Well," I said, "if you want to take the weekend that's fine with me, but one thing you guys are going to learn about me is that, when I make a commitment, I keep it. I can tell you right now that I'm not backing off. I won't back off on Monday, and you can give me until Christmas and I won't back off."

The meeting adjourned, I had a wonderful Thanksgiving Day with the family and received a call from Senator Mickey Steinberg from Pikesville on Friday. "Are you still with Clark?" he asked. "Yes," I said. "Well, so am I now," he said, "and Clark is going to win. I just found out that the entire city delegation is backing Clark. I told them you and I would join them, and that will give Clark enough votes to win."

"You can count on me," I told him.

"Look," he went on, "the winner gets the spoils. What kind of position would you want?"

I hadn't given a thought to anything like that. "I don't know," I said, "how about the budget committee?" I thought that would give me the best opportunity to promote the fiscal responsibility I ran my campaign on. Everybody wants to be on the budget committee because that's where the influence is, and freshman senators rarely get a seat on it, but Clark was elected Senate President and appointed me to the budget committee.

Word got around that, *This guy Kelly is really independent; he calls his own shots, and he can't be bought.* When people know you're honest and independent, the word gets out and they don't mess with you or tempt you. That was one of the ways God protected me for the next twelve years.

'Wow, he's unforgettable'

I remember the day and the hour when I first met Frank. It was January 1979. I was a 22-year old freshman in the Maryland House of Delegates and Frank was a freshman Senator. We were both mingling with our new colleagues at Fran O'Brien's restaurant in Annapolis.

After spending about 20 minutes exchanging information about our backgrounds and our early experiences in the legislature, I walked away thinking, *Wow, he's unforgettable.* I was impressed immediately by how much interest he showed in getting to know me, his Irish vigor, and his charm. I knew right away that Frank was a high-impact person. What I didn't know then is that I would work alongside Frank for hundreds and hundreds of hours over the next several decades.

-Tim Maloney
Principal
Joseph, Greenwald & Laake, PA

CATCHING ON QUICKLY

From my seat in the back row, I looked around on my first day in the Senate at a room full of people who, a year ago, I had been watching on television! They were more politically savvy and experienced than I was, and some were better educated. I said to myself, *OK, Lord, what am I doing here? I'm not sure I can handle this.*

I followed the wise advice that a couple of veteran Senators gave me: to be seen and not heard for a while until I established myself. I felt the Lord telling me that my peers would judge me on how I lived my life, not by anything I had to say. They knew I was a Christian and they knew I did not drink, so they would be watching closely. Even though I love to talk, I can be quiet and assess a situation when I need to.

The session lasted 90 days, and I did not stand up on the floor to speak until somewhere around day 70, but I did not pick the best time to ask my first question. Senator Malkus from the Eastern Shore, known as "The Dean of the Senate" for his many years of service, and one of the most powerful members, was droning on about some issue, and I stood to ask a question. Malkus started to answer, but I was so nervous that, in the middle of his answer I interrupted with a follow-up question—a rookie mistake that annoyed Malkus. He turned to the President of the Senate and asked, "Mr. President, is the Senator from Baltimore County on the subject matter?" It took me one second to plop back down into my seat. Not that I had to sit down, because technically I had the floor, but that was Malkus' parliamentary way of telling me to sit down and shut up, and I was not about to take on the Dean of the Senate in my first speech. As I left the session with my tail between my legs, some of my colleagues offered their condolences: "Welcome to the Senate, Kelly."

My initial approach was to listen, listen, listen.

A week or so later, Malkus was up again, going on and on about one of his bills. I stood. "Will the Senator from the Eastern Shore yield to a question?" I asked. The President of the Senate answered, "The Senate recognizes the Senator from Baltimore County." I asked a question, "Mr. President, is the Senator from the Eastern Shore on the subject matter?" and sat down. The Senate chamber erupted in laughter. Malkus put down the microphone and moseyed toward me. He was at the front of the chamber, and I was in the back row, so it was a long, slow walk, and every eyeball followed his steps. He stopped at my desk. I held my breath. Malkus knelt down on one knee, grabbed my hand, and kissed it. "Welcome to the Senate," he said. More wild laughter burst out across the chamber. I had passed his test.

For the rest of the years Senator Malkus and I served together, we respected each other and worked well together. He gave me one of my most cherished gifts from a colleague—a beautiful Irish Shillelagh walking stick, hand carved out of mahogany, that had been in his family for generations. "You're one of the only Irishmen I've ever respected or liked," he laughed, "so I want you to have this."

As I gained confidence on the Senate floor, my approach was to listen, listen, listen, and then be up-front about where I stood. "I heard what you had to say, and I have not yet made up my mind," I might have told my constituents.

Or, "Right now, the way I feel, here is how I am probably going to vote on this." People appreciate a politician who levels with them. The voters in my district sent me to Annapolis to control taxes and spending, so I was proud to serve twelve years on the Budget and Taxation Committee, eight as vice-chairman.

One of the first pieces of legislation I worked on was the creation of the Spending Affordability Committee, which recommended that the state budget should not increase faster than the growth rate of personal income. I went to work on that bill before the session even started, first by serving on a legislative commission to study the issue, and then convincing various newspaper editorial boards to endorse the concept. In the end, I brought together 26 co-sponsors, out of 47 Senators. My colleagues commented that I had learned legislative strategy quickly and noted how passionate I became when I believed something was the right thing to do.

I believe God put me in the Senate to help people, to correct injustices, and to speak for those who could not speak for themselves. The opportunities He gave me to do so came in many ways, shapes, and forms.

CREATING A WORLD-CLASS MEDICAL SYSTEM

The University of Maryland Hospital, which was part of the University of Maryland, Baltimore campus and governed by the Board of Regents of the University of Maryland, was always an excellent academic medical center. But chronic debt problems hampered it through the early 1980s. Every year the management of the hospital came to our committee to report cost overruns and ask for additional funds above what we had appropriated to them. It was evident to our committee that the hospital was not managed properly, and we got tired of hearing their requests for more money. It was on a path to bankruptcy when we told them, "This isn't working, and you have to do something about it. Maybe you should consider separating from the University and the state."

No state legislature in the country has ever privatized a university hospital, but the Board of Regents worked with the state House of Delegates, led by Joseph Tydings, to introduce a bill to convert the hospital into a private entity.

As chairman of the Budget and Tax Subcommittee on Health, Education, and Welfare, the bill came to our committee when it passed from the House to the Senate. I helped write the final legislation that took the hospital out of the University of Maryland's and the state's control and converted it to the University of Maryland Medical System (UMMS), a private, not-for-profit corporation.

UMMS receives no operating funds from the state, though the state can use its bonding authority to help fund capital improvements. The governor appoints the UMMS Board of Directors, which by law always includes one member of the House of Delegates and one member of the Senate. The first board included me and some of the most prominent business leaders in Maryland.

Over the years several community hospitals across the state have recognized the benefits of affiliating with UMMS. For those that fell into financial difficulties, UMMS offered financial resources and economies of scale. Also, a multi-hospital system offers all its members the ability to provide more diverse health services and handle almost any kind of case. Since its creation in 1984, UMMS has grown into a thriving $5 billion system of fourteen hospitals providing world-class medical care and clinical research.

It has been my privilege to serve on the board since

its inception in 1984, and to Chair the committee that has overseen all its acquisitions.

HEALTH INSURANCE, DRUNK DRIVERS, AND LEMONS

I put my health insurance experience to work on the State Employee Health Insurance Plan. The plan always lost money, and we constantly heard about it in budget committee hearings. After a few times, I lost my cool with the plan administrators. "Do you even know what you are doing when you're negotiating for health benefits?"

The ineptitude became so frustrating that Larry Levitan, the chairman, suggested, "Frank, why don't you take over? Why don't you put together a committee to investigate this and see what we can do?" I brought in Hal Cohen, who had started the Healthcare Cost Commission, two other Senators, and people I respected in the insurance business, and we completely redefined the benefits and made sure they went out for a competitive bid. We saved the State $22 million per year.

Because I chaired the Subcommittee on Health, Education, and Welfare, and served on the Gubernatorial Commission on Drunk Driving, I worked closely with Mothers Against Drunk Driving (MADD). I sponsored 25 drunk driving laws, which helped reduce the drunk driving death toll. One bill required alcohol offenders to attend Alcoholics Anonymous or another rehabilitation program and provided for monitors to track their attendance. If offenders failed to attend, they faced jail time; most of them attended. Now, it is standard practice for alcohol offenders to attend a rehabilitation program on their first offense.

Another popular law arose out of Janet's frustration

with the wood-paneled station wagon she drove. During the gasoline shortage of the 1970s, General Motors converted some of their gasoline engines to run on less expensive diesel fuel. We bought a brand-new Chevy diesel wagon, and every time Janet turned a corner, it stalled out. She and the kids almost got killed a couple of times. As much as we complained, the dealer refused to fix it, so I introduced a bill that required auto manufacturers to fix their "lemons." That touched off a chain reaction; dozens of legislators recounted their horror stories with their own lemons.

A Senior Vice President from GM came to my office and offered me a new car. "So, I get a brand-new car," I said, "and then you want me to withdraw the bill. Meanwhile, everybody else continues to get screwed by you guys. No way." We passed the first Lemon Law in the country, which protects consumers and requires manufacturers to repair or replace vehicles that meet certain problem criteria. I got my new car, and so did scores of others.

AN HONORARY PISCATAWAY

I was a member of the Executive Nominations Committee which approves the governor's nominations to various state boards and commissions. We held a hearing for a Piscataway woman nominated to head the Maryland Commission on Indian Affairs, and I asked her what her goals would be for the Commission. "Senator," she said, "my number one goal is to have Native Americans recognized as a minority in Maryland." She recited the list of groups who were already recognized and received the economic advantages that come with it and saw no reason why Native Americans shouldn't have the same recognition.

I wasn't aware that Native Americans were not recognized. "But you were here first! That's not fair," I said.

"That's right, Senator," she agreed.

Our committee approved her as Commission Chair, and I spoke with her after the hearing to learn more about the Native American situation in Maryland. She told me that legislation to recognize Native Americans had been introduced a number of times in the past, but the bills were always killed—because of prejudice, in her opinion. "Really?" I said, "How can anyone be prejudiced against Native Americans? If I introduce legislation to recognize them again, could you work with me to get the support we need to get it passed?"

"You would do that?" she asked.

"Sure, I will," I said.

"Oh yes," she said, "I can get you a lot of support."

I knew that some Senators questioned the need for the bill. They thought that intermarriage with other ethnic groups had left very few pure-blooded Native Americans remaining in Maryland. We pulled together a team that included the Maryland Historical Trust and a Native American history expert from the University of Maryland to get the facts and presented data at the hearing confirming thousands of pure-blooded Native Americans living in Maryland. It was easy to establish the contributions they made to the state and the reality of the discrimination they suffered. The Executive Nominations Committee passed the bill 11-0.

We invited eight pure-blooded Native Americans to the committee hearing on the bill and could have brought in many more if we had to. We also had the support of Majority Leader Clarence Blount. "I want to thank Senator Kelly for recognizing this injustice," he said during the discussion of the bill.

But what blew my colleagues away was the little tin

box that the Commission Chair's grandmother brought to the hearing. She was dressed in traditional beadwork and stitching, and read from letters she had saved in the tin box written by her Piscataway tribe ancestors who lived on Chincoteague and Assateague Islands. One letter—from the 1600s—recounted the time a European ship crashed off the Assateague coast. The Piscataway saved the lives of the passengers, only to be raped and pillaged by those same passengers soon afterward. You could hear a pin drop. She went on to describe the struggle they've had trying to adapt and integrate into a new and often hostile culture without giving up their Piscataway heritage. The bill passed, 47-0.

To show their appreciation for my efforts, the Native American community invited Janet and me to their next annual Pow-Wow in Cumberland. They dressed us in native headdresses, blankets, and beads, and designated us honorary Piscataway. Janet and I saw for ourselves how many Native Americans lived in Maryland and stood to benefit from their home state's recognition.

REINVENTING HIGHER EDUCATION

"We want College Park in the top five in the country," I urged my colleagues on the Senate floor in 1988, rallying votes for Governor William Donald Schaefer's plan to overhaul Maryland's higher education. "We're talking about projecting our system into the stratosphere."

Every year, the presidents of the state's twelve public colleges each made a trip to Annapolis, talked to our budget subcommittee about how they wanted to become the next Harvard, and requested a Harvard-sized budget.

While we couldn't support twelve Harvards, we did

want to raise the overall quality of higher education throughout the state in an efficient and affordable way. Our subcommittee drafted a charter to reinvent higher education by creating a school system based on the pillars of quality, accessibility, diversity, adequate funding, efficient and effective management, and capable and creative leadership.

But Senate President Mike Miller wanted to kill the bill. He was concerned that it would diminish the stature of his alma mater, the University of Maryland at College Park. I asked him if I could re-work the bill. We established a lead role for each school. We wrote into the law that College Park would be the flagship, public research university within the system, and the other schools would specialize in their own niche subject areas. Mike Miller was pleased, and the bill passed unanimously. College Park is now one of the finest public universities in the country and one of the most difficult to get into. College Park and many of the other schools in the system are nationally ranked and recognized.

THE DAWN OF MBNA

In late 1970s, inflation was out of control and the banks in Maryland wanted to raise their credit card interest rate above the 18% maximum allowed by Maryland law. One of those banks was Maryland National Bank, where my friend Charlie Cawley ran the credit card division. A bill was introduced in the Senate to raise the maximum rate, but it didn't go anywhere because legislators didn't want to raise their constituents' interest rates. But then the banks stopped extending credit.

Meanwhile, the state of Delaware had no interest rate limit on credit cards and was wooing banks to relocate there.

Charlie set up a meeting with two other Maryland National executives and me, who told me they intended to move to Delaware if Maryland didn't change its law. "We'd appreciate anything you can do to help us stay in Maryland," they told me.

I took the information to my colleagues, but most of them were afraid to lift the rate cap. Charlie called me almost every day. "Are you getting anywhere with the bill?" he would ask. "Charlie, it doesn't look good," I would say, "but I'm doing everything I can to help you." I tried to explain that when people need credit and can't get it, that's a problem too, but I got booed on the Senate floor for supporting the banks. Pushing for this bill was certainly not going to help me get re-elected!

The bill came up for a vote and lost. I was still in the Senate chamber when Charlie called me, burning mad. "Charlie, I just shed blood for you over this," I told him, "and I don't need to hear this right now. And besides, I have a feeling this could be the best thing that ever happened to you." The next day, he called me to apologize for getting so angry with me, and two weeks later, he called again to tell me that Maryland National Bank was going to spin off his credit card operation into a separate company, MBNA, incorporated in Delaware. The rest, as they say, is history.

SAVING THE SAVINGS AND LOAN

It was like the scene out of *It's a Wonderful Life*. In March 1985, hundreds of customers of Old Court Savings & Loan lined up to withdraw their money. Within a week, hundreds of customers lined up at several more of the state's 102 savings and loans to try to save their nest eggs and life savings.

Governor Harry Hughes declared a state of public emergency, imposed a $1,000 per month limit on withdrawals from state savings and loans and called a special session of the General Assembly to address the crisis.

We saw a warning sign earlier in the year after a savings and loan in Ohio failed, so during the annual budget hearings, my committee grilled our state savings and loan commissioner on his plans to prevent a collapse in Maryland. He did not inspire confidence, and a colleague turned to me during the hearing and whispered, "I don't know about you, Frank, but if I had my money in a state S&L, I'd get it the hell out."

A total of $10 billion of people's savings was at risk. I felt strongly that we needed not just a bailout using taxpayer dollars, but a two-pronged solution—immediate financial assistance to save as much of the deposits as possible, plus a plan to strengthen the entire regulatory system and prevent the kinds of abuses and criminal practices that sent several unscrupulous savings and loan executives to jail.

In the short-term, we guaranteed the deposits, which calmed the public and stopped the run on withdrawals. The lesson learned here is the importance of instilling confidence. Lacking confidence in any situation, the people will panic.

The trade-off for guaranteeing the deposits was requiring depositors to leave their money in the savings and loan, without interest, for four years before getting it all back. Their response taught me a lesson in human nature. For many customers used to earning 18% interest, the thought of no interest for four years—even though we had just saved their nest eggs—was an abomination, and they let me know it. Senate President Mickey Steinberg and I held a public meeting in Pikesville to explain the plan to a group of S&L customers, and they wanted to string us up. We needed a police escort out of the meeting. Sometimes, when it comes to money, people can never have enough, even if a short time before they were dangerously close to losing it all.

For the long-term, we helped create a savings and loan oversight commission, modeled after the FDIC, to provide stronger controls to assure the stability of the S&Ls, and protect the customers.

Looking at the big picture, the crisis resolved quickly, the losses amounted to only 2.5% of the $10 billion at risk, and the regulatory reforms we enacted have kept Maryland's financial institutions, and their customers, safe and sound.

BUILDING CAMDEN YARDS

Fans of the Baltimore Colts remember where they were and what they were doing on March 29, 1984. At 2 AM that snowy night, under the cover of darkness, with no forewarning or public announcement, owner Bob Irsay and a convoy of moving vans cut and ran to Indianapolis.

Irsay had asked Mayor Schaefer and the city of Baltimore to pay for improvements to Memorial Stadium. For a variety of reasons, the negotiations did not go well, and on March 27, the Maryland Senate passed a law allowing the city to exercise eminent domain and seize the team from Irsay. Irsay already had a deal on the table from the city of Indianapolis, which he quickly accepted that day and then packed up everything except the marching band and pulled the team out of Baltimore. He had to leave before the next morning when he knew the House of Delegates would approve the eminent domain bill, and the governor would sign it into law.

When Schaefer became governor in 1987, his top priority was building two new stadiums—one for baseball, to make sure the Orioles remained in Baltimore, and another for football, to attract a new NFL team to Baltimore. Since the proposal involved taxpayer money, it came to me in the budget and tax committee, where Senator Cathy Riley and I worked closely with Alan Rifkin, Governor Schaefer's Chief Legislative Officer and Counsel, to pass the legislation that authorized the new stadiums.

Frank demonstrates his characteristic humility when he says he "worked closely" with the Governor's office and me to help pass the stadium bills. I would say that without Frank, Oriole Park at Camden Yards and  M&T Bank Stadium might never have become a reality.

Even before Governor Schaefer's inauguration in 1987, he had made the funding and development of two new stadia—one dedicated to baseball and the other to football—his top legislative and policy priority. That was a visionary initiative and an enormously complex public policy issue. At that time, most sports facilities were dual-purpose baseball and football venues and were built in the suburbs. The governor strongly believed that to retain the Orioles and attract a new NFL football team, the state needed to authorize and fund two dedicated stadia and that the facilities needed to be located within the Baltimore City limits.

As soon as the word got out that the former Mayor of Baltimore and now Governor of the State of Maryland wanted to build not one—but two—sports facilities, it immediately triggered heated debate in every corner of the state. Legitimate questions were raised, including whether it would be cheaper and better just to update Memorial Stadium, where the Orioles then played, and if two stadia were to be built, how would they be funded? Many policy makers, principally from outside the city limits, were skeptical and concerned whether taxes on their constituents would have to be raised to pay for the facilities. It was a heated debate and many questions needed to be answered, but with the memory of the Colts fleeing in the middle of the night indelibly etched in the governor's mind, only one thing mattered to William Donald Schaefer—keeping the Orioles in Baltimore. His explicit direction was, "Get it done!"

For the first two months of the three-month legislative session in 1987, there had been plenty of emotionally charged discussions and a war of wills between the Governor and many in the General Assembly. The bills languished. The President of the Senate, Mike Miller, who represented Prince George's County, did everything he could to help move the legislation but faced strong headwinds from legislators around the state who opposed it. They were concerned about the need for two stadia and apprehensive about spending so much of their constituents' tax dollars on a project in Baltimore City. As the legislative session wound down, the bills were still stuck in the Budget & Tax and Senate Finance Committees in the Senate and their counterparts in the House.

Having worked with him previously as Counsel and Chief Legislative Assistant to the Senate President, I knew I could go to Frank and ask for his candid advice. Frank could always see the big picture, and even though he represented a portion of Baltimore County that had reservations about the stadia project, I knew he would always do what was best for the state as a whole. As I recall, with only a few weeks to go in the legislative session, I met with Frank in his office to seek his advice. Frank was seated behind his desk and graciously asked me to come in and sit down. I asked him what we had to do to get the stadia bills out of his committee with a favorable vote before the legislative session ended. Frank stood up, came around from behind his desk and sat in the chair next to me as a sign that we're in this together. As a longtime friend and advisor, Frank went straight to the point—"You need Edward Bennett Williams to address the Senate. The Governor is speaking for the Orioles, but the Orioles aren't speaking for themselves. Until Mr. Williams commits the team to the state on a long-term lease, I don't think it will ever make it out of the committee."

Frank's understanding of the political dynamic was, as usual, exactly right. I had been hearing similar comments from others in the Senate, including Senator Larry Levitan, Chairman of the Senate Budget & Tax Committee, Senator Tom Bromwell, Chairman of the Senate Finance Committee, and Senator Cathy Riley—all of whom were supporters of the stadia and keen observers of the stadia politics.

Edward Bennett Williams owned the Orioles at the time and was one of the best-known trial lawyers in Washington, DC. He had purposely stayed out of the debate because he did not want "to become the next Bob Irsay," who threatened to leave and then took the Colts to Indianapolis. Mr. Williams did not want the people of Baltimore to believe that he was threatening to move the Orioles. Mr. Williams knew, however, that his health was declining and that the Orioles needed a new stadium to best ensure that the club stayed in Baltimore for the long term.

I relayed Frank's comments, which the Senate President and other key leaders supported, to the Governor. The Governor quickly reminded me that Mr. Williams had told him directly that he would not publicly speak on the issue. Surprisingly, at least to me, at the conclusion of the Governor's next weekly press conference, when a reporter asked whether Mr. Williams would ever testify on behalf of the stadium bills which were languishing in the legislature, Schaefer said: "Yes. He'll be there." The Governor said that Williams would answer all the legislators' questions. The press conference then ended.

I hurried into the Governor's office and thanked him for reaching out to Mr. Williams and for persuading him to publicly support the stadia bills. Immediately, the Governor responded, "I haven't called him yet. You better get ahold of him." I was surprised in one sense but, knowing the Governor, there was a certain genius in what he had done. Following Frank's thought process, the Governor had put the onus squarely on Mr. Williams to answer the legislatures' call to hear directly from him or lose the opportunity for a new stadium.

That reality was not lost on Mr. Williams. When I got back to my office, my deputy counsel, David Iannucci, and I placed a call to Mr. Williams who was in Florida with the Orioles at their spring training facility. His secretary told us that Mr. Williams was out of the office watching the club on the back fields. When Mr. Williams returned the call, he said, "What the hell is going on up there? I couldn't be there next week if I wanted to be, which I don't. I'll be in Boston for medical treatment." Later that day, I received a call from Larry Lucchino, one of Mr. Williams' partners and later President of the Orioles, who asked what Mr. Williams might be asked at the hearing "if he was able to come."

We had our breakthrough. I told Mr. Lucchino, "We'll send you a memo."

I recall making a beeline to Frank's office and then to the offices of the Senate President and Senators Levitan, Bromwell and Riley to let them know. I told Frank what had happened and thanked him profusely. I asked if we could work with him, Senator Levitan and others to coordinate the parameters of Mr. Williams' testimony before the committee.

Frank, along with Senators Levitan, Riley and Bromwell, then suggested that they hold not only a joint Senate hearing on the stadia bills but also include the House of Delegates in the hearing, which would expedite the legislative process since the legislative session was winding down. In preparation for the hearing, Frank was an instrumental liaison between his committee, the Finance Committee, the House Committees, and the Governor's office. We discussed every aspect of the hearing in advance, and Frank's advice was critical to the success of the hearing.

When Mr. Williams arrived, David Iannucci and I held a short, private briefing in the Governor's mansion before the hearing. Mr. Williams appeared to be very weak, and I actually wondered if he had the strength to even walk over to the joint hearing room. But as the great litigator and orator he was, he girded himself, gathered his energy, walked into the hearing room, sat down at the table, and gave the speech of a lifetime.

For two-and-a-half hours, Mr. Williams presented the case for a state-of-the-art stadium for the Orioles and why the city of Baltimore and the state of Maryland needed a new stadium. He waved a copy of the most recent *Sports Illustrated* magazine over his head, which coincidentally that week pictured the three Ripkens on the cover in their Orioles uniforms, and said, "This is why the stadium is important to Maryland....All across this country, this city and this state stand tall with publicity they couldn't buy...we have an opportunity...to have one of the most exciting attractions...in America...a sports complex [that] will be the equivalent of anything in the nation."

That hearing—which Frank, Senate President Miller, Senators Levitan, Bromwell, and Riley had promoted and championed when all seemed lost—changed the entire dynamic and tone of the debate. In many respects, it saved the day, and the entire package of stadia bills were finally put up for a vote. But, the vote was still razor thin and, once again, Frank stood tall. The bill passed in committee by the narrowest of margins 7-6, with Frank Kelly and Senator Levitan casting the deciding swing votes in favor of the bills.

I think it's fair to say that without Frank's kernel of an idea to invite Edward Bennett Williams to address the legislature, and without his vote, it is doubtful whether Oriole Park at Camden Yards—the best baseball stadium in America—and M&T Bank Stadium—the finest football venue in the country—would ever have been built. And, one can only wonder whether the Orioles would have stayed in Baltimore and whether we would have ever seen another NFL franchise.

Does Frank ever take the credit for playing such a pivotal role in such an important project that changed the landscape of the city and professional sports in the region? No. Not at all. In typical Frank fashion, he saw a problem and only asked, "How can I help?" He intuitively understood what was right for the city and his state, disregarded partisanship, and stood in the forefront of solving a complex public policy issue. That's Frank Kelly.

-Alan M. Rifkin
Managing Partner
Rifkin Weiner Livingston LLC

TALES FROM THE WHITE HOUSE

There was a side benefit to being active in politics in the state next door to Washington, DC. Occasionally, when a president wanted to rally grassroots support for a federal initiative or an election campaign, he invited nearby supporters and legislators to the White House. I've had the privilege of meeting presidents spanning from Nixon to the Bushes.

My first visit to the White House came in 1972 when President Nixon invited 300 or so of the Democrats for Nixon to the White House for a "thank you for your support" reception. I had no idea where to park when I arrived, so I drove my car right up on the White House grounds and parked on the circle where the Presidential motorcade parks on inauguration day and walked over to the reception. Can you believe it? And I didn't even get a ticket! President Nixon was not very personable, so I had little interaction with him during the reception.

Heroes of the Faith

I've been blessed by opportunities to share in the ministries of two of the most impactful Christian leaders of our generation: Charles Colson of Prison Fellowship, and Franklin Graham of the Billy Graham Evangelistic Association and Samaritan's Purse.

'Lord, I'm not comfortable with this.'
On Fridays during my Senate career, I met with a group of fellow-legislators for prayer and Bible study, and since I was the chairman of the group, I helped book the speakers for the Governor's annual prayer breakfast. I usually relied on my friend, Doug Coe, who helped start the National Prayer Breakfast back when Eisen-

---

hower was president, and lead the Fellowship, a ministry to political leaders around the world, focused on prayer.

One year, Doug connected me with Chuck Colson, President Nixon's "hatchet man" who served time in prison for his role in the Watergate scandal, met the Lord while in prison, and founded the Prison Fellowship outreach ministry. After I met Chuck at the Governor's prayer breakfast, I invited him to Annapolis for our Friday legislative prayer meeting. About half the House and Senate showed up to hear him.

We kept in touch through notes and letters, and every year when Chuck came back to the area for the National Prayer Breakfast in DC, he invited me to join him on his annual after-breakfast visit to the Jessup Correctional Institution, where he told his story to the prisoners. But that was always at the height of the legislative session, and I had trouble getting away from all the budget hearings and votes. But in 1988, for some reason my calendar was clear, and I agreed to join him at Jessup. "Can I bring my son, John, with me?" I asked. "Sure," Chuck said.

For the entire week leading up to the Jessup visit, I had disturbing dreams of going into the prison, being kidnapped by the prisoners and held hostage until I met their demands for additional prison funding. Irrational, yes, but I hadn't felt that kind of fear since my drinking days. Before John and I stepped inside Jessup with Chuck, I prayed, *Lord, I'm not comfortable with this, but I believe this is where you want me today. I'm trusting you, I'm with Chuck, and I'm going in.* But my trust wasn't complete, because I pleaded with Chuck, "Will you do me a favor? Don't introduce me. I don't want these people to know that I'm Senator Frank Kelly from Maryland. I'd rather stay in the background and listen to you." "Don't worry about it, Frank," Chuck said, "we'll see how the Lord leads us."

Oh boy, here we go!

We entered the prison through a set of steel, barred doors,

which locked behind us. Then through another set of barred doors, and, CLANGGGG, they reverberated behind us. I think we went through four or five sets of crashing barred doors before we entered a gym filled with 400 or 500 prisoners. John and I sat next to the stage; Chuck stepped to the podium and delivered his usual inspiring message, to the cheers and applause of the prisoners. At the end of his talk, Chuck turned and looked at John and me. "I brought a couple of guests with me today," he said, "Senator Frank Kelly, from the Maryland State Senate, and his son, John. Frank and John love the Lord and wanted to be here today to encourage you in your faith." After a few more stirring words, he finished. I was so thankful that he didn't ask me to say anything!

I stood to leave, and ten steps from my chair, a prisoner came up to me. He told me his name and where he was from, then asked, "Sir, could you please sign my Bible?" "Happy to," I said, and wrote, "Dear Joe, God loves you, and so do I. Senator Frank Kelly." Before I could take another step, another prisoner walked up to me. "Could you sign my Bible?" Within seconds, the prisoners surrounded me, each one holding out a Bible for me to sign. Chuck and John left the gym, so there I was, standing in front of hundreds of prisoners in the Jessup Correctional Institution gym, by myself, and feeling no fear. God relieved my fear by appealing to my ego...though later I realized that most of the prisoners were probably more interested in delaying going back to their cells than getting my autograph.

A half-hour later, one of the prisoners told me, "Everybody else has left. We'll help you get back." He told the guards I was ready to leave, and then called a few dozen other prisoners to form a circle around me and escort me safely to the door. The people who I feared wanted to kidnap me became my protectors. I think that was God's way of showing Himself to me through the prisoners to make the point, *See, Frank. I'm always with you to protect you.* I also learned that the best way for me to overcome my fear is to do the very thing I'm afraid of.

"What happened to you?" Chuck asked when I caught up with him and John, and I told them about the Bible signing line. "That's great," he said, "that's why you're here. They need all the encouragement they can get. I can see that God has His hand on you, and you're going to be a strong and effective leader in Maryland."

'Franklin will call you.'

Before the 2016 presidential election, Franklin Graham, the son of Billy Graham and president of Samaritan's Purse and the Billy Graham Evangelistic Association, embarked on a tour of all 50 statehouses in the country "to challenge Christians to boldly live out their faith and to pray for our nation and its leaders." But Franklin was having trouble getting cooperation from the city of Annapolis to hold a prayer rally there.

One night in February 2016 I got a call from John Coale, a close friend of Franklin's who served with me on the UMMS board. He told me about the problems Franklin was having in Annapolis and asked if there was anything I could do to help clear the way. "Sure, I can try to help," I said.

"Thanks. Franklin will call you," he said, and gave me his cell phone number.

Franklin called and told me how important it was to pray in Annapolis: the country's oldest statehouse still in use, the place where George Washington resigned his commission as commander in chief of the Continental Army in 1783, the site of the nation's capital for a year, and the building where the precursor to the United States Congress had met to govern the country. He told me that every state capitol in the country was cooperating with him, except Annapolis.

I made a few phone calls, and Franklin had everything he needed. He called me from his personal retreat cabin in Alaska to thank me. "You'll never know how much this means to me," he said, and we talked for almost an hour.

When Franklin came to Annapolis for the prayer rally in October, he invited Janet and me to join him, John Coale, and his wife, news commentator Greta Van Sustern, for dinner the night before. The five of us sat and talked for four hours about faith, politics, and the news media.

Over the following months, we exchanged occasional notes and calls. I texted my condolences to Franklin when Billy Graham died in 2018. He texted back his appreciation, and a few days later, called me at six in the morning. "Did you receive the invitation to the memorial service?" he asked. "No," I said. He said, "I'd really like it if you could come." "Thank you," I said, "I would consider that a great honor."

I was among 100 guests who had the honor of meeting the Graham children and grandchildren and praying over the casket before the memorial service in the Billy Graham Library. At the memorial service, I was seated in a section of elected officials, five rows behind the Graham family and President Trump.

After the memorial service, I exchanged a few words with Franklin, who greeted a long receiving line of guests. I'm amazed at his capacity to reach out to so many people, just like his father.

Best wishes to Francis Kelly
Jimmy Carter

In 1979, President Carter faced a tough re-election challenge because of skyrocketing inflation and unemployment during his first term, so he invited state-level Democratic legislators to briefings at the White House to woo their support for his campaign.

I rode down to one of the briefings with Mickey Steinberg, the President of the Maryland Senate. He asked me, "Where should we park?" I pointed to the White House. "I came here years ago for Nixon. Just pull right up to the gate and we will park next to the White House; that's where I parked before."

A Secret Service agent with a clipboard met us when we pulled up. "Can I help you?"

"I am Senator Steinberg, and this is Senator Kelly from Maryland. We are here to see the president."

"I don't see your names on the list," said the agent.

"Here's the telegram with our invitation."

The agent pointed towards the White House. "Park over there."

We parked right on the portico in front of the White House. We got out of the car—this is the God's truth—and knocked on the front door of the White House as if we had just been in the neighborhood and stopped by to see the president.

A Marine opened the door, "Who are you? What are

you doing here?"

We showed him our telegram.

The Marine pointed across the grounds. "You are supposed to be over at the old State House building; that's where briefings are held."

"Sorry, we didn't know."

"That's fine," said the Marine, "I see your telegram; you're fine."

As we walked over to the briefing room, we stared over at the West Wing, and could not resist. We walked right into the West Wing, waved hello to Vice President Mondale, and walked out. Today, we would be shot!

At the briefing, every cabinet secretary came out and spoke to us. Also, Alfred Kahn, a Cornell professor and Carter's inflation advisor, gave us a lecture about inflation. He kept it clear and simple, and he definitely helped me better understand the problem of inflation, but he lost all credibility when he talked about how he woke up every morning trying to figure out how to climb out of the economic mess we were in but could not come up with an answer.

Mickey turned to me and whispered, "Carter's done; he's dead. If this is his chief advisor, I'm not voting for him." We walked back over to the White House after the briefing, where they properly escorted us through the front door, into a receiving line to shake hands and snap a photo with President Carter, and then took us up to the second-floor veranda above the West Wing for lunch.

Governor Hughes looked out towards the front of the White House. "What is that car with Maryland Senate tags doing down there?"

Mickey boasted, "That's my car; Frank and I parked there!"

"How did you do that? I parked five blocks away.

How the hell did you park there?"

Mickey piled on. "Governor, you need contacts, you have to know how to maneuver your way around this town. Kelly and I are important."

After lunch, when it was time to leave, Mickey whispered to me, "Let's get down there first and really stick it to them." We stood next to the car grinning like Cheshire cats as our colleagues walked past us, shaking their heads and sneering in disbelief, "How did you guys pull that off?" "Mickey," I crowed, "aren't you glad I came with you today?"

THE GIPPER AND THE BUSHES

I met Ronald Reagan several times. I had joined the American Legislative Exchange Council, a national group of conservative legislators from both sides of the aisle—blue dog Democrats, southern Democrats, and Republicans—who supported Reagan. President Reagan invited us to the White House frequently for briefings.

Cutting taxes was one of Reagan's first priorities. I was in my office in Annapolis one day, and the phone rang at around 11 in the morning. "This is Ms. Simmons from the White House." I thought, *yeah, sure, sure.* "The president asked me to call you. We need your help."

I could tell she was serious. "What for?"

"The tax bill is on the floor this afternoon, and we are 14 votes shy."

"You're kidding me; I can't believe it!" A major tax reduction should pass easily.

"Well, we have to turn around some votes, so we are calling legislators who we feel have good relationships with their Congressperson. Do you know Roy Dyson?"

Roy Dyson was a Representative from Southern Maryland who had been in the Maryland legislature for years before his election to Congress.

I said, "I know Roy well—you think he is going to vote against this bill?"

"That's the word. We need you to call him and turn him around."

I called Roy right away. He was on the House floor at the time, so I left a message with his aide to call me—"It's very, very important."

Roy called back ten minutes later. "What's up, Frank?"

I got right to the point. "Roy, what are you doing down there?"

"What do you mean?"

"Am I hearing right? You are going to vote against this tax cut?"

"Well, Frank, I don't know, I don't know. We need the revenue—we have all this debt."

I warned him, "Roy, you represent southern Maryland—you understand how conservative they are. If you vote against this tax cut, your career is over. And another thing—if you do it, I will spend next summer knocking on doors in your district telling everyone that you voted against it. That is how strong I feel about this."

"You wouldn't, would you?"

"You know damn well I would." I said, "Roy, I need your commitment. The White House called me, and they need your vote. I am asking you, will you give us your vote?"
"Alright, Frank. You have my vote; you've got it."

That was one vote, and the tax cut passed by four. Ronald Reagan was a master at working through personal

THE WHITE HOUSE

WASHINGTON

April 30, 1981

Dear Senator Kelly,

I am pleased you could attend today's White House briefing on my Economic Recovery Program.

No issue is more important to the future of our nation than the rejuvenation of our economy. As a state legislator you are a pivotal opinion maker as well as an elected representative of the people. I hope I can count on your support for our efforts in restoring a vibrant economy and returning to the states the powers and revenues usurped by the Federal government.

I appreciate your serious consideration of our proposals, and look forward to working with the state legislatures as we move forward. I hope you agree that protecting our citizens from the ravages of inflation and unemployment should be the number one priority for all public officials.

Sincerely,

Ronald Reagan

relationships. He had asked everyone in the American Legislative Exchange Council to work on Congresspersons they knew, and they turned the vote around.

That same afternoon, Donald Regan, the president's chief of staff, stopped by Roy Dyson's office about six o'clock at night with a handwritten note from President Reagan. *Congressman Dyson, I cannot thank you enough for your vote. It was important for America, and it was a good vote for you. Please join me for breakfast at the White House Thursday morning.*

Roy called me afterward, all giddy. "Man, I can't believe this. I voted for one bill and I had breakfast with the president. He said I could call him any time I want! I get along better with the Republican White House than I ever did with any Democrats, all because you called me!"

"Don't you forget it, you son of a gun."

President Reagan wrote me a letter also, thanking me for my help, but he did not invite me to breakfast.

My Favorite Presidents

The only presidents I admire more than Reagan are George Washington and Abraham Lincoln.

George Washington led by example and demonstrated profound wisdom. After leading the Continental Army to victory in the Revolutionary War, he could have consolidated his personal political power. Instead, to give the young democracy latitude to form a representative government, he voluntarily resigned as commander in chief and returned to private life. He gave his resignation speech at the Maryland statehouse in 1783.

On Washington's birthday every year the Maryland Senate commemorates his speech by meeting in the old Senate chamber where Washington delivered it. On the 200th anniversary of that speech, my colleagues honored me by asking me to give the Senate address that day. I spoke from the same spot where Washington stood and recounted his historic act of statesmanship, humility, and wisdom.

Lincoln's leadership style was equally admirable. If I were the president or a governor, I would do what he did. I would bring the smartest people into my camp, even if they were on the opposing side of the political aisle.

Lincoln's character was exemplary. He never gave up. He was thoughtful and prayerful, and never bragged about himself.

*Janet and Frank with
President George H. W. Bush*

That is an example of how Reagan accomplished so much. Politicians today do not seem to know how to work that way.

I will never forget the day in the early 1990s when I was up at Charlie Cawley's home in Maine, about 80 miles from where President George H. W. Bush had a home in Kennebunkport. It was a Saturday afternoon, and we heard a knock at the door—it was President Bush and Hugh Sidey, the presidential historian and one of Mr. Bush's best friends.

"I thought I would come up and eat lunch with you—I outran those Secret Service turkeys," Bush gloated. He loved his cigarette-style speedboat, and always tried to give the slip to the Secret Service when he took it out on the water. I found him to be a kind man; a down-to-earth person. I've met his wife Barbara on other occasions—what a pistol; she did not suffer fools at all.

In 2000, the Republican Party asked me to raise money for George W. Bush's election campaign. I told them I could not raise money for someone I did not know personally. They called me back and asked, "Can you be in Austin on Monday at noon for lunch with Governor Bush?" *Certainly!* There were only two tables and a dozen guests at the luncheon. Then-Governor Bush sat at my table, and I sat right next to his college roommate from Yale.

After Bush became president, I met him quite a few more times when he came to Maryland for fundraisers. He always invited me to the VIP room with a hundred or so others, and sometimes I would bring the boys. Somehow, he remembered us. "Oh yes, the Kellys from Baltimore!" He did not leave office with the best reputation, but I believe history will treat him well for the way he handled the

"The Kellys from Baltimore" meet President George W. Bush

events after the terrorist attack on September 11, 2001.

BLAZING THE TRAIL

Not every bill I worked on was popular, at least not at the beginning.

The North Central Railroad (NCR) hike and bike trail stirred up more controversy than almost any issue I ever dealt with. People in northern Baltimore County feared that motorcycle gangs would invade their backyards if we built the trail. They packed a hearing at Hereford high school, ready for a fight. A

The 20-mile NCR (Torrey C. Brown) hike and bike trail stretches from Hunt Valley to the PA Line.

scary looking guy with a beard and a red and black checkered shirt started the meeting with a threatening rallying cry, "The first thing we need to do is kill all the politicians!" His outrage whipped the crowd into a cheering frenzy.

I listened to all the yelling and screaming, and at the end, they asked me what I was going to do. I stood up and told them I planned to vote in favor of the trail. They wanted to tar and feather me then, but I didn't give in to the crowd and voted for the trail, which is very popular. No gangs invade the trail, but I do know of families who have moved to the neighborhoods along the trail to be closer to it.

The light rail that runs from Baltimore to Hunt Valley is a similar case. Not many people liked the idea, but I worked hard on it, and it has reduced traffic congestion along the York Road and I-83 corridors.

CREATING CAVE'S VALLEY AND
PRESERVING GREENSPACE

Sometimes it's what you don't build that counts. I have always valued preserving green space in Baltimore County. I opposed building 3,500 townhomes at Hayfields in Hunt Valley, and when a developer wanted to build estate homes at Oregon Ridge, I sponsored a bond bill to preserve it forever as a park.

And sometimes the best way to preserve greenspace is to build something that protects the land from something else. In the late 1980s a group of Baltimore's top business leaders, including Bernie Trueschler of BG&E, Furlong Baldwin of Mercantile Bank, and Les Disharoon of Monumental Life Insurance, approached me with their vision to build a private golf course. They wanted a new club that catered to businesses, where the executives they hired from out of town could play. Remember Baltimore's reputation of not being kind to outsiders—if you weren't a Baltimore blue blood, it was difficult to get a membership at the established clubs. They had a location in mind: over 900 acres of the estate of Buzzy Krongard of the Alex. Brown investment banking firm (who in 2001 became Director of Central Intelligence at the CIA) in Cave's Valley near the intersection of Park Heights Avenue and Caves Road.

Their obstacle was the Valleys Planning Council, which represented community associations throughout that corridor between the Baltimore Beltway and the Pennsylvania line, and did not want any kind of growth or development in the valley. The County Council always went along with Valleys recommendations, so the golf course was doomed if Valleys didn't like it. With this backdrop, the business leaders asked me, "Will you help us?"

The golf course would certainly be good for the Baltimore business community. I believed it would also help the Valleys Planning Council achieve its goal of preserving greenspace because a beautiful golf course would enhance the aesthetics of the valley and prevent any other kind of development on the Krongard property. A substantial portion of the 900 acres was deeded in perpetuity to the Maryland Environmental Trust, ensuring its protection from other development. The Planning Council knew that I valued their greenspace as much as they did, and as I presented my case to them over the next year, they trusted me and supported the golf course. The Cave's Valley Golf Club opened in 1991 and is ranked among the Top 100 courses in the U.S. by *Golf Digest*. I finally had enough time and extra money to join myself in 2005!

SHOCK TRAUMA: 'I MADE A PLEDGE'

Janet celebrates the approval of the new Shock Trauma Center building with Dr. and Roberta Cowley

I was first elected on two major promises: one to the voters, that I would fight for fiscal responsibility in state government, and the other to my friend Dutch Ruppersberger, that I would take care of Shock Trauma. I scheduled one of my first meetings after entering office with Dr. R Adams Cowley, the founder of Shock Trauma, and John Ashworth, the Chief Operating Officer. "I don't know either of you," I said, "and you don't know me, but I am going to help you in every way I can to help Shock Trauma because it's all my buddy Dutch ever talks about. I made a pledge to him, and I am going to keep my word."

Shock Trauma was housed at the University of Maryland Hospital, and when the work on the UMMS bill was introduced, Dr. Cowley expressed his preference that Shock Trauma operate independently, and not as a part of the newly privatized UMMS. But based on the research I conducted and the people I talked to about the issue, I concluded that for its own long-term financial sustainability it was better off as part of a larger entity so it could share costs and resources.

"You don't see it now," I explained to Dr. Cowley, "but you've built something great and I want to make sure it lasts well beyond your tenure. I'll protect your independence by making Shock Trauma its own separate department in the hospital, and give it control over its own budget."

Dr. Cowley told me that his biggest need was for more space. At the time, Shock Trauma occupied only three floors in the hospital and could handle only a fraction of the state's total trauma cases, which he estimated

The eight-story R Adams Cowley Shock Trauma Center opened in 1989.

at 3,500 admissions per year, and headed towards 7,500. I worked on a preliminary cost estimate for a new building to handle 7,500 admissions. The cost was $100 million, a jaw-dropping amount for state legislators who had their own projects to fund. I stated the case for saving lives to my Senate colleagues and insisted, as Dr. Cowley put it, that not a single Marylander should be denied the state-of-the-art treatment available at Shock Trauma. We ran into strong resistance to the price tag but kept pushing the case for nearly seven years. We had enough votes in the Senate, but the House balked, so we worked out a compromise, a $50 million bond bill for a building that could handle 3,500 admissions. The bill passed, and Governor Hughes signed it into law, creating the R Adams Cowley Shock Trauma Center at the University of Maryland Medical Center, an eight-story, state-of-the-art hospital building.

The night the bill was signed, the Cowleys, Janet, and I went out to dinner to celebrate. Dr. Cowley had just finished climbing one mountain and was ready to scale the next one. "Now we need new helicopters," he told me. Shock Trauma relied on the state police's aging Bell JetRanger helicopters to bring patients to the Center. "They're too small," he told me, "and the pilots can only fly by sight. They don't have instruments to guide them in bad weather automatically, and they don't even have locator beacons. If one of them ever crashed, it could take a long time to find it." Dr. Cowley explained how a fleet of faster helicopters, with room for a co-pilot, a second patient and additional medic, and equipped with high-tech IFR (Instrument Flight Rules) equipment to help pilots navigate in bad weather, could respond more quickly and save more lives.

"Are you crazy?" I said. "How much are they going to cost?"

"I don't know," Dr. Cowley said, "but we'll probably need twelve of them. Maybe $2 million to $3 million each."

My voice raised an octave or two. "It took us seven years to get the building, and now you're asking me to do this? How are we going to pay for it?"

He had obviously given it some thought and done the math. "We could raise automobile registrations by $5."

My voice returned to normal. "That's not a bad idea," I said, "that might work." It did not seem like an excessive amount, and at that time, most of the patients at Shock Trauma were auto accident victims. At the next legislative session, I introduced a bill for the helicopters. Several colleagues came up to me and said some variation of, "Look, Frank, you got your building, now lay off. We're going to kill this helicopter bill; it costs too much. Save yourself the embarrassment and withdraw the bill."

"It's not about me," I said. "I'm fine if someone else wants to introduce it; we just need the helicopters." But they didn't budge, and I agreed to withdraw the bill.

About a year later, on a Sunday morning after I got home from church, the phone rang. It was Dr. Cowley. "Frank, we have a major problem. We just lost two of our finest this morning. A Bell JetRanger delivered a patient and then crashed in the fog on its way back to Frederick. It took six hours to find it, in Leakin Park. We lost the pilot and the medic."

I re-introduced the helicopter bill on Monday morning, and this time, the governor and the Senate leaders realized we had to act. They appointed me Chair of a Joint Legislative Committee to study the issue. We recommended the purchase of twelve twin-engine helicopters with room to carry a co-pilot and a second patient, and equipped with instrument navigation, a locator beacon and a hoist for water rescues. To this date, since Shock Trauma deployed the new fleet, they have never had a helicopter equipment failure.

Every day I was in the Senate, and every day since I've been out, I've done all I can to protect, support and enhance Shock Trauma's standing within the University of Maryland Medical System. In 1997, the Dean of the University of Maryland School of Medicine came to me with the idea of establishing Shock Trauma as its own department within the medical school, separate from the department of surgery. But to accomplish that required raising $2.5 million to give the Director of Shock Trauma a permanently-endowed Professorship.

When John Ashworth of the University of Maryland Medical Center and Dr. Seamus Flynn from Shock Trauma heard about the need for the endowment, they approached my friend Charlie Cawley at MBNA. I knew nothing about what they were doing. Charlie and the officers of MBNA told John and Seamus they were willing to contribute the entire $2.5 million needed to create the first endowed Professorship in trauma at a U.S. medical school, but on one condition: that it was named after me. It's called The Honorable Francis X. Kelly Distinguished Professorship of Trauma Surgery. I am honored, but the real significance is the assurance that the Professorship will always be filled, and the life-saving work of Shock Trauma will always go on. I think my dad would have been proud.

The number of admissions to Shock Trauma continued to rise, and by 2014, the Center needed to expand again. The state legislature approved a second building, at the cost of $150 million, which would raise capacity to the 7,500 level that Dr. Cowley had originally requested. There was one twist to the financing plan for this building: Shock Trauma needed to raise $35 million in public donations. The board designated me as Chair of the capital campaign. I started by finding seven people to each contribute $1 million or more, and from that base, we raised the $35 million and opened the new building in 2015.

Today, if someone in Maryland is in an accident, falls, or is the victim of an act of violence, and flies to Shock Trauma, they have a 96% chance of living, no matter how serious their injuries. Maryland's Shock Trauma Center is recognized as the world leader and trains trauma surgeons for the U.S. military, and at trauma centers around the world. Other countries have requested teams from Shock Trauma to come and assist them after earthquakes and other natural disasters.

I made a pledge. I championed Shock Trauma in the Senate, and for 35 years as Chairman of the Board of Visitors, and I will continue to take care of Shock Trauma.

'That's a really cool helicopter'

I met Frank for the first time in 1996 after I was promoted to the head of operations at Erickson Retirement Communities. We were customers of Kelly Associates, and John Kelly invited me for a tour of their headquarters in Hunt Valley.

We stepped into Frank's corner office along the way, just to say hello, and I happened to see a picture of a Medivac helicopter on his bookcase. I launched into a monologue about my knowledge and experience with emergency response systems.

"Wow, that's a really cool helicopter," I said. "When I was in college, I read a book about Shock Trauma, and I had an internship there." I had no idea that Frank knew everything about Shock Trauma.

"I just moved from the Detroit area," I went on, "where the locals tell you that if you're ever in an accident, make sure you crawl across the border into the Dearborn district, because the average emergency response time in Detroit is something like 45 minutes, compared to just a couple of minutes in Dearborn."

I told Frank about how the people in Maryland don't realize how valuable their emergency management system is. "They have no idea that no matter where you are in Maryland, you have access to the finest emergency care in the world," I informed him.

Frank smiled, listened, and nodded as I continued lecturing him about Shock Trauma. "They assess your situation and decide where you'll go and what kind of transportation will take you, based on your injuries."

When I finally stopped for breath, Frank said, "Well, I happen to be the Chairman of the Shock Trauma Board of Visitors."

You know those cartoons where a normal size person shrinks down to the size of a thimble? That's how embarrassed I was for shooting off my mouth.

I braced for what Frank might say next, but there was no way I could have been ready to hear this: "I can see you're very

181

knowledgeable and a big supporter of Shock Trauma," he said. "How would you like to be on the Board of Visitors?"

That's Frank—so focused on the goal of saving the lives of Marylanders that he looked past my gaffe.

The reason that emergency management is so much better in Maryland than in Michigan is that Frank is committed to the vision that Shock Trauma will provide the best possible clinical care for the citizens of Maryland. He will defend that vision against any private or political interests that might compromise it. Shock Trauma is a case study in how the politicians do the right thing for the citizens.

I describe Frank's leadership style as a "passionate coach." He builds relationships with all sides, and at the same time directly and honestly confronts any weaknesses and challenges. Because of Frank's passionate and committed leadership, I'm part of a talented corps that wants to do our best to give Marylanders world-class emergency medical care.

-Rick Grindrod
CEO
Provider Partners Health Plan

REFLECTIONS ON POWER AND INFLUENCE

Sitting sheepishly in the rear of the Senate chamber those first two months after I was elected, I thought back to what the Franciscan monk and AA had taught me: enjoy the gift of the present moment; whatever happens next is out of my control. Those principles guided my approach in the Senate, as it guides my approach to every endeavor. My best hope for success in anything is to turn every day over to God, show up, and use the gifts He gave me to deal with whatever He puts on my plate.

Holding God in awe, rather than the people around me, lets me look at anyone I meet in the same way, no matter what their status. They put their pants on the same way I put on mine, whether they are the CEO of a large corporation, or

As a first-term State Senator, I sat in the back row and turned every day over to God.

a college president, or the president of the United States. That perspective eliminates fear and intimidation and gives me the freedom to be myself in my dealings with my colleagues.

I like people, so holding conversations and building relationships come naturally to me. Living in the present moment means I do not always have an agenda when I meet someone, so people are relaxed with me. High profile people are sensitive to others always trying to get a piece of them in some way or another. When I meet someone, I am not looking for anything from them, so they will talk to me; they will return my phone calls. I don't smother them; I respect their privacy. I try to get to know them. I ask questions, figure out what drives them, learn what their needs and goals are, and find out how I can help them.

REAL POWER DOESN'T CORRUPT

Of all the aphrodisiacs, power is the most potent and addictive. Power will corrupt if you use it to advance your own cause. But I believe our founding fathers expected government representatives to prayerfully and thoughtfully do their homework, listen to as much input as possible, and then decide based on what they judge as right and best for the citizens. I learned that the real power is God Himself, and that my power comes from surrendering my will to His, and praying for wisdom.

I saw the thirst for personal power destroy many people in Annapolis. One of my colleagues, I'll call him Senator C., served on my committee for years. He had a different girl every night. Janet called them Jezebels—women who stalk after men of power and influence, suck them in and destroy them. I made friends with Senator C., and one Saturday he came to me with a disturbed look on his face. "Frank, I need to talk to you. It's really important. I need your advice."

We found a quiet spot in the Senate lounge, and he continued, "I lost everything down here—my wife, my kids—between my drinking and the women. I have watched you for eight years. How do you do it? I don't know how to deal with it all."

How did I deal with it all? I am not a goody two shoes, but my parents gave me a keen moral compass, which helped to keep me on a straight path. And, I had a prayer partner, Stelman Smith, who helped me understand that I was engaged in spiritual warfare, and prayed with me about everything I worked on for all my twelve years in Annapolis. I also had AA; if I had been drinking, I would not have known what I was truly up against or been equipped to handle the temptations, and probably would have succumbed.

God gave me a window with Senator C., and I simply told him my story and advised him, "You have the problem half licked if you admit you have a problem. Go to AA and work the twelve steps. But you are the one who has to make the decision."

He entered treatment, got sober, and ended up happily married to one of his counselors. Lung cancer cut his life short, but he spent his final years making nationwide public service announcements, warning others not to repeat his mistakes.

Sometimes avoiding temptation is a matter of knowing who and what to stay away from. Harry McGuirk, who served in the State House for 22 years, offered me excellent advice during my first term: be careful with any legislation where cash is involved, because where there is cash, there is a high risk of corruption.

I watched how certain lobbyists manipulated legislators. Senators made only $22,000 a year back then, so some of them wanted to be wined and dined. We had a term for it: *looking for a sponsor.*

There was one lobbyist in particular who I avoided like the plague because I knew how shady he was. In my last year in office, he came to me and asked, "Why won't you ever meet with me? Why don't you talk to me?"

I stated plainly, "We don't have anything to talk about."

"Yes, we do. I want to talk to you; I want to be your friend."

I agreed to talk to him, but I made it as inconvenient as possible for him. "OK—eight o'clock Friday night, in my office. Not at a restaurant!"

I didn't want to discuss any legislation with him, and I didn't beat around the bush when he came to my office. "Here's the deal: you're a nice guy, but your way of doing business is different from my way of doing business. My job is to represent the people of my district, to evaluate every issue objectively and vote in the best interest of my district. I see the way you operate; you are going to try to convince me to do things that may not be in the best interest of my district, and I don't want any part of that. One day a tree is going to fall on you and I don't want to be sitting next to you when it falls." A year later, he went to jail.

Tempting offers don't come only from lobbyists. A prominent businessperson called me one day. "I want to come out and talk to you." I knew exactly what he wanted. He wanted to develop a project in Timonium that the community did not want, and I thought was unfeasible.

"I need your help," he pleaded. "Timonium is the best spot for this—it's perfect. I need you to convince the community."

"No, there is no way I am going to support this."

"You know, Frank, you have a nice business here. I buy a lot of insurance, and if you can see things my way, I can make it very easy for my business to come your way."

I said, "Why don't we just shake hands and say goodbye?"

'My intuition was accurate'

Frank and I would walk into a function together, and people would come up to him right away, "Frank! Frank! How are you?"

Frank would introduce me, "This is my wife, Janet."

"Oh, hello. So Frank, I'd like to talk to you about...." and they would go on to talk about some bill they were working on. Frank thought those people were foolish; if they wanted to get through to him, they should talk to me.

Was I going to stand there for an hour while they talked politics? I don't think so. I had a decision to make: either sit in the corner and pine, or get mad (I saw many wives do both) or mingle and say hello to people. I chose to introduce myself to as many people as I could, talk to them for maybe 15 minutes and learn a little about their lives. I met many lovely people that way.

When Frank walked into a room, he was ready to hug anybody and spend time with anybody, until they proved untrustworthy. I am more reticent. Too many people had ulterior motives, so I liked to stand back a little bit, watch and listen for a while. Frank could pick out most of the people that he should avoid himself, but I had an extra degree of intuition he did not have. There were times when someone spoke to me about something they wanted to do with Frank or for Frank, but I sensed it would end up hurting him in some way. Usually, I could not even put a specific handle on why I felt that way, but in many cases, my intuition was accurate.

On the way home, I would tell Frank what I thought. "I don't trust so-and-so; he didn't even give me eye contact." Other times it worked the other way around. Someone would impress me, and I would tell Frank that I thought he should schedule a meeting with him or her.

We made many lifelong friends and met quite a few influential people during those years in the Senate, and the experiences certainly opened doors for the future for both of us.

We learned valuable lessons that are applicable to every aspect of life: we need to work hard, plan the day, plan the campaign, and do the best job we can, but the results are not always in our hands. We need to surrender the outcome to God.

-Janet Kelly

THE POWER OF PRAYER

Doug Coe, who helped me arrange speakers for the governor's prayer breakfasts when I was organizing them, taught me the power of prayer for bringing about social change. Doug believed that if two or three local leaders in every city in every country prayed for their local and national leaders, more good would come about in our states and communities.

Doug encouraged me to find a prayer partner and begin praying for the state of Maryland. Around 2010 he even called me to say, "I've got a prayer partner for you—Timmy Maloney." I thought it was a great idea, and Doug had mentioned it to Tim, but I didn't act on it right away.

A few years later, at a dinner sponsored by the Fellowship, former Democratic congressman and UN ambassador Tony Hall spoke about how over 200 years ago William Wilberforce and his circle of social reformers prayed and campaigned to abolish slavery in England. Who was sitting at the table next to mine? Timmy Maloney. We looked at each other.

I said to Tim, "I think Congressman Hall was talking to us! I think the Lord is convicting you and me that we should be praying together."

"I'm with you, Frank," Tim said.

Our prayer group expanded recently. At a dinner event, I sat with a retired federal judge, The Honorable Ben Legg, who also knows Tim Maloney. I mentioned that Tim and I pray together every week. "I'd love to do that," he said. "Could I join you?"

"We'd love to have you," I said.

For where two or three have gathered together in My name, I am there in their midst. (Matthew 18:20)

> **Every Tuesday Morning**
>
> Frank and I pray together on the phone on Tuesday mornings at 7:30. It doesn't matter where we are, we've hardly missed a week in four years or so. On a recent Tuesday morning, Frank was in Israel and I was in Cincinnati, but we still called and prayed.
>
> We spend the first few minutes catching up on what's going on in each other's lives and what's going on in state and national politics. Then we get down to business. We pray for the people we know who are sick and suffering, and then for political issues facing the state and the country. Lately, we've been praying for a return to civility in government and public discourse, a healing of the divisions in the country, and an end to the corrosive effects of too much partisanship. We end our time, which typically lasts 15-20 minutes, with a prayer of thanksgiving for the ways we've seen the hand of God answer previous prayers.
>
> My prayer with Frank is one of the highlights of my week. We keep praying because we're both still involved with public issues in one way or another, and we both believe in the power of prayer to help solve them.
>
> -Tim Maloney
> Principal
> Joseph, Greenwald & Laake, PA

MALICE TOWARD NONE

I loved our debates in the Senate. They taught me the importance of doing my own homework, listening to other people's views, and respecting their opinions. My initial instincts usually proved right, but in some instances, I changed my position based on new information. Some bills looked good or looked flawed when first introduced, but after a more thorough analysis, I would see it the other way.

The motorcycle helmet law is one example of when I changed my view. My first impulse was that motorcyclists have a constitutional right to make their own decision about whether or not to wear a helmet. But at the hearings, I learned about the high human cost and societal cost of the deaths and injuries caused by motorcycle accidents, and how the damage extended far beyond the individual motorcyclist. Dr. Cowley told me about specific cases he had seen. In the end, my respect for life, interest in the medical system and fiscal conservatism all drove me to co-sponsor the bill that required motorcyclists to wear helmets.

Most politicians will respect colleagues who fight for what they truly believe in, even if they disagree. My willingness to listen and my straightforward approach helped me get along with both sides of the aisle. One of my most treasured honors came during my last year in Annapolis when my peers voted me one of the five most effective members of the Senate.

Way back during that budget debate in my rookie year in the Senate, one of my colleagues told *The Washington Post*, "Frank's very dedicated, but he thinks spending limits are some sort of biblical pronouncement." Yes, spending limits were important, but I laid everything on the line to defend the sanctity of human life. My passion for standing up for what I believe propelled me into the Senate, and that same passion ultimately ushered me out.

'He's all about bringing people together'

I was on the House budget committee, so I negotiated late into the night in many House and Senate conference committees against Frank on taxes, spending bills and budget cuts. Some days we were on the same side, and some days not, but we always maintained our mutual respect for each other. He's a smart and tough negotiator, but he's all about bringing people together. His friendships and alliances crossed every dimension—party, geography, race—you name it. He had people in every corner that he could talk with, pray with and negotiate with. He was an effective and moderating voice in the legislature because he worked to understand the views of the other side and kept his eye on the long-term economic benefits of every bill.

But he's willing to fight when he has to. In the late 2000s, there was a power struggle involving the CEO of UMMS and the hospital physicians. The tension drew in the Governor and the UMMS board, which included Frank. Frank assessed the situation and believed that the best solution was a change in UMMS leadership. For a long time, he was the lone voice in the wilderness and faced tremendous pressure to back off. But he saw the situation as a threat to the survival of the UMMS system, stood firm in his convictions, led the push for the leadership changes, and eventually, the state leadership came to see that his concerns were well-founded. UMMS would not be in such a strong position today if Frank's courage and Irish stubbornness had not carried the day.

-Tim Maloney
Principal
Joseph, Greenwald & Laake, PA

PRAYER FOR THE CITY
Jeremiah 29:7, 11-13

Also, seek the peace and prosperity of the city
to which I have carried you into exile.
Pray to the LORD for it,
because if it prospers, you too will prosper.
"For I know the plans I have for you," declares the LORD,
"plans to prosper you and not to harm you,
plans to give you hope and a future.
Then you will call on me and come and pray to me,
and I will listen to you.
You will seek me and find me
when you seek me with all your heart."

9

Sixteen Speak Up

Speak up for those who cannot speak for themselves
Proverbs 31:8

As a man or woman of God, there will be times in your life when you have to stand up, draw a line in the sand, and fight for what is important and for what God wants you to defend. My time came in 1990 when God called me to defend the sanctity of human life.

My Senate career was going strong. I had been elected three times, each time by a landslide, and I was cruising towards a fourth term. One evening, while watching the news on television, I saw a report that the Supreme Court passed the *Webster* decision, which meant each state had the right to set its own laws regarding the use of state funds, facilities and employees in performing abortions.

The Federal Government had legalized abortion in *Roe v. Wade*, but now each state could set its own guidelines for enacting it. *Webster* gave the so-called "pro-choice" side, the pro-abortion side, the ammunition they needed to get language in the budget to allow abortions under any circumstances.

Sitting in my chair, I felt the hand of the Lord on my shoulder. I believed it was the Lord because it was gentle. I heard His still, small voice—not screaming, not intimidating—but encouraging me: "This is why you are in the Maryland Senate. This is the issue you have been waiting for."

I did not start out my career in politics thinking about abortion. The subject makes many people uncomfortable, and it should because it's murder. Intrinsically most people know that, and they're uncomfortable.

The Declaration of Independence asserts that "...all men are created equal, that they are endowed by their Creator with certain unalienable Rights, that among these are Life, Liberty and the pursuit of Happiness." This is what the government is supposed to protect. I believe that a baby in the womb is a life, and we are obligated to protect it like any other life.

The pro-abortion side introduced a bill permitting unrestricted rights to abortions any time until delivery and birth, even for minors without their parents' consent, which made it by far the most liberal law in the country. Those of us in the Senate who believed abortion is wrong and that there are two lives to protect, led by Senator Jack Cade and me, banded together with Cardinal Keeler, Catholic Charities lobbyists Dick Dowling and Pat Kelly, and others in the pro-life movement. We held meeting after meeting in our offices to plan the strategy to prevent the further legalization of abortion. We met with the representatives of the other side and tried to work out a compromise. But how can you compromise life?

Senator Cade and I introduced our own bill that allowed for abortion only if the life of the mother was threatened, and in the cases of rape and incest. It prohibited abortion for sex selection and birth control and contained a long chapter on informed consent.

The major media outlets totally opposed what we were doing and editorialized against it. The media focused mainly on the right to choose and the *Roe v. Wade* decision. I could sense their bias when they interviewed me and anyone on the pro-life side.

The media, the majority of the Senate, the majority of the House, and a majority of the public all aligned against us. The Senate wanted to bring the pro-abortion bill to a vote, and it was certain to pass. Our best chance at preventing passage was to invoke the "unlimited debate" procedure, a rule designed to give the minority an opportunity to express its views through ongoing debate—a filibuster. We could talk forever and kill the legislation unless 32 members of the Senate voted to stop us, which meant we needed 16 votes on our side to keep talking.

'WE WERE NOT GOING TO FOLD'

Jack Cade and I organized the team. We had 18 people willing to fight the bill, but two of them told us that if Mike Miller, the President of the Senate, called them personally and asked them to vote for the pro-abortion bill, they would change sides. That left 16 votes I considered solidly pro-life, so we alerted the other side that if their bill came out on the floor, we would filibuster it.

Even on the day the pro-abortion side intended to introduce their bill, we hoped to avoid a filibuster by offering amendments restricting the permissible circumstances for performing abortions. I began that morning by reading from the Old Testament book of Proverbs. I was reading in Proverbs because, before the legislative session had even begun

Sixteen spoke up for life

that year, Frank III had recommended that I read a chapter a day as a way to discern God's wisdom. As God worked it out, I read Proverbs chapter 31, verses 8-9, which says, *"Speak for those who cannot speak for themselves, for the rights of all who are unfortunate and defenseless."* What better confirmation to proceed with the filibuster could I have asked for? After the opposition voted down our amendments, I knew without any doubt what God wanted me to do. On the Senate floor I announced, "Ladies and gentlemen of the Senate, we are in for a long siege," and read Proverbs 31:8-9 aloud to everyone.

Those verses address the heart of the issue. A baby in the womb cannot speak for itself, but we could filibuster on its behalf. I told them about the circumstances of my own birth, "I would not be here today if my parents had believed in abortion."

We set up our team and sent one person out at a time to talk—twelve talkers for one hour each per day—while the rest of us pulled together in what was the old House Appropriations room in the original State House, where we had food, drinks, and prayer. We could have talked for two years. The more hours we held the floor, the more irritated the opposition grew.

On day three, I wanted to make sure we still had our votes, so I checked in with everyone individually. One colleague divulged, "Frank, you know I am with you and you know I am pro-life, but I have to tell you I have just been offered a position on the Workman's Compensation Commission. It's a lifetime job at $100,000 a

"We could have talked for two years."

year. If the governor were to call me and say, 'Senator, if you want to go on this Commission, you had better back off your stance on this filibuster and let this bill slide,' I would do it."

Immediately I called Governor Schaefer, who gave me an earful. "Frank, what are you doing down there? You are tying up the whole state! What are you doing? Why don't you just vote against their bill? You are going to lose your seat over this. You're a great Senator, and I need you."

I reminded him, "Governor, people seem to forget that we are talking about life and death here. Two lives are at stake, and this bill allows abortion right up until birth."

He admitted, "I am torn. I have people in my office for it, and people against it. I don't know what to do."

I asked, "Do me a favor, promise me you'll stay out of this, and don't call anybody in the Senate. One person is worried you are going to call him and he is going to lose his appointment."

He gave me his word, "I will stay out of it, tell him not to worry, and I won't call him."

I went back to my colleague and assured him, "I just talked to the governor; there is no problem, and he is not going to call you. Hang with us. You can speak forever on this and you don't have to worry about your appointment."

Within an hour, he stood up on the Senate floor and gave one of the most inspiring pro-life speeches I ever heard. He was all in, and we had our sixteen; we won. From then on, the question was when the other side would decide to fold because we were not going to fold.

While all this went on, our team continued praying in the House Appropriations room. Most of those on the other side sat idly in the lounge, read books, or watched the NCAA college basketball tournament. I saw qualities emerge in my colleagues that they had never seen before in themselves, and I saw God working through them, and strengthening their hearts. *O God, how great is the power of prayer! If everybody in the Senate would pray together, we would do the right thing!* Sadly, that was not the case.

Mike Miller broke the unwritten rules of the Senate: never ask somebody to do something against their conscience, and never ask someone to do something that would hurt them in their own district. But the gloves were off, and he persuaded two on our side to switch their votes. Hoping for one more convert, Miller took a chance and called for a vote. At eight o'clock that night, the tally came in, and we held our 16 votes to continue the filibuster. "Hell will freeze over before they get that last vote," I declared to a *New York Times* reporter.

At 11 PM on Saturday night, Tommy Bromwell rushed over to tell me that one of our colleagues who had voted against us was across the street at the bar in Harry Browne's Restaurant, distraught and conscience-stricken over what he had done. I grabbed two of the state troopers who were assigned to the Senate building and sent them over to bring him back. Tommy and Jack Cade stood with me, and I assured our colleague, "You are still with us. We know what you had to do, we understand you did not want to do it, and you will be with us until the end of this thing. When we meet to pray, you are going to be with us, and you will be with us forever. Nobody has a problem with you. We all understand why you did it."

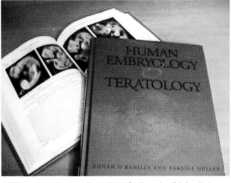

"The book used at the School of Medicine says life begins at conception."

After losing his vote, Mike Miller knew it was over. On the fourth day of the filibuster, he called me up to the podium and confronted me, "What the hell are you trying to do, ruin the Senate? You are holding up the whole state. Nothing is moving. We have to end this thing; how are we going to end it? This is going to cost you your seat."

"I know," I replied, "but it's not going to cost me my soul."

I had them ring the bells, and I asked everyone in the Senate to come into the chamber. I brought a book on human embryology I had researched at the University of Maryland Library, and the Bible. I read Proverbs 31:8-9, then began my speech.

"Ladies and Gentlemen of the Senate, if you don't want to believe this book, the holy word of God, then believe this book, a human book taught in the school we fund every day, the University of Maryland School of Medicine. It says life begins at conception, and I am at my wit's end trying to understand how all of you don't see it, and why we are blinded, and why we cannot write legislation that defends the life of the unborn."

Dead silence. No one reacted, and then somebody stood up from the other side and said, "Look, our bill gives the woman the right to choose. In the old days, there were coat hanger abortions, and we have to stop all that kind of stuff from happening."

All I could muster at that point was a prayer of dejection, *OK, Lord, you gave me the gift of persuasion, but I am not being very persuasive because I am not winning any votes.* The next day the newspaper criticized me for reading the Bible on the floor of the Senate. After that, we stopped trying to reason with the other side.

We were five days into the filibuster. We talked for another full day, and when we got to the seventh day, Mike Miller was beside himself. He called me into his office and said, "We have to end this thing. We're holding up the entire state." So, we offered a compromise. "I have a solution: you pass our bill and then pass the other bill, and we'll take it to referendum and let the voters decide." It was one of my most gratifying moments in the Senate when Mike announced the eight-day filibuster would end on the condition that the Senate passes our bill. It passed indeed, with 24 votes! Not one of our team voted for their bill, which passed with 29 votes. Eight days before, the opposition rammed one of the most liberal abortion bills in the country down our throats, but we stood firm, and now the voters would decide.

With our work on the Senate bill completed, the issue moved to the House of Delegates, where Tim Maloney led

---

When the filibuster ended, I invited the sixteen senators to the House Lounge to speak to the pro-life House delegates, about 50 of us. When they walked in the room, we were so impressed with their courage, stamina and commitment that we broke into a 10-minute standing ovation.

-Tim Maloney

the pro-life cause. The opposition lobbied the House to kill both bills. They planned to attack me, defeat me in the upcoming primary election to get me out of the Senate and pass their bill the following year.

Tim Maloney and the other pro-life members of the House prayed for us and stayed with us out on the Senate floor throughout the entire ordeal. The ovation they gave us when the filibuster ended felt as if it went on for an hour! That was an uplifting experience none of us have ever forgotten.

'I WOULD NOT DO IT ANY OTHER WAY'

When the time came to start my re-election campaign, Dick Bennett, who was then the leader of the Republican Party and is now a highly respected federal judge, invited me to lunch at the Valley Inn on Falls Road and made me an offer. "Look, you are going to lose the Democratic primary. We would love you to be a Republican, and you are really a Republican at heart anyway. If you change parties, we will make a big deal of it and announce it to the world. You will be re-elected because you will win in the general election, but if you remain a Democrat, you are going to lose in the primary." Then he made a promise I will never forget. "If you run, if you change parties, I can assure you that we will run you for governor or the United States Senate."

I was skeptical. "Dick, you don't have the power to do that; you are only one person."

He answered back, "I am chairman of the state party now, and I spoke with the chairperson in every county in the state. They all agreed that if you change parties, we will support you if you decide to run for governor or U.S. Senate."

*Frank III, John, David and Bryan on
the campaign trail in 1990*

I could tell he was serious. "Let me think about it."

I talked to Janet, prayed about it, and felt that if God wanted me in the Maryland Senate, He could get me there regardless of my party. As a Democrat, I would be among the leadership of the majority party, and in a position to impact legislation to help Marylanders. As a new Republican, it would have been difficult to gain a leadership position.

There were pros and cons to running for Governor or the U.S. Senate. With my experience in Annapolis, I would be a strong candidate, and with the backing of the Republican Party, I would receive the necessary funding. Dick Bennett thought I would certainly win, but I wanted to run for the right reasons, and it became clear to me that God did not want me to change parties just to win an election.

I met Dick for lunch again. I thanked him for thinking so highly of me, and told him, "Dick, I will be a Republican someday. When I change parties, it will be at the right time for the right reason, but changing parties to get re-elected, that's not me."

"I don't like it, but I think I understand," he said.

I kicked off my campaign, and Planned Parenthood and the National Organization for Women kicked off theirs. They flooded the phones and told every lie in the world about me. They dialed every female registered Democrat in my district and swarmed the polling places with a vengeance. When my sons and daughters-in-law distributed my literature at the

'Only God can see to the end of the road'

After my brothers and I and our wives worked the polls all day, where angry voters barked at us and some spat on us, we headed to what was supposed to be our victory party at the Timonium Fairgrounds. My dad was nothing but gracious in his concession remarks, and I felt led to stand and say what was on my heart.

"Who wouldn't be proud to have a father who was willing to pay the price for standing up for what is right?" I said. "Dad, we can see to the bend in the road, but only God can see to the end of the road."

Little did we know at the time the plans God had for our family. The business challenge we faced immediately after the election required the whole family's full focus and attention, and God brought us through.

Then, I believe that because my father stood up for life, God chose to bless him with new life in our family. First with David Jr., seven months after losing the election, and again six months later with his namesake, Francis X. Kelly IV. And since then God has filled the road of new life with 20 more grandchildren.

-Frank Kelly III

Controversy swirls over Kaos club from abutting communities
Page 6

Rookie coach at Dulaney grapples with lack of strong feeder program
Page 28

Patuxent Publishing Company

TOWSON TIMES

Volume 23, Number 43   Wednesday, January 15, 1992

LIFE AFTER POLITICS

Frank Kelly finds blessings in defeat / page 20

"Frank Kelly finds blessings in defeat" (holding Frank Kelly IV as David Kelly Jr. looks on)

polls, people spit on the literature, and on my sons and their wives.

I lost my seat, along with three others from our team that they also took out. In the subsequent session, the liberal abortion bill passed the Senate in about 45 minutes because there was nobody to filibuster, and not enough votes to sustain a filibuster even if someone had tried. The right-to-life supporters raised a petition and took the issue directly to the voters in a referendum, but the citizens upheld the liberal law by 60% to 40%.

The abortion vote was a watershed moment, and the state of Maryland—and the entire country—has paid the price. I don't think things have ever been the same in Annapolis since then. We don't value life as much anymore; look at our murder rate. Our country was founded on the principle of protecting life—all life. It's as clear as can be to me, and it's hard for me to understand why others cannot see it. Slavery split our nation's families, and abortion is doing the same thing.

I believe God is not finished with this issue yet. More and more, science is showing that life truly begins in the womb. Therefore, we must protect the rights of the baby as well as the rights of the mother. If I had to do it over again, I would not do it any other way, because I believe abortion is taking an innocent life.

After losing, I asked God for strength and for wisdom in dealing with the people who had hurt me so much, and friends who had turned on me. *What would Jesus do?* I always ask myself when I think about how to respond to my opponents. I hold no negative feelings toward anyone on the other side, none of them, and I hope they feel the same about me. I have no bitterness at all toward Mike Miller, even though, in the heat of one debate I had lost my temper and called him "the biggest liar I have ever seen in my life." "Just calm down," he told me, and later I apologized to him. I believe you can disagree with someone and still show love and respect.

I've supported Mike as President of the Senate his entire career, and we remain friends.

On one of the occasions when I met President Reagan, I told him I had registered as a Democrat when I lived in Pennsylvania because the Republicans in my town were corrupt, and besides, being an Irish Catholic, I wanted to vote for Kennedy. "I was a Democrat too," he joked, "and I changed, so it's never too late!" The Democratic party drifted more and more to the left, more pro-abortion and more anti-business, and I could not identify with them anymore. A few months after my Senate defeat, I switched to the Republican Party, still with no plans to run for elected office.

Over the years, I learned that I do not need to be out front to lead, I do not have to be in the Senate, and I do not have to be the center of attention to be effective. I look back and I know that God put me in the Senate for a reason, and He took me out for a reason.

'Nothing but praise for Frank Kelly'

The first time I ever saw Frank was in the Maryland House of Delegates. I was a member of the House and saw a group of citizen activists sitting in the gallery. The delegates from Baltimore County were pointing up at him. He was pushing his Operation STOP project and holding the delegates' feet to the fire to move it forward. I met him personally in 1978 when we bonded together as State Senators. Years later we worked together to help elect Mickey Steinberg as Senate President.

Frank was a brilliant advocate for change on the Budget and Taxation Committee. He is a leader in everything he does, and a very compassionate person. He always helped those who couldn't help themselves.

I chaired the Judicial Proceedings Committee before becoming Senate President, so we rarely worked on the same bills or issues. But as Senate President, my charge is to govern, to adopt bills and move the Senate forward, so the abortion debate was a difficult and trying time. Frank and the others who filibustered were ardent pro-life advocates, and there was no grey area. Others in the Senate supported a woman's right to choose, and still others thought that religion had no place in the Senate and said that we should not even be talking about abortion.

I will always remember Frank's tenacity. When he has a goal, nothing stops him from reaching it. For me, presiding over the Senate, I had to put my personal feelings aside and try to find what the majority will was, and move the body forward. The two-bill compromise Frank proposed was the only way to get off the dime. We gave the Maryland voters the opportunity to decide, and they reflected their desires in the next election.

I look at Frank's marriage to his beautiful wife, Janet, his wonderful children and grandchildren, the business he built and his philanthropic activities, and I see an honest man, a hard-driven man who overcame personal obstacles and helped others along the way. I'm proud to have served with him. He's a living example of what the Bible tells us to do here on earth—to help our neighbor. I have nothing but praise for Frank Kelly.

-Thomas V. Mike Miller Jr., President of the Maryland Senate

'Integrity'

The minute you lay eyes on Frank and hear what he has to say on any topic, you're struck with the thought that here is a man of intellect and integrity. Frank has core beliefs about what is right and what is wrong, and never waivers. The nature of politics is to follow where the political winds blow; the nature of integrity is Frank Kelly.

-Alan M. Rifkin
Managing Partner
Rifkin Weiner Livingston LLC

10

Living the Dream

Whatever you do, work at it with all your heart, as working for the Lord, not for men, since you know that you will receive an inheritance from the Lord as a reward.
Colossians 3:23-24

Everyone asks Janet and me the same question: *How do you keep your four sons working together without killing each other?* People seem more impressed by the family harmony than anything the business itself has accomplished.

After Janet and I started our business, I always dreamed that my sons would work with me some day, just as I had dreamed of working with my father. But when Frank III graduated from Cornell in 1986, he was not thinking about pooling small businesses through their trade associations. He served in Japan for a summer as a missionary. When he returned, he still wanted to impact the world for the Lord but believed that God was calling him to start from home, following the Acts 1:8 approach of reaching out locally, then nationally, and then to the ends of the earth.

I had an idea for helping him fulfill his calling. "Frank, give me a year working in the business," I suggested. "Our business is all about relationships, and through relationships, you can impact lives. And you can have the flexibility you want to lead Bible studies with your friends, coach and reach kids through lacrosse, start a ministry at Calvert Hall, whatever you want, and you can do it from your cubicle at Kelly-Chick."

Happy retirement, Janet!

"Alright, Dad, I will give you a year," he said.

When Frank III came in, Janet thought it was a good time for her to retire. She didn't think it would work having the husband and the wife, the mother and father and son all in the same business—too many different roles and dynamics to manage.

Frank III started working in association sales. John joined a year later after graduating from Washington College, also in association sales. David came in 1989 after graduating from the University of North Carolina, on the property and casualty side. Bryan followed out of UNC in 1991, selling to the brokers.

As each one came into the business, I reminded them that the most important thing is that the business is not the most important thing. Yes, we need to make money, but money is not our god. God is God. Though each of them already knew that and practiced it in their lives, I wanted to remind them that God has given us fertile land to plow in the insurance and employee benefits business. If we're faithful stewards of the resources and opportunities He has given us to help our clients solve their employee benefits problems, He will bless us with crops and growth.

Why do they work together so well? Because they

all put God first and put their unique gifts and talents to work for the good of our customers, our employees, and our communities. And they do it with passion. As Emerson said, "Nothing great was ever achieved without enthusiasm." Frank III is a strong leader, and when he sinks his teeth into something, he doesn't let go. He keeps the trains running on time. John is a true visionary. He has eyes to see what others can't see. David can do anything you ask of him, and he does it with a sense of humor that keeps everyone around him in balance. Bryan is a natural born coach. He gets to know people as individuals, and people know he's always there for them.

'TURRIS FORTIS MIHI DEUS'

Kelly-Chick adopted the Kelly family crest, which we had discovered on our trip to Ireland in 1989, as our company logo. The timing was perfect because we needed to hold on to its motto, *Turris Fortis Mihi Deus* (*God is My Tower of Strength*) for encouragement through the decade of transition and turmoil that followed.

The day after I lost the election in 1990, Frank III came into my office. "Dad, I'm glad you're back," he said, "I have a feeling something's not right around here." He didn't know exactly what it was, but a few months later the corporate auditor asked to speak to me. *This can't be good.*

I almost had a heart attack as he showed me the magnitude of an inadvertent accounting error. The premiums that one client paid us were supposed to go into a separate trust account for future payouts, but our accountant mixed them in with the regular bank accounts, so we were unknowingly spending money that was not yet ours to spend. It was simply a case of the business outgrowing our accountant. I would rather die a pauper than misuse one penny of a client's money.

This was the first major business challenge I encountered after standing up in the Senate and defending life, but I never asked, *"How can you do this to me, Lord?"* I stood up for life because that's what God wanted me to do. I trusted God then, and I had to trust Him again now. I didn't have time to feel sorry for myself. I immediately hired a new accounting firm, one run by a hospital finance committee chairman that I respected, to figure out how the mistake happened and how to prevent anything like it in the future.

We told the client that we could not make up the entire difference right away but would make sure we replaced the whole amount over time. They respected us for being upfront about it and gave us three years to replenish the trust account.

We needed cash quickly and decided to sell the property and casualty business which, demonstrating God's perfect timing once again, my son David had turned around from a money loser into a profitable line, so it had value. My brother Bob connected us with a prospective buyer in Pennsylvania, and David and I drove to his office to make our pitch. In the parking garage before walking in, I popped a couple of Rolaids and asked David to join me in a brief prayer. "Lord, I just ask You to give us wisdom, and to help us leave today with a done deal."

We presented our case for why our growing customer base and profitability justified our asking price. When we finished, the prospective buyer stood up, extended his hand, and said, "Done." As he showed me his financials that proved he had the cash to make the purchase—and much more—a thought occurred to me about how to raise the rest of the cash that we so desperately needed. "Would you consider a loan as well?" I asked, and he agreed.

We had a deal for more than we had even prayed for, and enough to cover our obligation to our client! David and I high-fived in the parking garage and celebrated the entire ride home.

A month later, the buyer, David, and I drove together downtown to our lawyer's office to settle on the deal. Once we had the check, we could put this financial emergency behind us. We pulled into the parking lot and got out of the car. That's when the buyer dropped a bomb: "There's one more thing I need to finalize the deal," he said. "I want David to come and run the company for me."

He brings this up now? I was sick at the thought of losing David and steaming over the buyer's last-second stunt. "No way I'm going to sell my son!" I told him, "the deal is off!"

"We have no choice," David said. "I'll do it."

We decided to go inside and talk it over with our lawyers. They pointed out that it's quite common for the buyer of a company to hire in key personnel as part of the deal, and they agreed with David that we had no better option.

"David, are you sure?" I asked him again.

"Dad, I'll do it," he said. For the next three years, David ran our former property and casualty company out of our

Hunt Valley office. He re-joined Kelly-Chick in 1994.

This close call with going under showed me that losing the election was the best thing that could have happened to Kelly-Chick & Associates. If I had continued in Annapolis, I would not have been home to deal with this and all the other changes and challenges we encountered. God's plan was for me to return to the company full-time and realize my dream of building a godly business and sinking roots deep into my community.

GAME ALMOST OVER

Through the early 1990s, we continued to grow with a boost from the Harford County Chamber of Commerce. A group of independent insurance agents and brokers from the Chamber approached Frank III and asked if we could design and administer plans that they could then sell to other Chamber members. This opened a completely new strategy and segment of customers. Not only were we selling "retail" to associations and employers, but now also "wholesale" to and through independent agents and brokers. Today, Bryan heads this division, which we call Kelly Marketing Services.

In 1994, I turned 55, and Frank III turned 30. Frank III had the sales and operations under his direction since taking over as Executive, and I thought it was time to take the next steps in the company's management succession plan.

I announced to Janet, "I am going to make Frank III the president, and I want to turn the day-to-day operations over to the boys."

She wasn't so sure the timing was right. "How do you know they're ready?"

"If they're not, I'll find out, but I want to do it while

I'm still alive and around to be here for them."

That was my training program, the "do or die" method that taught my father how to survive on the streets of Brooklyn, that I used to teach Pedro how to swim that summer in the Catskills, and the way I learned how to sell insurance and negotiate legislation. Giving them a chance on their own would be more effective than holding their hands all the time, and I would always be there if they needed me. Since they each have different strengths, the challenge for me was to put them in the right spots to maximize their gifts and talents.

I named Frank III the President and Chief Operating Officer, and I took the title of Chairman and CEO.

The boys faced an immediate challenge to the very core of the business when the Clinton administration decided to tackle Health Care Reform. Anticipating federal-level changes, Maryland's state legislature aggressively pursued its own reform measures, and, with one stroke of the governor's pen, our secret sauce became public policy, and our niche disappeared, only six months after Frank III became president of the company.

Because insurance companies could self-select the groups they insure and vary the rates based on each group's size and risk, our pooling service gave small employers access to health insurance at lower rates. With Maryland's reforms, however, all our association clients would automatically combine into one large pool, and insurers would be required to guarantee coverage at regulated rates.

At that point, we had around 20 employees and 1,500 clients, all connected to trade associations, but we supported the reform because we believed it was the best thing for the insurance markets, employers and employees. The new rules made the insurance market what it should be: one large pool of good and bad risks.

I could have sold the company then and retired, but what about the legacy for my sons? What about our impact on the community? Instead of cashing out, we sought new ways to create business by helping other businesses.

While we could no longer create groups to insure, we believed we could still enroll employees and administer the insurance plans more efficiently than the big insurance companies could if they tried to manage the plans themselves. Rather than pool people, we pooled multiple benefits—health, life, disability, dental, and vision—into a single integrated solution with a single point of contact and a single bill. CareFirst Blue-Cross BlueShield and other carriers understood the cost-efficiency of integrating all the benefits with one easy step and continued to outsource administrative services to us.

A major threat turned into a major opportunity and another growth spurt. *Turris Fortis Mihi Deus.* Frank III and Bryan developed the marketing services business with independent brokers and agents, John sold to large employers, and David oversaw all the direct small group business.

'ANOTHER SHOE DROPS'

"Every day, I come in and another shoe drops," was how Frank III once described the various operational glitches that our outdated technology caused in the mid-1990s. Various tech companies lined up to show us their solutions, and John took the lead in evaluating them. John and the boys decided, "We're not going to buy it, we're going to build it." They tackled the problem head-on, starting from scratch to design Kelly Associates' own software, and they did it with our in-house programmers and without millions of dollars from Silicon Valley venture capitalists.

We were the industry pioneer in online benefits administration and client portal technology and branded it as KTBS (Kelly Total Benefits Solution) Online. The transition was painful because for a year we had to do all the benefits administration work twice in parallel operations while we rewrote every system. Some employees quit under the pressure, and we had to let some others go because our expenses ran higher. It was a scary time, but what John and the boys ultimately accomplished positioned us with superior technology that is now the key driver of our growth and profitability.

LIVING THE DREAM

Ever since my friend Charlie Cawley opened MBNA, he had tried to hire me as his insurance expert. But I loved running my own business with my sons, and I had always declined his offers. I was MBNA's insurance broker all along, and now, with the boys running the daily operations so well, I had more time to help develop MBNA's insurance business on a consulting basis.

For the sake of my friendship with Charlie, I agreed to consult for MBNA on one condition: that I would never report directly to Charlie. Why? Here's an example. A decade earlier, Charlie had suggested that I open a Delaware office of Kelly-Chick to handle the MBNA business and establish a foothold for further expansion. He suggested that I hire Terry Flynn, my friend and colleague who I had introduced to Charlie and who Charlie respected, to manage the office. I agreed, only to have Charlie turn around just three months later and, without saying anything to me, offer Flynn six times the salary I was paying him to come work at MBNA.

I called Charlie. "You think you're my friend, but then you do something like this to me. That's not the way I do business." In fairness, Charlie did cover my expenses to close the office, but I vowed that I was finished doing any business with him.

We didn't speak for weeks, but eventually, he called me: "I hear you're upset with me."

"That's an understatement."

"What are you doing tonight? Julie and I will be there in an hour," Charlie stated, like I was supposed to drop everything for him. They came, and Charlie sent our wives out of the room (this was in my house!) so we could talk alone.

"So, you're mad," he said.

"Charlie, you and I just don't do business the same way," I told him. "It's either friendship or business for you and me. I'll take friendship; I just don't want to do business with you anymore."

"No," Charlie said, "we can be friends and do business at the same time; that's the way I want it."

"Well, only if I don't report directly to you," I said, "but to someone who reports to you."

Charlie pulled out a yellow legal pad and wrote out the scope of my engagement: "Broker for life." "Consult on all insurance matters." "For now, and forever."

Because of experiences like that, in my expanded consulting role I worked directly with Al Lerner, the Chairman of the MBNA Board (and one-time owner of the Cleveland Browns), an arrangement that worked well for all of us. I brought in David to consult with MBNA on the property and casualty side, and he saved them millions of dollars per year in commissions and generated significant profits for Kelly-Chick.

Al and Charlie included me in all their major strategy

meetings. At one meeting, Al noted that MBNA customers had lower credit losses than the industry average. He explained his theory that if we set up an automobile insurance company and marketed it to our credit card customers, our losses would be low and profits high because our clients had better credit.

He wanted me to run the auto insurance business, but I had reservations. "Al, there's no proof for your theory." I pointed my finger at Charlie. "See this guy here? He gets speeding tickets all the time. He pays his credit card bills on time, but he's a lousy driver! How many Charlies are out there?"

He listened to what I had to say, but then hired Goldman Sachs to prepare an initial public offering to start a new insurance company, with me as president. I sat in on the Goldman Sachs presentation. They wore nice blue suits and told Al he could make billions of dollars. Afterward, in a private meeting in Charlie's office, Al sat back puffing on a cigar, and Charlie turned to me and asked me to tell Al what I thought of the presentation. Charlie had no idea what I was going to say.

"Al," I said, "that was the biggest pile of horse---- I've ever heard in my entire life."

Al took another puff on his cigar. I thought Charlie was going to jump out the window. Al exhaled and said, "Frank, I agree with you 100%." I probably saved Al $1 billion, maybe $2 billion.

Another day—May 15, 1996, to be exact—I met with Al, Charlie, and Hank Greenberg, the CEO of AIG, one of the largest insurance companies in the world, to discuss how AIG and MBNA might collaborate on an insurance venture. Al introduced me as MBNA's insurance consultant and asked me to make some remarks about the business. I was honored to be in the same room with Hank Greenberg. I offered my advice, and Mr. Greenberg was impressed with my grasp of the industry.

Later during the meeting, I glanced over at Charlie and noticed him writing feverishly on a piece of MBNA letterhead. He folded it and passed it to me. The meeting continued, so I played it cool, put the paper in my pocket, and never looked at Charlie. After the meeting, I opened the note, and my jaw dropped to the floor. It was an offer to be president of MBNA Insurance Services, Inc. The offer was full of seven-figure dollar amounts: salary, signing bonus, annual bonus, stock grants, stock options, life insurance, and a pension. The smallest numbers on the page were $60,000 for a new company car every 50,000 miles.

He sweetened the offer with a note at the bottom: "Bryan comes with you." (Bryan is Charlie's godson.) He asked me to "seriously consider" his offer. I said, "OK, I'll pray about it and get back to you."

I showed the note to Janet when I got home. She had her doubts about whether I would be happy working for Charlie. The next day, I asked Dave Deger, one of our company's financial counselors, to look it over. His eyes popped. "This could be a $25 million deal for you. You can't turn this down."

I believed the $25 million number because I had seen how Al Lerner's investment in MBNA grew eleven-fold to $4 billion. Kelly-Chick was doing well, but I wasn't making anywhere near that kind of money. The days of me making $5 a week more than Charlie were long gone.

Deger persisted. "I'm telling you as your financial advisor, let your sons run the business, go up there and get your $25 million, and invest it back in Kelly-Chick & Associates."

For two weeks, I talked it over with Janet, Deger, and

7/27/96   Offer from Charlie Cawley
CHAIRMAN MBNA

This was tough to turn down. I am really flattered that Charlie has such confidence in my abilities to put this in writing.

God has blessed me so abundantly with four of the finest son's in the world. I am living my dream each and every day as I work with them in the KCA business which God has given to us. All the money in the world and all the power in the world couldn't separate me from working with my sons and being a wise steward of all the Lord has given to our family.

I praise God, thru his son Jesus Christ for the peace, faith and wisdom that he has freely given to me.

I thank God most of all for Janet who I love forever. Without her help, counsel, and support none of this would be possible. Praise God & Jesus Christ !!!

The explanation I wrote for declining Charlie's offer: "I am living my dream each and every day."

the Lord. My mind drifted back to the parking lot at Jackie Gordon's Men's Store, where my dad had taken me to buy my first suit and asked me to go into business with him. Now,

I had my sons in business with me; I was living my dream.

With the memory of my dad burning inside me, the last thing I wanted to do was sell out my sons. I didn't care about the $25 million. I called Charlie to schedule lunch, where I gave him my answer. "Charlie, I can't do it. Working with my sons is what I've always wanted, and you and I both know that we operate so differently, it could be the end of our friendship."

"Yeah, you're probably right."

Dave Deger thought I was out of my mind. But my decision was not about money; it was about quality of life and being where God wanted me. I wanted to be under His control, not Charlie's, or anyone else's.

That decision had such a profound impact on me that I wrote a note explaining my reasons. That note is the closest thing to a diary entry I ever wrote, and I've kept it for all these years in a manila folder along with the original piece of

'A positive influence'

It's very rare to see the kind of mutual respect and support that Frank and Charlie had for each other, how they trusted each other's judgment, lifted each other up, and celebrated each other's successes. They had different styles but lived by similar precepts: faith, family, respect for others, and living true to their beliefs. They were a positive influence on each other's lives.

-Julie Cawley

MBNA letterhead with Charlie's offer. In part, it says, *"All the money in the world and all the power in the world couldn't separate me from working with my sons and being a wise steward of all the Lord has given to our family."*

I have never regretted my choice. Since the day I stopped drinking and shifted my dependence onto God, He has always blessed my decisions to step out in faith and follow Him when I didn't know what the outcome would be. He has given me the strength to put temptations aside and live out my faith, and has proven to me time after time that following Him is the right way, not following the world.

'THE PURSUIT OF EXCELLENCE… HONOR AND GLORY TO GOD'

With all four sons in the company, I wanted to preserve it for them for the long-term. I had complete confidence in their abilities, and I wanted to put them in a situation where they could succeed and the business could continue without me. I believed God had given the business to our family to glorify Him, and that He wanted the four brothers working together to take the business to the next level.

Gary Chick was ten years older than I was, so I thought he might be open to selling his share of the business and retiring. My accountant called me crazy, but I knew that as we kept growing, the price of buying him out would only go up. In 1988, Gary gladly accepted our offer to buy him out over 20 years and was as happy as a pig in you-know-what.

Janet and I did not want to keep amassing owner equity ourselves and stick the boys later with a massive estate tax bill, so we began gifting stock to them, shares they had certainly earned. I kept the voting stock, but over the years transferred all the owner equity to them. Now, every year, I take my salary and the boys and I split everything else five ways. We have never fought over money.

Refining the mission statement in 1994

Frank III went to work on writing the company's mission statement. We wanted biblical principles to guide all our decisions, practices, and policies, and to be our benchmark for defining and measuring true success. Frank III had written the first draft after he and I attended Larry Burkett's "Business By The Book" seminar in 1991, but now, three years later, he wanted additional input from the entire family and me. We went away for a five-day retreat—all the husbands and wives—to refine the mission statement, which begins,

"Kelly Associates is an organization committed to the pursuit of excellence in an effort to bring honor and glory to God."

We display the mission statement prominently throughout our buildings, and on our website and collateral materials. An outside public relations consultant once suggested to Frank III that we remove the reference to God. Frank showed him the door politely, but also let him know, "If my father was here right now, you'd be out on the parking lot on your backside."

We need to be careful that the mission statement does not convey a "holier-than-thou" type of attitude. "We're far from perfect," Frank III explained to *Smart CEO Magazine*.

The Kelly Associates cycling team inspires our people to live a healthy and active lifestyle.

"Just because we have a mission statement that talks about God doesn't mean we're better than anyone else by any means."

We also make it clear that a person does not have to be of the Christian faith to work at Kelly Associates or do business with the company. Yet, as Frank III says, "If you show up on time and do what you say you're going to do, if you're honest with your coworkers and treat people with dignity and respect, you are living out biblical principles whether you believe the Bible or not."

ABUNDANT BLESSINGS

"God has blessed me so abundantly with four of the finest sons in the world," was another reflection in the note-to-file I wrote and saved in the manila folder with Charlie's MBNA offer. Over the next decade, they proved me right.

In 1998, we moved the corporate headquarters to a 30,000 square-foot building at 301 International Circle in Hunt Valley, opened our DC/Virginia office to penetrate further that fast-growing market, and changed our official corporate name to Kelly & Associates Insurance Group, Inc. In 2002, the *Baltimore Business Journal* ranked us as the largest employee benefits administrator in the metro area, and we have maintained our first-place position ever since. In 2005, we diversified our product line again, adding what today we market as Kelly Payroll, which David and his brothers built from scratch into a highly successful company where David serves as the president.

John's love for cycling led him to found the Kelly Benefit Strategies Pro Cycling Team in 2007. We continue to sponsor both an amateur team and a professional team. The teams ride for a greater purpose than winning races. It's part of the company's overall desire to inspire our employees to live healthier, more active lifestyles. We are proactive in offering our employees incentives, resources, and opportunities to improve their health, including gym discounts, smoking cessation programs, and healthy drink choices in the vending machines.

Also in 2007, I took the next step in our succession plan and handed my CEO title over to Frank III. Bryan became president of Kelly Marketing Services. John continued to serve as president of Kelly Benefit Strategies and to manage our technology. David remained president of Kelly Payroll and continued to oversee direct KBS sales to companies with under 200 employees.

GOD'S FAITHFULNESS: OUR CORNERSTONE

The Great Recession welcomed in the newly fine-tuned management team, but perhaps the company's biggest test ever came in 2009 and had nothing to do with falling housing prices. It was a multimillion dollar error by our Chief Financial Officer, which our auditors also failed to identify. *Not again!*

As a family, we immediately put our savings into the company, cut our salaries, and started looking for a new CFO. A priest friend of mine recommended Craig Horner, who has proven to be one of our best hires ever. We recovered from the error within six months.

Since then we've been audited by the IRS and came through it as clean as a whistle. We have an open invitation to our insurance carriers to inspect our books whenever they want, and they have always been satisfied.

God proved His faithfulness once again. It was a painful lesson, but it was His way of strengthening not only our financial team and accounting processes but the entire foundation of the company. The scare drove us down on our knees and into our Bibles. As we reflected on what God might be teaching us through the trial, five verses emerged which clarified our vision and undergirded our mission statement. We call them our Cornerstone and Four Pillars, and display them prominently in our lobby:

CORNERSTONE:	*Love the Lord your God with all your heart, and with all your soul, and with all your mind, and with all your strength.' The second is this, 'You shall love your neighbor as yourself.' There is no other commandment greater than these.* (Mark 12:29-31)
PILLAR 1:	*Unless the Lord builds the house, its builders labor in vain. Unless the Lord watches over the city, the watchmen stand guard in vain.* (Psalm 127:1)
PILLAR 2:	*Trust in the Lord with all your heart, and lean not on your own understanding. In all your ways acknowledge Him, and He will make your paths straight.* (Proverbs 3:5-6)

| PILLAR 3: | *But seek first the kingdom of God, and His righteousness, and all these things will be added to you as well.* (Matthew 6:33) |
| PILLAR 4: | *Whatever you do, work at it with all your heart, as working for the Lord, not for men, since you know that you will receive an inheritance from the Lord as a reward.* (Colossians 3:23-24) |

'I HAVE TO PINCH MYSELF.'

Back in 1994, I told Janet that we would find out soon enough if the boys were ready to run the company. Well, since they took over the daily operations, our corporate benefits client base of 1,000 employers has grown to more than 10,000. Annualized premiums and payroll administered has risen from $20 million to over $4 billion. The number of employees has

Cal Ripken Jr., Frank, Janet, Frank III, John, David, and Bryan

"Dad, I had this dream..."

grown from 20 to over 500. We are one of the largest administrators, brokers, payroll providers, and consultants in the country. In 2012, we incorporated Kelly Investment Services (trading as Kelly Advisory) to diversify into retirement plan consulting. In 2013, we received the Ernst & Young Family Business Award of Excellence in Maryland.

Yes, the boys can handle it!

With all the growth and diversification, optimizing workspace became an issue once again. Because of the logistical difficulties of working out of one building we owned and two other buildings we leased, the boys released David to focus on consolidating our operations into one building. David soon came to us with an idea. "I had this dream about the Fila building in Sparks. I know we didn't think much of it when we first saw it, but I'd like to go back and take another look," he said. I thought it was the ugliest building I ever saw, but I always try to support my sons and let them run with their ideas.

A couple of weeks later he called, all excited. "We've

been looking at that building the way it is now. I think God wants us to look at what it can become."

David developed the plans and managed the entire renovation project. We moved into our miraculously transformed 100,000 square feet at 1 Kelly Way in June of 2015. I go into the building and have to pinch myself when I see how God used David, Frank III, John, and Bryan to bring all the companies and divisions together in one people-centered campus, with collaborative workspaces, state-of-the-art security and technology, a gym, fitness studio, and café. There's more synergy now with all parts of the company collaborating in ways we never could when we were spread out over multiple buildings. In coordination with the move, we announced the unified KELLY branding and revised logo as the single face for all our divisions and subsidiaries.

As much as everyone loves it, I don't want to be judged by the size of the building. I want to be judged on whether I have the faith to follow what I perceive to be God's will, and how faithfully the company follows our Cornerstone and Four Pillars.

GEN 3

Sometimes, putting God first means seeking counsel from other godly men and women. John and Frank III brought in Keith Yoder and Jay McCumber from Teaching the Word Ministries and The Emporia Group to coach us with spiritual advice on leadership, teamwork, and succession planning. Keith and Jay have emphasized the importance of understanding our individual strengths and weaknesses, respect, constructive criticism, and getting all issues out on the table and quickly resolving conflicts.

The entire Kelly family at Frankie and Acacia's wedding in 2017. "Now we're planning for Gen 3 in the business."

With the boys working together, I feel sorry for our competitors. But it takes effort to keep their different gifts and personalities—and mine—in harmony. It was quite a feat for four brothers to work together and agreeably share ownership, but never in my wildest dreams did I think we would have to figure out how to deal with Generation 3, our 21 living grandchildren, in planning for the future of the company.

With counsel from several wise advisors, we have lately turned our thinking again to the long-term structure of the company. We need to decide what to do about ownership, policies for the grandchildren entering the business, and the role of any grandchildren not in the business. Maintaining family unity will be our top priority, even more important than any new business plan or financial goal.

There are external challenges to the business as well. In 2015, the ramifications of the Affordable Care Act and the fact that one of our largest clients shrank significantly caused us to make the painful decision to downsize by 30 employees. National health care policies are always in flux. A public, single-payer system, for example, would put the future of health insurance marketing and administration up in the air.

Threats and uncertainties are why holding fast to our Cornerstone and Four Pillars, and mission, is so critical. If we live and work by these unshakable truths, we will keep a positive attitude about change and our opportunities to create innovative businesses to help other businesses. Whatever happens after that is up to the Lord, and we trust that He will continue to amaze.

My primary contribution now is nurturing my long-standing relationships with some of our larger customers and vendors. At times, I've had to step in and smooth over problems, but as the boys lead the growth of the business, my role continues to diminish.

Frank III, John, David, and Bryan took the business to a level I never dreamed possible. I can't thank them enough for their hard work and dedication. Their success gives me the time for what I love most—public service.

11

Love Your Neighbor

"Love the Lord your God with all your heart, and with all your soul, and with all your mind, and with all your strength. The second is this, 'You shall love your neighbor as yourself.' There is no other commandment greater than these."
Mark 12:29-31

I cried three times delivering my five-minute speech, the speech I wrote on a napkin and gave at the 150th Anniversary Gala for the University of Maryland St. Joseph Medical Center. Janet, who CEO Dr. Mohan Suntha called "one of St. Joe's greatest ambassadors," co-chaired the Gala event, which celebrated not only its milestone anniversary but also its emergence from the brink of extinction.

A scandal involving St. Joseph's chief cardiologist in 2012 plunged the hospital into a tailspin. The previous owner, Catholic Health Initiatives, hastily, and probably unnecessarily, signed a Corporate Integrity Agreement with the federal government and paid a $22 million fine. Hospital admissions declined 20%, St. Joseph's owed $37 million in malpractice claims, and over one stretch was losing $3 million a month. Doctors and staff left in droves, either on their own or through layoffs. Many health care experts thought the best thing for St. Joe's to do was to close its doors, and it might have shut down if it had taken much longer to find a buyer.

I led the acquisitions committee of the University of Maryland Medical System (UMMS) which I helped form with legislation in 1984, so we immediately began the effort for UMMS to acquire St. Joe's.

I knew something about St. Joe's that others, looking only at financial statements, could not see. For years my kids kept St. Joe's emergency room busy, and eleven of my grandchildren were born there. As I said in my speech at the gala, there is something special about St. Joe's. Their motto is, *Loving Service and Compassionate Care.* Patients do indeed feel loved and cherished there, and they experience first-hand the value everyone at St. Joe's places on every human life, which they consider a gift from God. The hospital's value lies, not only in the quality of care it provides for Baltimore County residents but in its culture.

My top priority during the negotiations was to maintain St. Joe's long tradition of faith-based, compassionate, high-quality care. UMMS typically allows its member hospitals to remain autonomous, and they signed an agreement with the Catholic Church stating that St. Joe's would

Under Dr. Suntha's visionary leadership, all of St. Joseph's performance indicators quickly turned positive.

continue to follow the church's religious principles and beliefs. "All of the ethical standards of the church will be upheld," I affirmed to *The Baltimore Sun.*

I knew that holding on to the highly esteemed Towson Orthopedics practice would be crucial to the future viability of St. Joe's, and, therefore, to completing the deal with UMMS. But I had heard that most of their doctors were ready to sign on with another hospital system, so I had to act quickly. On Christmas Eve I met for breakfast with the group's Chief of Orthopedics, Dr. David Dalury. He wanted to make sure I could pull off the deal with UMMS. I assured him I could, but I wouldn't unless Towson Orthopedics remained part of our team. After that meeting, we held additional negotiations with Dean Reece at the University of Maryland School of Medicine and agreed to negotiate new contracts with the doctors at Towson Orthopedics to bring them in as employees of St. Joseph's.

UMMS was not the highest bidder, but St. Joe's

wanted our partnership to preserve its heritage and selected us as its new owner in December 2012. To my surprise and delight, UMMS asked me to chair the board of the new University of Maryland St. Joseph's Medical Center. I pledged to the Sisters of St. Francis that we would do everything in our power to carry on the mission they started in 1864.

Our first task was to find the right CEO to rebuild the hospital's reputation. The name that immediately rose to the top of the list was Dr. Mohan Suntha. Not only did he possess the skills and experience for the job, but he also leads through building relationships—the kind of leadership the hospital needed.

Within two years, under his visionary leadership, all the important performance indicators turned positive, and the patients and the doctors returned. Our consultants said it would take a minimum of five years to return to profitability. I said we could do it in three, and we did! St. Joe's has the highest possible rating for quality and safety from the U.S. Centers for Medicare and Medicaid Services (CMS), all thanks to Dr. Suntha, Dr. Tom Smyth, the current CEO, and Chief Medical Officer, Dr. Gail Cunningham. God has indeed placed his hand on St. Joe's for 150 years, and my prayer is that He will continue to protect it forever.

'Belly-to-Belly Diplomacy'

The naysayers thought it would be best for St. Joseph's to close its doors. But the naysayers did not know about our secret weapon—a man whose passion for St. Joe's is unmatched—who had the vision to see beyond the problems of a few years and understand that 150 years of faith-based tradition and history would sustain us well into the future.

Like everything else Frank does, it was his faith that drove him to help St. Joe's. He understood the value of faith-based health care in the community. He had experienced first-hand St. Joe's loving service and compassionate care many times, especially after the unspeakably tragic stillbirth of his granddaughter, Faith, two weeks before her delivery date. Frank knew the difference that faith-based health care makes to patients and their families and knew that maintaining a faith-based mission and culture was the key to St. Joe's turnaround.

Frank Kelly casts a big shadow. I don't think any other single individual could have pulled off a deal where a secular hospital system takes over a Catholic hospital and runs it as a faith-based institution.

Frank took his classic "belly-to-belly diplomacy" approach with the negotiation process. He believes that sitting down in a room together is the best way to solve problems, not sending emails. Frank is never afraid to meet with someone whom he knows he completely disagrees with; he seeks out opportunities to hear and understand their point of view.

Frank's unique ability to move and influence people who disagree with each other to find common ground is a talent few possess. He could have pushed the UMMS deal through solely by the power of his personality, but he did not do it that way. He engaged with others who cared about St. Joe's and Baltimore County, such as Dutch Ruppersberger, former Baltimore County Executive Jim Smith, the doctors and staff at the hospital, and Archbishop Lori.

Archbishop Lori was the final decision-maker on St. Joe's side. If he had any doubt about St. Joe's freedom to operate according to the values, ethics, and guidelines of the church under UMMS, he would not have allowed St. Joe's to maintain its designation as a Catholic hospital. Archbishop Lori was new to Baltimore at the time. He had no relationship with the health systems; he had only a blossoming relationship with Frank Kelly. Frank made a commitment to him on behalf of UMMS that St. Joe's could maintain its faith-based mission and sanctity of life approach to health care. The Archbishop's trust in Frank as a man of conviction and a man of his word gave him the confidence to write a letter to Rome recommending approval of the acquisition. The union has worked so well that we are a national model for Catholic and secular health care partnerships.

Frank has supported me on every step of the journey. When I started as CEO, he held up his cell phone and promised me, "Mo, I'm a 24/7 guy. If you need me, you call me, anytime, anywhere, and I'll talk to you. You will never bother me. If you leave a message, I'll call you back as soon as I can." I've challenged him with all kinds of calls at all kinds of hours, and he has kept his promise.

I talk to Frank almost every day, sometimes multiple times a day. I usually don't ask him for anything, but I want him to hear about what's going on at the hospital from me, and I like to run ideas past him. I appreciate his willingness to listen and offer advice without dictating what he thinks I should do.

Frank is the most active and engaged board chair I have ever seen. He attends meetings with the state regulatory bodies and the rate commission to show his support. That's unheard of; you don't see other board chairs advocating for their hospitals at those meetings. He comes to watch surgeons in the operating room and asks the doctors and nurses what they need to do their jobs better.

On Monday of a Memorial Day weekend, a pipe burst in the hospital—a big pipe—and by 2 AM Tuesday morning we shut down the operating rooms to bail out the water. Frank was at the beach in Bethany for the holiday, but he was here in our operations command center by four in the afternoon on Tuesday to tell us that the board is here with you, how can we help? Volunteer board chairs of community hospitals just don't offer that level of commitment, but that's how Frank is wired. He lives his creed. When he is passionate about something, he goes all-in. St. Joe's is fortunate to be counted as one of his passions.

Our families became personal friends over the years. My family had a place in Avalon on the Jersey shore one summer, and Frank and Janet came to visit for a weekend. What a joy to walk down memory lane with Frank, though "memory sprint" is a better description.

We squeezed more activity and more eating into those 48 hours than my family is used to in a week! No downtime at all. We stopped at all the pizza places, the bakeries, the beaches, and the churches on the Kelly's old circuit, and Frank was disappointed he couldn't stop to see more people he knew. "But Frank," Janet pointed out, "we're only here for a day and a half!"

Janet was like everybody's Fairy Godmother, so sweet, and she knew exactly how to engage my young daughters. She instinctively knew what to talk to them about, the kind of t-shirt my 13-year-old would like, and that my 11-year-old would want something different.

Recently the Kellys have invited us to attend Christmas Eve Mass with them, and we appreciate their kindness in sharing such a special celebration with us.

Never in my lifetime will I be able to thank Frank for everything he did for St. Joe's and for me. I cannot communicate the depths of my gratitude enough to him. When these next few chapters about St. Joe's are written, there will be many people standing in line to take credit. But hear me clearly: when it's time for recognition, there will be only one man worthy: my friend, Senator Kelly.

-Dr. Mohan Suntha
President and CEO
University of Maryland Medical Center

'Ripples of Service'

Senator Kelly was one of the first people I met when I came to Baltimore. On my desk was the merger of the University of Maryland Medical System and St. Joseph Hospital, and that's a pretty

Archdiocese of Baltimore
MEDAL OF HONOR
Presented on November 3, 2016

to

Senator Francis Kelly
For outstanding service and ministry to
University of Maryland Saint Joseph Medical Center

ARCHBISHOP WILLIAM E. LORI, S.T.D.
ARCHBISHOP OF BALTIMORE

tall climb when you're brand-new. I was just a country bishop from Connecticut. I was willing to go out on the limb because I knew from the start that I was dealing with a man of high principle, Frank Kelly, and it was not a hard decision to make. Anybody that would stand up as he has stood up for what he believes in, for his faith, for life, for service of others, it wasn't hard to do. As I think about his life, and think about his service, I recognize how broad and how wonderful it has been: service to our country, service to our state, service to our business community, and, of course, service to St. Joseph's. And so, the ripples of his service have gone all across the Archdiocese and affected people that not even Frank Kelly knows. Because of that, I thought it was a wonderful thing to honor him with the Archdiocesan Medal of Honor.

-Archbishop William E. Lori
Archbishop of Baltimore

'I HAVE A JOB FOR YOU':
RESOURCES FOR MORGAN STATE

When I worked on legislation in the Senate that gave birth to something new, I enjoyed following through and helping it grow, and I had that privilege as a board member of the University of Maryland Medical System. After I worked on the legislation to create the University System of Maryland, I had hoped Governor Schaefer would appoint me to the Board of Regents, but the offer never came. Two years after I left the Senate, I met Governor Schaefer at a social event. "I have a job for you," he said.

"I appreciate you for thinking of me," I said, "but I'm running my business; I'm not looking for a job."

"I want you to go on the board at Morgan State," he said.

"But I helped draft the legislation for the new university system. I'd rather you put me on the Board of Regents."

"I could, but Morgan needs a Kelly kick-in-the-butt," he insisted.

I remembered from my days on the Budget and Tax Subcommittee on Health, Education and Welfare how dysfunctional and disorganized the Morgan board had been. They couldn't answer basic questions about their cash flow and operations. I told my Senate colleagues, in front of Morgan's president at the time, "I can't support any more budget requests until they get things straightened out."

Morgan appointed a new president, Dr. Earl Richardson, and a new board. Within two years, the new administration turned things around, and I offered to take my subcommittee on a tour of the campus to see first-hand what their needs were.

We were shocked. The campus was dirty. The auditorium flooded when it rained because the roof leaked. I've been in prisons that looked better than some of the dorms: tiles were falling off the walls, there was no air conditioning and no ventilation in the showers. I wouldn't have want-

"The state needed to fund Morgan properly."

ed to go to a school with a campus in that condition, and I wouldn't have wanted my sons—or anyone—to have to live on a campus in that condition.

I immediately called Senate President Miller, House Speaker Mitchell, and Governor Schaefer to tell them they needed to see it for themselves, and that the state needed to fund Morgan properly.

So now, knowing my history with Morgan, Governor Schaefer thought I could help their board continue making progress, even though I was no longer in the Senate.

"I don't know, Governor, I don't think I'm interested," I answered.

"I'll call you next Tuesday at noon, and you can tell me what you've decided. But I expect you to do this."

Next Tuesday at noon, my assistant came into my office to tell me the Governor was on the line.

I picked up my phone. "How are you doing, Governor?"

"Well?" he asked.

"Well, what?"

"You know well what! Are you going to do it?" he asked.

"OK, Governor, I'll do it."

"Thanks."

Click. End of call.

Over the next fourteen years—twelve as vice chair and two as acting chair—I helped Morgan further define and implement its mission as ordained in the 1988 legislation. And because I still had close relationships with many of my former legislative colleagues, I helped Morgan's presidents navigate the political waters, and I advocated for Morgan in Annapolis. With Morgan's new-found financial stability and my reputation for fiscal responsibility, legislators listened when the president and I made a case for the funding Morgan needed to grow and compete, including a performing arts center, and new dorms that students were proud to call home.

'THE MAN WHO SAVED THE SYSTEM':
MAKING EDUCATION MORE ACCESSIBLE

In 1996, when Dutch Ruppersberger was Baltimore County Executive, he called me to ask a favor.

Enrollment and resources in the Baltimore County Community College system were declining rapidly. Using the University System of Maryland as a model, Dutch wanted to consolidate the three colleges—Catonsville, Essex, and Dundalk—into a more effective and cost-efficient multi-campus system. The State passed the legislation, but the board was too dysfunctional to accomplish anything. Dutch asked me to be Chairman of the Board. I knew that half the board was incompetent at best, and maybe even corrupt. I told him, "No. I have enough on my plate, and that's a big job."

He kept calling me. I told him "no" three times, but

Dutch and the leaders in Annapolis practically begged me. I finally agreed to give them a proposal: I would take the job, but for me to clean up a mess like that, they would need to trust me completely to get it done the way I saw fit; to let me act as a benevolent dictator. "If the faculty or anybody complains about me, and you back them, I'm gone." We shook hands, and I went to work on another volunteer challenge.

I did not know what I would find, but I knew it was a sticky situation. There were eleven board members, all appointed by state senators who do not like to admit mistakes. My job was to work with the existing members until their terms ended so I would not make the senators look bad.

The good news was the board was not corrupt. The bad news was it was incompetent and highly political. Before the official board meetings, a subset of members would meet by themselves for lunch at the Sparrow's Point Country Club and decide what they wanted to do, and then ram their decisions through at the official evening meeting. They never included two members in their lunch: the sole female member, and another whom they just did not like.

I had to shake up the culture and their practices, so I made the woman they had shunned the chair of one committee, and the person whom they had disrespected the chair of another. The rest of them, I iced completely; I did not talk to them at all. The senators who appointed those members did not want me calling out their person, so they instructed their appointees to vote for whatever I wanted, whether they liked it or not.

I also needed help with the academic side of things. Though I was vice chair of the Morgan State University Board of Regents, I had no experience with the daily operations of an academic institution. I hired Jim Fisher, a former president of Towson University and one of the world's top consultants in higher education, for analysis and advice. I admitted candidly, "Look, Jim, I am a businessman, I am a politician, and I am a leader, but I am not an academic. I need to know if we are good or bad, and what our strengths and weaknesses are. I need you to conduct an institutional review and give me a roadmap to formulate an academic plan."

Jim's report, which made the Metro Section front page of *The Baltimore Sun*, stated, "an inept and political board of trustees led Baltimore County's three schools to 'near chaos.'" He added that the task before me "may not approach the cleaning of the Augean stables, but it is daunting."

The faculty was so dissatisfied that they wanted to unionize. The maintenance workers and administrative staff were already unionized, and I promised to work with their unions. I sat down for pizza with the union leaders, made friends with them, appointed some of them to various search committees, and kept them involved with everything I did as part of the team. We gained respect for each other, we worked things out, and never fought. But I strongly opposed a faculty union because I did not think it would benefit the schools or the students. Still, I wanted to hear their concerns.

I mentioned to Fisher that I was going to meet with the faculty at the Dundalk library.

"You can't do that," he said.

"Why not?"

Fisher raised his right hand above his head like a church cantor. "A Chairman of the Board has to be up here. You are the leader. You need to be up here. Leaders cannot be with the masses. Leaders have to be up here. The people need to see a clear separation."

I disagreed completely. "I don't believe that. If I am a leader, and they get to know me, they will follow me. The one thing I do not want them to say is that I never listened to them. I am going to make some big decisions, and when I make decisions, I want to be able to say that I listened to everyone and gave everyone in this system the opportunity to tell me what they think I should do." (Even though I had a pretty good idea of what I should do.)

We debated whether leaders are born or made. I believe the charismatic leader is born. Leaders can be made, they can develop charisma and succeed, but in some people, leadership is there, and you can see it. My definition of a charismatic leader is one who inspires trust and confidence. People will follow them even if they don't know why they are following them, and even if they disagree with them.

I spent a whole day with the faculty and wrote everything they said on my yellow legal pad. I just listened; I did not say a word. Within the first hour I discovered exactly what I was dealing with: they loved the colleges, they were committed to the colleges, and they felt the colleges did a lot of good, but they did not feel loved, respected, or appreciated. They felt like nobody listened to them and they had no say in how the schools were run. And they wanted to be paid fairly.

Toward the end of the day, I addressed their concerns and unveiled my plans.

"What I understand from listening to all of you is that you don't feel appreciated and you don't feel respected, and you are probably right. I will tell you right now that I appreciate you, but my respect—you must earn it. I appreciate the fact that you are here, that you care, and you are trying, but I will respect you as you learn how to do your jobs with excellence."

"So, here is the deal: there will be no union for the faculty. None. If you want to go to Annapolis and try to form a union, it is not going to work. The legislators gave me their word that my job is to run this place, and I told them there would be no faculty union. We will offer you three-year contracts. They will renew every year, subject to a performance evaluation. Everybody in this room knows who is doing their job and who isn't. Whoever is doing their job, they will be rewarded. Whoever is not, they're gone."

"Another thing you'll learn about me is that I am not in favor of automatic cost of living raises. I am going to bring an expert in to review every position in the college and tell me what each position is worth. If we are underpaying for any position, we will bring it up to where it should be. I want our salaries at the 75th percentile of all colleges in the United States."

"How do you feel about all of this?" I asked.

"This is the first time management has ever talked to us," someone said. They also liked the sound of above-average salaries and applauded my plan.

We redefined the community colleges' mission and goals. To improve both quality and efficiency, we transformed the three separate colleges into a single college, multi-campus system, and renamed it the Community College of Baltimore County (CCBC).

The consultant's compensation study showed that most positions were indeed underpaid, and, due in part from the consolidation, some positions could be eliminated. The upshot was that I asked Dutch for $4 million to fund salary increases for the newly reclassified positions.

"Isn't this better than a 3% cost-of-living increase?" I asked.

As we made progress and improvements, I gained support from every corner. The faculty appreciated the changes, never bucked me, and stopped talking about a union. Dutch

The Francis X. Kelly Center of CCBC in Hunt Valley

and the state legislators kept their word by not interfering in the way I did my work. They also backed me when I was up for reappointment for another term, and the Governor wanted me out because I had supported his Republican opponent in the election. Even *The Baltimore Sun* endorsed me in an editorial they titled, "Man who saved the system." With so much support, I was reappointed for a second term.

It's an honor to have played a role in making education more affordable and accessible to Baltimore area students and to have my name on the Hunt Valley Center building. Today, CCBC enrolls over 60,000 students, about half of which receive some form of financial aid, and employs over 5,000 full-time and part-time staff. Jim Fisher told me he had never seen a turnaround like that before. He later coauthored a book on leadership entitled *Born, Not Made*.

Man who saved the system

■ **Community college:** *Governor should reappoint Kelly, who led transformation in Baltimore County.*

IF EVER A member of a community college board deserved reappointment, Francis X. Kelly does. The former state senator from Baltimore County was instrumental in transforming Maryland's largest community college system from a directionless, competing group of campuses into a cohesive, smoothly operating institution that offers thousands of students a less-expensive gateway into higher education.

Mr. Kelly has been an enthusiastic booster of community colleges. He understands their mission to provide opportunities for students who have the desire but may lack the academics or income to enter a four-year institution, as well as for older workers looking to improve their skills.

Mr. Kelly's term is about to expire. Political insiders believe that Gov. Parris N. Glendening may not reappoint him. Mr. Glendening should not let Mr. Kelly's support

of Ellen R. Sauerbrey, his opponent in two campaigns for governor, outweigh Mr. Kelly's invaluable contributions to improving the governance of Baltimore County's community college.

When Mr. Kelly became chairman, the county's community college campuses in Catonsville, Essex and Dundalk were reeling from a report that gave a startlingly frank assessment: The schools were in pandemonium, they suffered from weak management, and classroom technology was badly outdated. A skeptical County Council slashed the colleges' budgets. Mr. Kelly took control of a warring board, melded three campuses into one system and lured an impressive new chancellor, Irving Pressley McPhail.

In the past, appointments to the college board were plums doled out to political supporters. As the blue ribbon panel pointed out, a number of these appointees were "unenlightened [and] hostile." If the board once again becomes a haven for political cronies and payoffs, the system's recent gains may be undone.

DOING MORE WITH LESS:
RAISING ACADEMIC STANDING

In 2003, Maryland elected Bob Ehrlich as its first Republican governor since Spiro Agnew back in 1967. Two years later, Governor Ehrlich granted my long-standing wish and asked me to serve on the University System of Maryland Board of Regents. But state law required me to step down from my positions at CCBC and Morgan State. I had served fourteen years at Morgan and nine at CCBC, and both schools were headed in the right direction, so I felt at peace about moving on to nurture the University System of Maryland I had helped give birth to when I was in the Senate.

I served on the Regent's finance committee for eleven years—eight as chairman—having been reappointed for a second term in 2009 by Governor Martin O'Malley, a Democrat. It was a tricky period for managing college finances. O'Malley came into office on a pledge to freeze tuition, which he did for four years. At the same time, the Great Recession was squeezing every family, business and governmental budget. By the end of O'Malley's second term in 2015, state budget deficits were so high that he proposed a $40 million cut to the higher education budget.

How could the Regents help keep the systems' national academic standing high at the same time we brought tuition down from one of the highest among our public university peers to the middle of the pack? Many of us had business backgrounds, so we started by pointing out to the schools' administrations that bigger budgets are not the only path to higher quality, and they needed to manage the funds they had more efficiently and effectively. We also recommended that the schools raise more private funds through grants, and from foundations and private donors.

The Regents also helped turn the University of Maryland University College (UMUC) around from the brink of closing to the fastest growing school in the system, thanks in large part to granting UMUC more independence, and the growth of its award-winning online program. The Regents also supported College Park's move to the Big Ten Conference, for both financial and academic reasons.

UMB'S 200ᵀᴴ COMMENCEMENT ADDRESS

There aren't very many 200ᵗʰ anniversaries of anything, so one of my greatest honors as a regent was being chosen to deliver the keynote address at the 200ᵗʰ commencement of the University of Maryland, Baltimore. "Through words and deeds, Senator Kelly has shown he is a true believer in the University's mission," UMB President David Ramsay kindly said in his announcement.

How special it was to address a university, almost as old as our country, with professional schools in medicine, nursing, dentistry, pharmacy, law, and social work, plus a graduate school. I wanted to do something that the students would remember, so in my speech, I told them, "When you come up here for your diploma, I'm going to hug every one of you!" I slowed down the line, but I hugged all 1,200 graduates.

'YOU CAN'T DO THAT!'

Though my second term on the board expired in 2015, I asked to remain for another year to finish the work I had started to improve the sports medicine program. The University of Maryland Hospital at UMB provides orthopedic and other sports medicine services for the teams at College Park, but Kevin Anderson, the Athletic Director, was not happy with the quality of the care and service. He called to tell me he wanted to outsource sports medicine to MedStar Health.

"You can't do that!" I pleaded, "you can't go to a competitor. I can fix it."

I pulled together the presidents of UMMS, College Park, and UMB to work together on a plan—a collaboration between schools that had never happened before because of their simmering rivalry. We implemented the necessary changes, and now UMB has the largest sports medicine program in the Big Ten, one that doesn't stop with treating the players. The hospital also provides sports medicine education and conducts research on brain trauma and other hot-button issues, and we are on our way to raising over $100 million of private donations to open a state-of-the-art sports medicine center in a newly renovated Cole Field House.

With the sports medicine initiative near completion, I told Governor Larry Hogan that I was ready to finish my term and step down. I am no longer on the Board of Regents but still serve on a special Regents committee that oversees the implementation of the sports medicine enhancements.

My experience shows that God can use anybody for

'A force for good'

Frank,
I can't begin to thank you adequately for all you've done to support the entire State of Maryland—from its higher education system to health care. You have been, and continue to be, a powerful Force for Good.

I am especially grateful for all the support you've given to UMBC—my colleagues and students—and to me personally. You have always shown us how much you believe in our ability to support the State's citizens and families.

Dr. Martin Luther King Jr. once said that "darkness cannot drive out darkness: only light can do that." You have been that light for so many of us in so many ways. We will be forever grateful.

-Freeman A. Hrabowski III
President
UMBC

anything when they just show up and make themselves available. I chuckle to myself when I think about my work in higher education—me who squeaked by at Villanova, and spent more hours working part-time jobs than studying. But I love challenges, and I love to bring people together to work for the common good, and often organizations need that kind of catalyst more than a subject-matter expert.

GETTING THE MESSAGE OUT TO AT-RISK YOUTH

Sometimes giving back means working on complex health and education systems, but other times it simply means being a friend and a mentor to someone trying to help kids. One evening in 1996, Channel 2 News interviewed Ernie Graham, the University of Maryland basketball star (he holds the school record with 44 points in a single game, and played professionally for twelve years in Europe), talking about *Get The Message*, the after-school program he developed to teach life skills, drug prevention, and basketball in elementary and middle schools.

I said to Janet, "I like what he's doing. He turned his life around and is taking his message to young people. I'd like to meet him some day and see if I can help."

I was hoping the publicity from the Channel 2 interview would help me get into more schools and raise more money for *Get The Message*. I was also hoping to make another connection the next morning in a meeting that Glenn Norris set up for me with someone he knew from his club lacrosse days, Frankie Kelly, who ran a company with his brothers and father. I tried not to get my hopes up too high—I had met with so many people who promised, "I'll get back to you," or, "I'll have so-and-so contact you," but never heard another word.

The next morning, after talking with Glenn and Frankie, Frankie walked me over to Senator Kelly's office. "This is so ironic," he said, "I just saw you on Channel 2!"

Frank put me at ease right away when he let me know that he was there to help *Get The Message*—that very day—and just needed to know how. While I was explaining my vision to expand into more schools, Frank asked his assistant to make a call, and a few minutes later, handed me a note with the day and time for a meeting with Mike Gimbel, the "Drug Czar" of Baltimore County. Frank introduced me to his accountant, Dave Deger, who helped me manage our books over the years. At the end of the meeting, Frank opened his checkbook, opened his phone book, and went to work for *Get The Message*. Mike Gimbel opened the doors of several Baltimore County schools for me.

Frank joined my board and impressed upon me the importance of a good name, always doing what I say I will do, and being a faithful steward of our finances—the kind of responsibility and accountability it takes to run a successful organization. He invited me to various business and civic affairs and introduced me to influential leaders who became key sponsors. He visited our summer camps at the University of Maryland Eastern Shore. Kelly Associates was a corporate sponsor, and their communications staff designed and printed our collateral materials.

Thanks to Frank, I learned to navigate the business world, and learned to play golf. In return, I've helped him understand more about the world where I come from (though he could never learn to shoot a basketball!).

The Kelly family became personal friends with my wife Karen and me, and our son Jonathan. I see how close, loving and respectful they are toward each other, and I'm a better husband and father from watching how they raise their families. Jonathan's friendship with several of the Kelly grandsons began when they all played on the youth basketball team I coached, and their friendship was a big influence on Jonathan's decision to attend Calvert Hall. I see how kind and generous all the Kellys are to so many people, and that motivates me to do whatever I can do to help others in similar ways.

Whenever I need advice, I can still turn to Frank. What he thinks about me, matters to me, and that will never change. Whatever good things happen to Frank, he deserves them all!

-Ernie Graham

Ernie has been like a fifth son to me, and I've had the thrill of watching his dreams come true. I was glad to put in a word to the Maryland Athletic Director Kevin Anderson about hanging his number 25 jersey from the rafters in the Xfinity Center, where it was raised in 2011, and I'm happy that he got to see Jonathan also wear number 25 for the Maryland Terps. I look forward to one more of Ernie's dreams fulfilled: finishing his degree. In the meantime, I pray that Ernie continues to share his heart with young people, and those young people continue to get his message.

SO MOUPH CAN STAY IN AMERICA

If Ernie is like a fifth son, Mouph is number six. Villanova basketball coach Jay Wright called me in 2013 with a request regarding his team captain, Mouphtaou Yarou, who is from Benin in West Africa.

Mouph told me, "I want to marry a woman like Janet some day."

"Frank," Jay said, "I need some help for Mouph. He wants to play in the NBA but will be starting out in Europe. The problem is, he's not a U.S. citizen. If he leaves the country, he can't come back. The only way he could come back is if he has a job with an American company. Would you be willing to give him an interview and see if you might have a spot for him?"

At 6 feet, 10 inches tall, with a smile just as big, and fluent in six languages, Mouph immediately impresses. We invited him for an interview, and he continued to impress us with his love for God and his desire to always do the right thing. We hired him part-time at Kelly Associates and helped him hire an agent to manage his basketball career—he's playing professionally in France.

I talk with him 3 to 4 times a week while he's playing in Europe. During the off-seasons, he lives in our home—he has to duck when he comes in the back door. Our family loves having him; all the grandkids have a blast with him. He's fond of us as well. We went out for dinner recently before he left for a basketball camp in Benin, and he told me, "BF, I just want you to know, I want to marry a woman like

Janet someday. Thank you for showing me how God wants a family to be." Mouph and I both hope that he has a long, successful basketball career, but both of us are also looking forward to the day he settles down in Baltimore, joins Kelly Associates full time, and finds his "Janet."

I'm proud of my alma mater and happy to help as I'm able. In 2018 my sons honored me with gifts to Villanova in my name that dedicated a study room in the School of Business and enhancements to the lounge outside Coach Wright's office in the Davis Center for Athletics and Fitness.

'You inspire me'

Frank is the kind of person who, as soon as you meet him, you love him. We first met in 2004 when Frank and his friend and fellow Villanova alumnus Frank Culotta introduced me to Joe Ehrmann, the former Baltimore Colt who I later invited to speak to our athletic department. Frank and I quickly became good friends and started working together when he invited me to become involved with the Cal Ripken Sr. Foundation.

By the time Mouph ran into his visa problems, I knew Frank well enough to know he would be sympathetic to Mouph's situation so I asked him if he could help. Now, this shows the kind of person Frank is. He didn't look at my request as a bother or take an, "I

---

guess I have to figure out a way to help this kid" type of attitude. He looked at it as an opportunity for him and his family to develop a relationship with someone by helping them with a need.

In life, it's not about what happens to you, but how you approach each challenge. When there's a problem, like Mouph's, Frank faces it with a smile and figures out a plan to overcome it. Frank is a great example of approaching each day and every situation with a positive, can-do attitude.

Once Frank met Mouph, he was intrigued by his story. Whenever Frank came up to see a game, he would talk to Mouph—another demonstration of his love and concern for people—and they became friends. Frank hired Mouph at Kelly Associates, and their relationship took off. Now Mouph is like part of the Kelly family. As much as Frank has done to help Mouph, which is a lot, Frank will say that Mouph has done even more for him and his family.

Frank clearly values his friendships, and I'm impressed by his loyalty to his friends. Almost everyone I meet who knows Frank says something along the lines of, "I've known Frank for 40 years. He's a great friend; always been there for me." Once he's your friend, he's your friend for life.

More than anything, Frank values his faith and his family. They are part of everything he does. Even with all of his success in business and politics, his family is without a doubt his #1 priority and his #1 source of pride. I know he has a very successful insurance business, but he doesn't talk about it much. He'd rather tell me about his grandkids. Then he always asks about my family.

Frank, thank you for your friendship and your example. I love the values you live by. You inspire me to stay committed to my family and friends first, and to run our basketball program the way you run your business.

-Jay Wright
Head Basketball Coach
Villanova University

BRINGING BASEBALL'S LIFE LESSONS TO
THE CITY WITH THE IRON MAN

At the 2001 Super Bowl
Ravens 34 Giants 7

I met Cal Ripken Jr., the Orioles' Hall of Fame "Iron Man" who broke Lou Gehrig's streak by playing in 2,632 consecutive games, the way I met all the important people in my life—purely by the Lord directing our steps.

Charlie Cawley invited Janet and me to his MBNA suite in Tampa to watch the 2001 Super Bowl—Baltimore Ravens vs. New York Giants. Cal was also at the game, and though he loves to mingle with his fans, at one point he wanted a break from the steady stream of autograph and photo seekers. Security brought him up to the suites, where he found MBNA, one of the many companies he had worked with previously. He recognized Howie Long, the former Villanova and Oakland Raiders' football star and now a Fox NFL announcer, who was sitting at a table with me trading Wildcats stories. Cal and his family sat down with us.

"I hate to tell you, but the Giants are going to blow you right off the field," Howie teased us. (So much for being an expert. The Ravens won 34-7, which equaled the largest margin of victory in Super Bowl history.)

I spent the rest of the evening simply having fun with Howie and Cal and our families—no agendas, no ulterior motives. I didn't think about our serendipitous get-together much more until I received a letter from Cal a couple of years later, after he had retired from baseball:

Dear Frank, I really enjoyed meeting you at the Super Bowl, and I would love to get together some day for lunch. How does the Oregon Grille sound to you?

He gave me eight dates to choose from.

I wrote back, *I would love to get together with you. Let's make it November 5.*

We ate lunch in the back room, and we hit it off right away. Cal impressed me as genuinely sincere, a deep thinker, and inquisitive, as he asked me how I got into politics, how I started my business, and on and on. I looked at my watch, and it was five o'clock. I had to drive up to the Villanova basketball game at eight, so I cut to the chase. I was thinking to myself, *he is looking for something; he must want something,* so I asked him, "Is there anything I can do for you? Is there any particular reason you wanted to meet?"

He paid me one of the most heart-warming compliments I have ever received in my life. "Frank, when I was in baseball, for 21 years, I met a lot of people, and every once in a while, I would meet somebody that I wanted to get to know better when I finished playing. It's tough to build relationships when you are on the road so much playing Major League Baseball. I wrote your name down at the Super Bowl and told my wife on the flight home that I would like to get to know Frank Kelly better someday. I haven't met many politicians I respect, but I have heard nothing but good things about you. So, no, there's nothing in particular I wanted, other than to get to know you better."

I invited him to the Villanova game with me, but he couldn't go on such short notice.

A few weeks later, he invited me to Aberdeen to see his baseball operations. He drove me around the whole complex in a golf cart, and then mentioned the Foundation that the family started in his father's name. "I would like to tell you about it."

We sat in the stands for two hours discussing Cal's vision to use baseball as a hook to teach at-risk youth the same life lessons that his late father taught him and his brother Billy: integrity, responsibility, hard work, teamwork, respect, and leadership. I could identify with those values, and I could identify with wanting to carry on the legacy of a father who taught them and who died too young. Then Cal asked me, "Are you hungry?"

"I am always hungry."

"What do you say we go for lunch?" Cal asked.

"That sounds great. Where's Billy?" I asked.

"Do you want to meet Billy?"

"Yes, thank you, I would love to meet Billy."

Cal called Billy on the phone. "I'm with Frank Kelly. Meet us at your favorite place for lunch."

What a dive that place was, but Billy loved the hot roast beef sandwiches. We sat there until three o'clock getting to know each other better and listening to Billy complain about all the players on steroids. It bothered him how he played cleanly for 13 years while so many others cheated.

In the fall of that year, Cal called me again, on a Sunday night. "Frank, it's Cal. I want to ask you a favor. I told you all about the Foundation; we held our first fundraiser and raised $750,000. Another fundraiser is scheduled for February, and I would love it if you and Janet would get involved and chair this one for me."

The fact that he mentioned Janet enticed me, and I asked him, "Why do you want Janet?"

"I really like Janet," Cal said.

I said, "Cal, you've got damn good instincts! I need another responsibility like I need a hole in my head, but since you included Janet, we will help."

The first decision Janet and I made was to charge $25,000 per table to attend the gala. Cal and his board thought we were nuts. Most tables at Baltimore area fundraisers went for around $1,000, and some were as high as $2,500, but $25,000 was unheard of. Even so, Janet and I felt the buzz that was building in town with Cal only a couple of years away from entering the Hall of Fame. There was no question he would be elected on the first ballot, and fans were starting to make their reservations for Cooperstown. We also solicited major sponsors, and raised about $500,000 through them, and moved the venue to the Baltimore Convention Center, which overlooked Camden Yards as it gleamed in its night lights. The gala raised about $1 million.

In the spring of that year, I organized a fundraising golf tournament that was also very fruitful. Then Cal asked if I would join the Foundation board, which at the time consisted of his mother Vi, Billy, Cal's lawyer, and a couple of others who Cal had known for a long time. I told him that I would be honored to be a part of what he was doing.

He also brought on Robbie Callaway and Steve Salem, national fundraisers for the Boys & Girls Club of America, who have taken the Foundation to a whole new level. Frank III joined the board, and it has evolved into a national lineup of the biggest hitters you can imagine, with Steve serving now as CEO. Janet and I led the fundraising for six years, and together with Cal's talented team, consistently raised more than $1 million each year.

I chaired the Foundation for two years, and at what turned out to be one of the most consequential fundraising trips during my term, Robbie, Steve, and I sat with Charlie Cawley in a hotel lobby in Naples and turbo-charged the Foundation's signature initiative. We told Charlie about the

Frank and Janet receive the Cal Sr. Award from Cal Jr. and Billy Ripken.

Foundation's mission, and he wanted to support it. "But is there something I can wrap my arms around?" he asked.

That started our wheels turning. I mentioned the turf field we were building at Calvert Hall. Doris Buffet had pledged $1 million to the Ripken Foundation to build a youth baseball and softball complex in Fredericksburg, VA. The lightbulbs went off. What about expanding our reach by installing all-purpose turf fields in some of the most disadvantaged communities we can find?

We started in Baltimore at the former Memorial Stadium site, with a field on the exact spot where Cal stood at home plate for his first eleven seasons with the Orioles. Frank III supported the FCA Park Heights Saints football and cheerleading program, so we built there, and Under Armour helped us with a field at Patterson Park. We would not put a shovel in the ground until all the money was in the bank. Cal was learning how to operate a grassroots community program, and the Foundation honored Janet and me with the Cal Sr. Award in 2011.

A year or two later I was the leadoff speaker at a fundraiser back in Naples. "As a matter of fact," I told the guests, "we're going to build 50 fields in 5 years."

It just came out of my mouth. I had not discussed it with anyone before then. Cal and the other board members gasped and nearly fell off their chairs. But we all embraced

50 fields as our goal, pushed and pushed to the max, and reached 50 in less than 5 years. In 2018, there are 71 completed fields and another 30 under development.

HALL OF FAME MOMENTS

Janet and I were thrilled to join the Ripken family for Cal's Hall of Fame Induction Weekend. I could hardly believe it was happening as we joined the Ripkens at the various ceremonies, dinners and receptions. Plus, I played golf with baseball leg-

Terry Flynn (MBNA), Cal Ripken Jr., Frank Kelly, John Cochran (MBNA), and Dutch Ruppersberger at Cal's Hall of Fame Induction, 2007

ends Mike Schmidt of the Phillies and Bill Mazeroski, whose walk-off home run in the bottom of the ninth of game 7 won the 1960 World Series for the Pirates.

But my Hall of Fame moments with Cal got even better the following year when he invited me as his guest for another Hall of Fame weekend. Talk about the A-list—the only people allowed to stay in the same hotel as the Hall of Famers were their wives and kids—and me!

Cal showed his playful side all weekend. "There is one guy we are going to have some fun with," he said.

"Who?" I asked.

"Reggie Jackson. He'll see you with me and want to know who you are, but we won't tell him. We'll avoid him. If he comes toward us, we'll walk the other way. It will drive him crazy. We will have fun with Reggie."

At the Friday night reception, I met Ernie Banks, Wade Boggs, and dozens of players I idolized as a kid. Reggie stood about ten yards away from us, looking in our direction. Cal said, "He's looking at us. Let's go over there." We walked in the opposite direction and talked with a few more players. Everybody wanted to talk to Cal. Reggie moved toward us again, so we kept moving away, and avoided him the whole night. It was hilarious.

On Saturday morning, Cal invited me to play golf—just the two of us (and the security guard assigned to him by the Hall of Fame).

At dinner on Saturday night, I met Doris Kearns Goodwin, who wrote *Team of Rivals*, about the genius of President Lincoln bringing his rivals into his cabinet. Doris was born in Brooklyn and loves baseball, so we had plenty to talk about.

While we waited in the hotel lobby for the bus to the Hall of Fame, a young girl in her twenties came up to Cal. "Can I take my picture with you?"

"Sure," Cal said.

Then she introduced herself. "I'm Kim Jackson."

Suddenly Reggie appeared. "Hi, Cal, how are you doing?" He had sent his daughter over as a decoy! Cal still played it cool and did not introduce me.

Reggie looked at me and held out his hand. "I'm Reggie Jackson."

"Hi, I'm Frank Kelly; it's nice to meet you, Reg."

There was silence for a few awkward moments. Finally, Reggie spoke up.

"Yeah, so Frank, how long have you known Cal?"

"A good bit of time."

"How do you know him?" he asked.

'He's just a big kid'

What I'll remember the most about my dad is that in many ways, he's just a big kid. He comes to the Carolina lacrosse games, all decked out in his UNC gear, proud as a peacock, and asks me a million questions: What's going on? Why isn't [fill in a grandson's name] in the game more? Are you going to talk to the coach?

We went to Disney World when my kids were little. On the Boardwalk, there's a waterslide designed like an old-fashioned wooden roller coaster. The kids are walking up and riding down, walking up and riding down; I'm catching them at the bottom. All of a sudden I see the whole thing sway to the left. CREEEEAAAAK! Then it sways back to the right. The slide's ready to break! Then out comes BF. "Let's go again!"

By 3:30 in the afternoon, Missy, the kids and I are sweaty and tired. Mom is sweaty and tired, but BF is still going strong. "Where are we going next?"

"We're going to take the kids back for a nap," I tell him.

"Want to go to the ESPN Zone for some wings?" BF asks.

"The kids need to cool off and take a nap. Missy and I might even take a nap."

We get the kids asleep, and then we hear a knock on our sliding glass door. "Your mother wanted to take a nap," BF says. "Let me see your room." He looks around for a few seconds. "Very nice. Want to go swimming?"

We go to dinner at a place famous for their milkshakes. "This is a great milkshake!" BF says. "How did you know about this place? How do they make these milkshakes? Where do they get their ice cream?"

There's no one like BF.

-David Kelly

"We are just close friends," I said.

"Oh really?" he said, "I've never seen you before."

"It's not intentional."

More silence.

Cal wouldn't bite; I wouldn't bite. I'm sure Reggie was wondering, *What the hell are you doing here at this hotel with Cal Ripken where only family is allowed? Who the hell are you?*

Someone near us told Reggie I had been in the Senate. Reggie asked, "You were in the Senate? You're a politician?"

I said, "I'm not a politician. I'm a statesman."

"Oh, is there a difference?"

"Yes, there is a big difference. Look it up when you go home tonight. Read the Bible and check the dictionary; you'll find out what a statesman is."

Cal finally ended the game. "Reg, we were just having fun with you," he said.

I introduced myself properly. "Cal and I have been friends for a long time, and I am chairman of his foundation board. I am just honored to be here."

Reggie laughed. "That damn Ripken! He was always pulling practical jokes when we were playing."

'HE'S THE REAL DEAL'

I asked Cal if I could meet one more person, my favorite Brooklyn Dodger pitcher of all time, Sandy Koufax. The next day at breakfast, Cal introduced us, and we reminisced for ten minutes or so about the glory days at Ebbets Field.

After breakfast, Cal said, "Let's play golf again, just you and me." At the end of the round, the security guard asked Cal when he planned to leave. "Frank and I are going to play golf again tomorrow, and then we're going home. Would you like to join us?"

The security guard's face lit up. "Are you serious? I would love to join you."

"Great. We tee off at eight o'clock."

Then the guard nervously cleared his throat and said, "Mr. Ripken, I have a nephew who lives around here. He is 16 years old and loves to play golf, and he would love to play with you."

"Bring him along!" Cal said. That showed me the kind of person Cal is. He's at the Hall of Fame Weekend, and he chooses to play golf with only me for two days, and then with a security guard and his nephew who he has never met. The kid gaped in awe the whole time. While we waited at one of the holes, the security guard came over to me and whispered, "I have been in this business a long time and served protection for a lot of famous people, but I have never met anybody like Mr. Ripken."

How many people who love baseball would kill to spend three days at the Hall of Fame with Cal Ripken? And he picked up the tab for everything, which he always does every time I'm out with him.

"He is the real deal," the security guard also said to me back on the golf course.

"I spend a lot of time with Cal," I said, "and I can tell you, he is the real deal."

Cal and I love each other like father and son. He's not a hugger, but I am, and we hug every time we see each other.

'It was great being with you'

You can take Frank anywhere.

Our friendship had grown quickly, I was grateful for all that he had done for me, and I knew he would enjoy the Hall of Fame weekend experience. I also knew that he would be fine mingling with the Hall of Famers on his own while I was away at my obligatory functions.

But the part of our trip that I cherish the most was not at the Hall of Fame. It was the hours in the car driving up and back. It reminded me of my hours in the car with my dad traveling around to minor league baseball games. Frank and I talked about life, direction, and how to help more kids and more people. I love the little phrase he uses when he says goodbye: "It was great being with you." When I dropped him off at his house at the end of that weekend, and every time I say goodbye to Frank, I think, *Yes, it was great being with you, too.*

-Cal Ripken Jr.

BETTER FOR EVERYONE:
OUR OWN DEAR CALVERT HALL

When it came time for Frank III to choose a high school, both Calvert Hall and Loyola recruited him to play football. I think he would have done well at either school, but we chose Calvert Hall because it seemed to be a perfect fit in every way. Calvert Hall turned out to be a good choice for John, David, and Bryan as well, and now the grandsons are continuing the Kelly legacy there.

With my family so heavily invested in Calvert Hall, they asked me to join their board. After declining twice, I eventually agreed on the condition that they would let me start moving on several campus improvements they had recognized as needs but had not yet acted upon. Calvert Hall has no additional acreage to expand, so the issue is always how to increase the usability and efficiency of the existing land. My first motion was to commission a campus master plan.

The first item on the plan was a stadium that could host football, soccer, lacrosse, and track (even though Calvert Hall had a track team that won championships, there was no track on campus, so the team never had a home meet). We immediately commissioned the architects and started raising funds, and in 1999 opened the 3,000 seat Paul Angelo Russo Stadium, complete with locker rooms, coaches' offices, and an athletic training center.

As beautiful as the stadium was, we soon recognized a major problem: so many games and practices made it impossible to keep the grass growing and prevent the field from turning into a dust bowl. I called my friend Charlie Cawley, and once again, he and MBNA demonstrated their generosity and contributed half of the funds to lay a synthetic turf field. I contributed the other half.

Calvert Hall's baseball program is one of the best in the country, but the field sloped so badly, the late sportscaster Vince Bagli joked that, "Unless your right fielder was 6 feet 7 inches tall, he couldn't see home plate."

Being a two-stadium man, I went to work on planning and fundraising for a new baseball stadium. Thanks to our generous donors, led by Carlo Crispino and John Carey, we were soon able to ask Cal Ripken to help with the design, and in 2008 we dedicated the Carlo Crispino Baseball Stadium.

We moved and upgraded the tennis courts, and doubled the number of parking spaces. We revitalized the campus, all on the existing acreage.

Even synthetic turf fields have limited lifespans. By

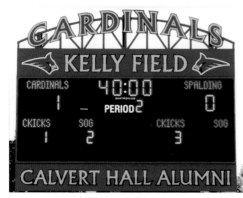

I told them not to, but...

2010, the turf in Russo Stadium was worn out and full of patches. After watching a lacrosse player break his ankle, I called Brother Zoppo to tell him I would contribute the funds for new AstroTurf. He didn't ask any questions!

Calvert Hall wanted to name it Kelly Field, but I told them not to, that I wasn't contributing for that reason. But they invited Janet and me to attend a game where there would be a "special announcement," which turned out to be the unveiling of Kelly Field.

Our next project was turfing the practice fields, which, with too many ruts and not enough grass, was unsafe for the players. The Ripken Foundation began the construction on the fields in 2018.

In 2017, Calvert Hall honored Janet and me as the

inaugural recipients of the President's Medal. We are thankful for the blessing that Calvert Hall has been to our sons and grandsons, and happy to do what we can to make it the best school possible for everyone.

Happy 4th of July from Bethany Beach!

IMPROVING THE NEIGHBORHOOD

We loved our condo in Ocean City, but every Sunday when we were there, we found ourselves driving north to the less crowded beaches in Bethany. Our dream was to own a home on the beach someday.

The daughter of a client sold real estate in Bethany, and I told her that if she ever found anything reasonably priced, to please let us know. She called us about a year later, in November of 1994, with two lots for us to see. They were right on the ocean with a private beach in a community called Sussex Shores, the first community north of Bethany. Janet and I prayed about it and made an offer that was well below the asking price, and a little below the maximum we could afford. The owner laughed; while we were making up our minds, one of the lots sold for the asking price. We countered with our maximum offer, but the owner wanted to hold out for the full price. But our agent had bad news:

"You've lost it. He has three other buyers."

"Well," I told her, "I guess it's not meant to be."

About a month later, in early December, the agent called me. "Are you still interested?"

"Oh yeah, we sure are. But we can't go over the price we already offered," I said.

She said, "I think I can get it for you if you can settle by the end of the year. The other offers fell through."

"Oh yeah, absolutely!" I said.

"Then the other broker and I will give up some of our commission, so you can pay what you can afford, and the seller will get his asking price."

Sussex Shores is a charming community, and we love it there, but it was built in the 1940s after World War II, so by the time we moved in, it was showing its age. The roads were full of potholes and so uneven that they flooded whenever it rained. It had the old-fashioned above-ground telephone and electricity wires strung between ugly poles, and during thunderstorms, we often saw sparks flying out of the transformers. Twice, houses caught fire. The underground water lines were narrow (only four inches, which meant weak flow out of the faucets and showers), rotting, asbestos-coated pipes.

Janet and I bought the house in Sussex Shores to have a place at the beach to relax and enjoy ourselves and the grandchildren. We consciously avoided involvement in any of the civic affairs of the community. "We have enough of that in Baltimore," Janet told me.

But year after year I attended the community association meetings every Memorial Day and Labor Day weekend, when most of the families were there at their beach homes. Year after year there was a lot of talk about replacing the water system, repaving the roads, taking down the telephone poles, but the same pipes, potholes, and transformer sparks never got fixed.

Finally, at one of the meetings I got so fed up with all the empty talk I stood up and gave them a piece of my mind. "I've been in this community sixteen years now. We all have a lot on our plates, but all we ever do is talk about these problems. Eventually, the dilapidated infrastructure is going to hurt the value of our properties if it hasn't already. I've had it. I don't feel like paying any more of my assessments if we don't get our act together and get something done." I turned and stomped out of the room.

Later that afternoon, Janet and I were sitting out on the beach, and two of the community association board members came up to me. "Frank, everybody is talking about what you said earlier. They realize that you're right; something has to be done. If we nominate you, would you be president of the association and help us get this done?"

I decided to put them to the test. "If you can convince my neighbor, Mark, to join the board with me, I'll do it." I said that half because Mark is smart and would be a helpful colleague, and half because he had told me over the years that he would never, ever get involved with the association. I thought for sure he would say no and get me off the hook.

The board members walked over to ask Mark. "Is Kelly going to be the president?" he asked.

"He said he would if you also joined the board."

"I'll do it," Mark said, "but only for as long as he's president."

The board members came back over and told me Mark had agreed to join the board with me. I had to keep my word. "OK, I'll do it," I told them. But I made the same stipulation with them as I had made with the community colleges years before: "You have to let me do it my way. The minute anybody complains, I'm outta here."

The biggest issue was how to pay for everything. We

worked out a deal with the county to issue bonds that residents could pay back with a modest increase in assessments spread over 15 years, and the residents overwhelmingly approved it. The local, family-run water company was more difficult to work with. All I heard in my 20 years living in Sussex Shores was how no one could ever get the water company to do anything.

Weeks passed, and then I learned that the water company president had turned the company over to his daughter. On the beach one day, I asked my neighbor and Sussex Shores native, John Neff, if he knew the daughter. "Sure. I went to school with her," he said. "Can you get me an appointment with her this week?" I asked.

John and I met with her later that week, and we hit it off right away. I gave her my pitch. "The water lines are 60 years old, and you're going to have to replace them sometime soon. Why not do it now, before we put in the new roads? If you wait, you'll be responsible for replacing the roads also."

"Let me think about it," she said. "We don't have the money in the budget right now. I'll have to take it to my board."

She got back to me with the board's answer. "We don't have the money for this. The only way we can do it is with a rate increase."

"If you ask the public service commission for a rate increase, I'll make sure our community supports it," I said.

With the financing in place, we were ready to roll. The County hired a consultant to manage the project and work with us. I asked Tony Moag, the COO of The Whiting-Turner Contracting Company and a Sussex Shores resident, to join the board and help me manage the work on our end. Ironically, though the water company was the last one in the project, they were the first to finish their job. But then we found out how hard it is for a tiny community of 120 households to get to the top of Delmarva Power and Verizon's project list. After delay upon delay, I worked my contacts at Constellation Energy in Baltimore and Verizon in Philadelphia, and two days later, the trucks showed up to start the work.

Our Sussex Shore neighbors thanked us for our help with the community improvement projects.

After two years of construction, the electric lines and fiber-optic phone and cable lines all ran through underground conduit, and there's not a telephone pole or electric transformer in sight. We have the best-tasting water anywhere and enjoy high-pressure showers through our eight-inch asbestos-free water lines. The roads, five inches of smooth as silk blacktop, don't flood anymore and are lined with beautiful new fences and landscaping. We replaced the short, stubby stop signs with new signs tall enough for drivers to actually see.

We finished on time and under budget. Neighbors came up to me and thanked me for my efforts, and the community threw a party for Janet and me to show their appreciation. One neighbor wanted to commission a statue in my honor, but I told him, "No way." This was the kind of challenge I love. It brought the community together, everyone supported me the whole way, and we accomplished something that had never gotten done before. On top of all that, so far the water company hasn't needed to increase their rates, so the whole project hasn't cost the Sussex Shores residents a dime.

CELEBRATING BALTIMORE'S BEST

In 2016 *The Baltimore Sun* established their Business and Civic Hall of Fame to recognize "those who have dedicated their lives to making this region thrive." I was humbled and honored to be chosen among the twelve inaugural inductees. It's an award I want to share with Janet and my sons because without them I would not have been able to get involved in so many community projects.

2016 HALL OF FAME RECIPIENT

Francis X.
KELLY JR.

Whether as a business owner, state senator or health care leader,
Frank Kelly is an accomplished problem-solver

(June 10, 2016, *The Baltimore Sun*)

Francis X. Kelly Jr. is such a familiar and omnipresent figure in the Baltimore region that you might assume there are at least three of him. One to build a hugely successful insurance company. Another to become a respected Baltimore state senator. A third to devote himself to his faith and to the community.

Yet friends and colleagues insist that there is just one: the happy warrior whose greatest success may be in raising a family—including quite a few highly successful lacrosse players. He and his wife, Janet, celebrated their 50th wedding anniversary in 2011, and they have four sons and 22 grandchildren.

Francis X. Kelly Jr. has been an active figure in business, government, health care and philanthropy.

Mr. Kelly's inclusion in the inaugural class of The Baltimore Sun's Business and Civic Hall of Fame might have been granted on his business success alone. The Villanova University graduate started Kelly Associates in the basement of his home in Timonium in 1976. It now employs 450 at its Hunt Valley headquarters and regional offices, making it one of the region's top health insurance brokers and administrators, with thousands of corporate clients.

But many also know him as the Democratic state senator first elected to the Maryland General Assembly in 1979 whose conservative views and deep Roman Catholic faith didn't always align with his party's leadership priorities. Yet he must have done something right because elected officials, Democrats and Republicans alike, have been calling on him ever since he left office to help advise public institutions on the state and local level.

That has most notably included his work with the University of Maryland Medical System and particularly the R Adams Cowley Shock Trauma Center. Not only did he help the system make the transition from state government to private, not-for-profit status, but he helped it grow from a single financially challenged hospital to a $3.5 billion network of 12 hospitals. Most recently, that included the acquisition of St. Joseph Medical Center in Towson at a time when the facility was facing a huge debt. Today, it's back in the black, and many there credit the indefatigable Mr. Kelly, who now serves as chairman of the hospital's board.

As a fundraiser and philanthropist, Mr. Kelly's legacy has spread far and wide. He has helped the Community College of Baltimore County, Morgan State University, the Children's Guild, the Cal Ripken Sr. Foundation and Calvert Hall College High School. He has been honored by the University of Maryland School of Medicine, the Catholic Business Network of Baltimore, the Baltimore Health Underwriters Association, the Maryland Motor Truck Association, the Baltimore County Chamber of Commerce, the American Trauma Society, and on and on.

Six years ago when Mr. Kelly, as a member of the Board of Regents, was interviewing candidates to serve as the University of Maryland, College Park's next president, he recalled falling for Iowa's Wallace Loh (who was ultimately hired) because of his can-do outlook, but he may have simply found a kindred spirit. "I want someone who looks at problems and sees opportunities to solve them," Mr. Kelly told a reporter. Surely, the same can be said for the 76-year-old chairman of Kelly Associates.

'TO THE ENDS OF THE EARTH'

As long as God brings opportunities to me and makes it clear to Janet and me when something is indeed His calling, I will continue to help people and serve the community every way I can. I don't ask for jobs or grovel for headlines, and I think that's why people from all sides—Republicans and Democrats, liberals and conservatives—say, "I'll call Frank Kelly about that."

The Baltimore Sun joked about there being three of me, but I count six, adding Frank III, John, David, Bryan, and Janet. They all have a heart for establishing roots and solving problems in the communities where they live. Each one serves on multiple boards and committees of professional, civic, social, faith-based, health care, and educational organizations. As our company mission states, *As good stewards, we believe this corporation should earn a reasonable return on its invested capital after it has given an appropriate share of earnings to charities committed to serving the least, the last and the lost.*

Like everything else the boys touched in the business, they took community service to new frontiers. They have truly impacted the world from their offices in Hunt Valley. They have far outdone me in the way they answer the call of Acts 1:8 by reaching out to our employees and supporting ministries around Maryland and around the world.

Kelly Associates offers scholarships for employees' children to attend summer camps, and for employees and their spouses to enjoy FamilyLife weekend marriage get-

In Zambia with World Bicycle Relief

aways. We established the Kelly Associates Green Cross fund to provide support to employees who suffer a sudden and severe financial hardship through no fault of their own.

The boys constantly lend the company's resources, such as our meeting rooms, technology, and design and printing services, to nonprofit organizations. The company financially supports dozens of charities, a standard business practice Frank III and I implemented after the *Business By The Book* seminar and writing our mission.

Kelly Associates adopted children in the poorest countries in the world, mostly in Ethiopia and Uganda but also in many others, through sponsorship with World Vision, and if an employee wants to sponsor a child, the company will match their giving. Through World Vision, the People of Kelly Associates help bring basic nutrition, wells for clean water, health care, and education to over 200 children.

John established a partnership with World Bicycle

Relief, which donates bikes to people in poor villages throughout the world, giving them easier access to education, health care, and jobs.

In 2018, Kelly Associates sponsored a Fellowship of Christian Athletes (FCA) lacrosse team, called FCA Team Serve to

Taking the good news to Israel: Frankie, BF, and Frank III at the Mount of Beatitudes overlooking the Sea of Galilee

attend the Federation of International Lacrosse Men's Lacrosse World Championship in Israel. Team Serve was not a USA national team so it could not compete for the championship itself, but Frank III wanted to assemble a team to go for the fellowship, to serve, share God's love and truth, and help inexperienced teams from countries where lacrosse is a relatively new sport prepare for their games. I was thrilled to go along on the trip and watch my grandsons Frankie, Stephen, Timmy, and JK share their faith, play against international competition, and coach young players from around the world.

One of those young and inexperienced players, Vova, was on our team. He is on staff with FCA in Ukraine and came to play with Team Serve. Most of what he knew about lacrosse he learned from watching YouTube videos. His first few games, he could barely catch a pass. Then Timmy spent hours with him practicing shooting attack moves around the goal. "Vova," Timmy encouraged him, "I think you're going to score a goal next game against the Russians!" Vova didn't score one goal; he scored three.

The games showed me how the Lord could use a la-

Team Serve shares with Team Russia before Vova prays with them in their own language

crosse field to break through political and cultural barriers to unite people who might otherwise be considered enemies. There we were, Americans, in Israel, playing with teams from Turkey and Russia. And Vova is from Ukraine, the country Russia invaded in 2014. Where else have people from those five nations come together in peace?

After every game, the players from both teams would come together, and Frank III would tell them about the ministry of FCA and then ask if he could end with a prayer. Every team agreed to pray with us, and I saw many players reach out for another's hand or shoulder.

After the game against Russia, Frank told the group, "We have a player on our team, Vova, from Ukraine who speaks Russian. Is it OK if he leads our prayer in Russian?" The Russian team loved the idea, and my heart swelled as I stood in a circle on Israeli soil, praying to Jesus with a group of Russians lead by a Ukrainian. From Baltimore to Vail to Israel and beyond, God has blessed multiple generations of the Kellys and lacrosse players around the world.

'ONLY IN AMERICA'

Only in America can two people come from entirely different backgrounds get married, move to a strange city, set up an office in the basement of their home, step out in faith to start a family business, and publicly proclaim that faith. Our dream, when Janet and I knelt to ask for God's blessing on our new endeavor, was to sink roots deep into our community, and then give back, give back, and give back, as much as we could. There have been busy stages of life and lean financial

Still dancing after all these years

periods when giving away time and money made no worldly sense. But we hold to a certainty that we have seen proven true over and over, in good times and bad: you can't out-give the Lord.

'Living the Kelly Way'

I know Frank is incredibly proud of his boys, now men, and his grandchildren. Frank's kids have all grown up to be successful in their own right, helping with the family business and living the "Kelly Way" of helping others, giving back to their community, and living their faith.

-Congressman C. A. Dutch Ruppersberger

'I'm grateful you're my friend'

Frank is a remarkable person; he and his entire family. They're close, they're smart and successful, yet they're all about others. They're spiritually motivated with deep Christian humility. You don't see such a combination in too many people.

Frank helps a lot of people in quiet ways and doesn't announce it. I was with him at the beach one summer, and he got a call from someone facing a medical emergency. Frank knows all the top experts and made arrangements for the person. He helps people in those situations all the time. Then he prays for them and follows up to see how they are doing. He changes many lives, but unless you're there to witness what he does for people, you'd never know about it.

Frank, you've been an inspiration and a guidepost for me over four decades. I'm grateful you're my friend.

-Tim Maloney
Principal
Joseph, Greenwald & Laake, PA

12

Surrender to Win

In conclusion, be strong—not in yourselves but in the Lord,
in the power of his boundless resource.
Ephesians 6:10

What could be better than watching my four sons play together in a lacrosse game known as the Miracle on the Mountain? Well, watching five grandsons play together at Calvert Hall, on a team coached by my son Bryan, and watching three of them play together at the University of North Carolina two years in a row are right up there.

There was a year at Calvert Hall when my grandsons, David Jr., Frankie, Patrick, Johnny, and Stephen, all played on the same team, with Bryan as their coach. David Jr. went on to play at Rutgers and Johnny at Ohio State (where he played in the 2017 National Championship game and was elected Captain in 2018). The others, plus Timmy a year later, all played at North Carolina.

Frankie, Patrick, and Stephen played on the same team at UNC in 2014. Two years later, Frankie had graduated, and Patrick (the team Captain), Stephen and Timmy played together. *The Baltimore Sun* referred to them as "The Kelly clan out of Calvert Hall." That team was on the bubble

6 THE BALTIMORE SUN | **SPORTS** | FRIDAY, APRIL 30, 2010   **VARSITY**

BOYS LACROSSE

MATT ROTH/PHOTO FOR THE BALTIMORE SUN

From left, Patrick, Frankie, Stephen, David and Johnny Kelly all play for uncle Bryan on Calvert Hall's varsity. "It's been a great experience," Bryan Kelly said. "They are very respectful of the boundaries I set here as their coach and outside of school as their uncle."

Hall in the family for Kellys

Cardinals coach has five nephews on this year's team, with more on the way

for the NCAA tournament, but they squeaked in, unseeded, caught fire at the right time, and played the #1 ranked University of Maryland for the 2016 National Championship.

There I was, in Philadelphia, on Memorial Day, 56 years after my father and I watched our last baseball game together. Coach Joe Breschi invited me down on the sidelines to watch my grandsons play, and to celebrate with Bryan and his 1991 UNC team that was honored at halftime in recognition of the 25th anniversary of their national championship. I'm sure Dad was also watching, and it turned out to be a game that neither of us would have wanted to miss.

UNC trailed 13-11 with less than four minutes to go. I looked up at the hazy sky and prayed, "Lord, maybe I shouldn't be asking for this, but this is Patrick's last game. Please let Carolina win, but if that's not in Your plan, please let Patrick go out in style." The sun broke through the clouds; I looked back at the game and Patrick was right in front of me. I watched him make a bad pass and Carolina lose the ball. *God, were you listening?* Patrick didn't stand there and pout though. He sprinted off the field to allow the long stick defenseman to get in the hole and stop a fast break and keep Carolina in the game.

UNC got the ball back, and Patrick ran back onto the field. He got the ball on the right wing, then threaded-the-needle with a pass through three defenders to an attackman who fired into the goal! *What a big set of cahoonas it took to make that pass! It's 13-12. We can do this!*

Stephen won the next faceoff, and 30 seconds later, Patrick took the ball to the cage and scored the tying goal. *We're going to overtime!*

I couldn't help but think back to the Miracle on the Mountain. It was "déjà vu all over again," to quote Yogi Berra. Three minutes into the overtime, God answered the rest of my prayers when UNC scored to win their fifth national championship, and their third with the Kelly clan.

I might have missed it all. If I had not surrendered my alcoholism to the Lord, I would never have quit drinking. If I hadn't quit drinking, I doubt that I would have been alive to see the game. People ask me, "How

Frank with 2016 NCAA Lacrosse National Champions Stephen, Timmy, and Patrick

did you do it?" I followed the simple principle that everyone can follow: *surrender to win.*

It's simple, but not always easy to do. Our society tells us to be tougher than everybody else, to be smarter than everybody else, and power ourselves to success. I think that's why, with many of us, God must use trials to bring us to the point of surrender when we realize that He is our true source of strength. It's painful to be honest with ourselves, but it brings true freedom and blessing. The Lord wants us to trust in Him when there is no other way; that's how He strengthens our faith.

My prayer for myself, my family, friends, colleagues, and anyone who reads my story is that we will surrender to God and find true peace and joy in life, the kind that goes deep into the soul and remains whether we sign a big contract or lose an election. May we surrender every day to God and then get busy with what we think He wants us to do. The key is to trust God and show up. There will be days when the challenges seem too big, and we don't want to show up, but God will always prove Himself faithful and give us the strength and wisdom we need.

When I see my mother and father again, I'll thank them for instilling in me the most important lesson I ever learned in life, to put God first, and for showing me how to surrender to Him. I'll thank them for being the best parents they knew how to be, and for planting their dreams in me. Then, my hope is that Mom, Dad, and my heavenly Father will each put a hand on my shoulder, look me in the eye, and say, "Well done!"

The Tradition Continues

All through my sons' sports careers, I prayed with them before their games, asking for protection from injury and that they would play up to the highest potential that God has given them. I've continued the tradition with my grandchildren. Someone snapped this picture as I prayed with Bryan's sons Jacob and Daniel before Calvert Hall's 2018 Championship game. Their younger brother Caleb ran up to our huddle to join in. I had prayed with Bryan—Calvert Hall's head coach—earlier that day.

Calvert Hall beat Boys' Latin, 8-6, for their second consecutive championship, and Bryan's fourth in 23 years as head coach. But more important than winning the game is the note Jacob texted me with the picture:

"This is us before the game as you prayed for Daniel and me. My favorite photo ever. Completely captures who we are as a family and who you are as a Godly and loving grandfather. I'm so thankful that I was able to have you on the sidelines with me four years at Calvert Hall and especially for your pregame prayers. Those moments will make these past four years some of the best memories of my life. Thank you, Pop Pop!!!"

Afterword

A Vision for the Future
By John R. Kelly

When I pitch innovative ideas to Dad and tell him about opportunities I see and what I'm doing about them, he gets it. Our gift is the ability to see a preferable future, and the path to getting there.

A vision begins with a hope. Dad's world revolved around caring for his wife and four sons, and he had the hope to do something special by bringing his family together into a business; a hope that sprang from his unfulfilled hope of working with his father.

Hope drives faith. Dad's faith was strong enough to say no to a $100,000 investor, and instead, borrow $10,000 at 18% interest on a credit card, panel the basement and start a business with my mother based only on a single client endorsement. He walked by faith each present moment to make it a reality.

Dad accomplishes so much because he acts on his faith and hope with his wisdom. He has tremendous intuition and instinct; a sense of what's right what's wrong and what to do in any situation. He might not be a Bible scholar, but he knows God, constantly reads and studies the Bible, and is full of wise advice when I need help with a problem.

My dad trusts his sons with running the business. He's the anchor of the business, but he gives us the space, freedom, and authority to set the strategic direction and run the daily operations. He never tells me what to do, but when I go to him with a challenge, he's there for me, and he's there with me.

I learn the most from him simply by being with him and watching him be himself in his world. When I was young, we often had guests for dinner. When dinner was over, we kids could be excused while the adults had coffee, but I would never leave. I absorbed Dad's wisdom sitting at the table listening to him.

It's the same when I'm with him in his office. We'll be discussing something and—this happens all the time—his phone will ring, and he'll say, "I have to answer this." I never leave. When I sit there and listen, I learn volumes, just from the one-sided conversation. (I do the same thing with my colleagues. When I'm meeting with someone and take a call, I tell them not to leave my office. They think it's being rude, but I tell them, "No, please stay.")

He's a master at navigating complex relationships. He can be friends with people who disagree with him and forgive people who try to defeat him because he can separate their personhood from their responsibilities to their constituents.

Dad's greatest strength is his capacity and willingness to solve problems. He loves problems because he's an optimist. He chooses to look at the positives in everything and everyone. Anyone can come to him with any kind problem—alcohol, finances, marriage, job—and he will help them; he will not judge them. He sees problems as opportunities to exercise faith and trust in God.

Love is the true mark of a follower of Christ. Dad loves by seeing the best in people and caring about them. Why else would he help anyone who comes to him? Why else would he work his butt off to improve the quality of life for people across the state of Maryland and beyond?

Because my dad knows God loves him, he loves others. Before he had any material resources, he gave himself away in public service. His motto all through his Senate career was, "Actions speak louder than words." Both he and my mother embody that divine flow of giving and receiving, loving and caring in everything they do.

Thank you, Dad, for the way you love me and care for me. Thank you for teaching me to put God first, and praying with me for my protection. Thank you for celebrating my successes. I know that you would do anything in the world for me; you would give me your eyes if you could.

Some of His Most Challenging Moments
By David E. Kelly

Vince Lombardi said that "Adversity doesn't build character, it reveals it." I've been with my father in some of his most challenging moments, and what he revealed to me in those moments was faith, generosity, and wisdom.

I came into the business shortly before my father stood up for life in the Maryland Senate. Some of his pro-abortion opponents spit on me during the next campaign, and I cried at the campaign staff dinner the night he lost the election. I could see that the loss hurt him, but I also saw that he trusted God and moved on quickly. It wasn't the end of the world for him. Then I watched him forgive his opponents. He still invites Barbara Hoffman, the leader of the pro-abortion side, to visit him and Mom for a weekend at the beach house every year.

My mother was sick the day in 1991 that she and Dad were scheduled to find out the bottom line on the accounting error that could have put us out of business, so he asked me to go with him. Months later, when it was time to sell the property and casualty business to raise the cash we needed, I drove to Pennsylvania with him to make a pitch to a potential buyer. He prayed with me in the car before we went in, and we came out with a deal. But, only weeks later at the settlement table, despite how much we had celebrated the deal and how desperately we needed the cash, Dad was willing to walk away from it rather than let the buyer hire me away from Kelly-Chick. I assured him that I was fine with going— it was the best (and maybe the only) option we had.

About 20 years later I called him on a Sunday to talk to him about another, even bigger accounting problem. He didn't overreact. Sure, he did ask, "How can this happen again?" But he also asked, "What is God teaching us?"

It seems that every few years something happens that threatens the business—health care reform, recessions, our own internal systems, regulations, talk of single-payer systems, on and on. "If we do the right thing, God will take care of us," Dad always says. He once supported legislation that eliminated group insurance for associations—our basic service—because he thought it was the best thing for the consumer. Our revenue tripled afterward. He has taught me not to worry so much, because no matter what the health care system looks like, somebody still has to sell it, administer it, and show people how it works, and that's what we do best.

For as long as I can remember, Dad has shown generosity to everyone, even when he couldn't afford it. When my brothers and I were little, he wanted to give us a nice Christmas, even though he was hurting financially. He borrowed $1,000 against the house so that Mom could buy us what we wanted, paid the loan back over the next eleven months, and then borrowed it again the next Christmas.

It doesn't matter who you are or whether or not you can return the favor, BF will be generous. One of our health insurance clients dropped us for a competitor, but did they call their new provider when their son faced a life-threatening medical emergency? No, they called BF. He values a life more than a commission, so he immediately got on the phone to the right people at UMMS, and they saved the boy's life.

Recently he decided at the last minute to hop on a plane and come to a Carolina lacrosse game. He invited Delroy to come along with him; Delroy is his caddie at the golf course in Vero Beach. It was a Saturday game—a busy day on a Florida golf course.

"Delroy," I said when I saw him, "you must be losing

a lot of money today."

He pointed to BF. "Senator is taking care of me." He didn't let Delroy spend a dime and even gave him a Carolina blue shirt to wear to the game.

He loves being in the middle of the action. He wants to know everything that's going on—with our families, the business, Carolina lacrosse, the hospitals, Calvert Hall, everything—because he's excited to serve people and help solve problems. He'll help in any way he can—with his time, his advice, his money, and often by providing access to other people who can help directly. He won't hesitate to reach out to other people for you. And when BF says he'll help, when he says he'll make some calls, you can count on him to come through for you. I've had a problem with my dried-up well. I tried to get the county to fix it, but they said nothing could be done. Dad heard about it, made some calls and talked to some people, and the next day it was fixed.

If you ask for BF's help, he might ask you tough questions—the who, what and why of the situation—but that's his way of discerning if and how he can help. Then his compassion and energy will take over, and he'll agree to do whatever he can for you.

Wisdom, the book of Proverbs says, begins with the fear of the Lord, so it doesn't surprise me that my father has made wise decisions throughout his life. He always tries to put God first in everything he does. He prays for wisdom in the situation, discerns what God wants him to do, and then goes at it full speed ahead.

He never shies away from giving glory to God, and it's always at the appropriate time and in the appropriate way. He doesn't preach. He likes everybody, he likes being with people, and most people like being with him. Often someone will comment along the lines of, "there's something different about you; a sense of peace about you." If he senses the Holy Spirit moving, he simply explains that his faith makes him who he is, and his faith is the reason he does what he does. He follows the wisdom often attributed to St. Francis: "Preach the gospel at all times, and if necessary use words."

His wisdom wouldn't be much good if he weren't so approachable. Throughout my life, I've been able to come to him with any problem, confess any mistake—even when his public reputation is at stake—and feel secure that he will listen calmly and react in love and compassion. He not only tells me he loves me, he shows me he loves me.

Dad, I want you to know that even though I joke around a lot and it might seem like I'm not paying attention, I have been paying close attention to the way you live your life, and I hope that I can be as wise, as passionate and loving, and as generous as you have modeled for me.

Living His Faith
By Bryan J. Kelly

Two visions of my father from my childhood paint the picture of who he is for me. First, I see him sitting on his bed, reading the Bible.

Some people talk a good game about their faith, but my father lives it. In the world's eyes, he was done after losing the election and returning to a struggling business. But in the midst of defeat, he trusted God. He might not have understood it at the time, but God had an even greater ride planned for him, and he's even more influential now than he was in the Senate.

My father sees the good in people. He treats everyone the same—with love and respect. When he's with you, he's with you. He doesn't put anyone up on a pedestal and doesn't put anyone down. Whether you're a CEO or the custodian who cleans the gutters, he'll give you the same eye contact and the same amount of time. I've watched him mentor a down-and-out drug addict, help him financially, offer him advice, and make phone calls and contacts to find opportunities for him. That former addict is now sharing his story with countless city kids, helping them to avoid his same mistakes.

I've seen him love his enemies. If you disagree with most people (this is especially true with many politicians) you're a bad person in their eyes. But there's not a judgmental bone in my father's body. He met Dutch Ruppersberger when they ran against each other for the Senate, and they disagree on almost everything politically, but they're best friends. Many of the pro-abortion opponents who campaigned to defeat him became his friends. He loves people and cares about people whether they believe the same way he believes, or not.

In a summer league lacrosse game, I was racing for a

loose ball on the sideline and laid out the kid from the other team who was racing against me. I stood over him, glaring down at him like Muhammad Ali over Sonny Liston. Then I heard a growl from the stands. "Bryyyyaaaan!!!" I turned, looked up and saw Dad. *Oh, crap; that was wrong.* I looked back at my opponent, asked him if he was OK, and apologized.

"You don't do that," Dad told me in the car.

"I'm sorry."

"Just learn from it," he said.

The second image of my father is in church, when the collection basket is being passed. At times during my childhood we shopped at second-hand stores, we rarely ate out, and we needed scholarships to afford Calvert Hall, but every Sunday I watched Dad put money in the basket. Some people are generous because they have so much. My dad was generous when he had nothing, and it meant sacrifice. He instilled in me, even as a child, that your first 10% goes to God.

My father is generous even to people he doesn't know. When I was a senior at Carolina, I had three roommates. I don't think I was ever invited out to dinner with any of them when their parents came to visit. But when my dad came to visit me, even though he had just lost an election and the business had yet to take off, he always invited my roommates along and treated them to dinner. He would never leave one back by himself. Regardless of his circumstances, he always thinks of others.

I've called my dad to ask his help for a friend of a friend who got in trouble at college, and he made calls to help him get a second chance at another school. I've called him late at night for the son of a friend who was hit by a car. He called ahead to Shock Trauma and went to visit the family and help them through their tragedy.

He was generous to offer me a job at Kelly Associates. I had decided to work at MBNA in Wilmington after graduation, but also had a yearning to coach lacrosse, and would not have had the opportunity to coach in Wilmington. At the time, Kelly Associates couldn't afford to take on another salary. But late in the summer, Dad pulled me aside. "We can't pay you a lot, but you can work at Kelly Associates and coach if you want."

My first job was in telemarketing. Dad sat me down at the phone with the instructions, "Make 50 calls a day and see what you can do." I started calling, lived at home for two years, and began my coaching career at Calvert Hall.

Watching how my dad interacts with people has helped me to learn the business and grow in the business. He always sees the positive in everyone and offers reassurance and encouragement even when things don't go well. He gets so much accomplished because he listens to all sides and builds consensus.

Whether it's managing people at the company or coaching a team, I've learned what my dad also learned: the most important leadership principle is to know your flock. I need to know who they are as individuals, and what's going on in their lives that can affect their performance. And they need to understand that I am here for them to talk to if they are hurting.

In whatever he does, my dad wants to honor God. He has overcome his demons, and overcome a lot of challenges, by surrendering to the true power that comes from God. I've seen him trust the Lord and do the right thing in many challenging moments. He knows that God will take care of us, but he also knows that we have to work hard and fight through the challenges to find the answers.

Afterword

Dad, I want my kids to know that I love them, so I will show them in the same ways that you showed me. I'll tell them I love them, I'll hug them, I'll pray with them before their games and events, and I'll be there for them if they get in trouble. Most of all, I'll try to instill in them the importance of putting God first, and do my best to model what that looks like. Thanks for giving me so much love to pass on.

I Gained a Best Friend
By Congressman Dutch Ruppersberger

It's hard to put into words the impact our decades-long friendship has had on my life. Frank and I met when I ran against him for State Senate. It was hard to dislike Frank—he was smart, honest and it was clear that his passion for helping people was genuine. I was impressed by his straight-up style. After our debates on the campaign trail, we would go out for pizza and debate some more. In the end, Frank beat me. It was the first (and last) election I ever lost, but I gained so much more. I had gained a best friend.

When I became County Executive, Frank became one of my most trusted advisors. I remember a time when Baltimore County Community College was poorly managed—there was a lot of bickering and politicking going on—I went to our State Senate delegation, which agreed that Frank was the guy to step in and straighten it out. Frank has a way of identifying a problem, analyzing it, determining his best option and, finally, implementing the solution. Like me, he is an end-game guy. As Board Chairman, he consolidated three separate colleges into a single institution that is now considered one of the best in the country.

It was Frank who sponsored the law creating the Shock Trauma system at the University of Maryland and we have worked together to make it the top trauma system in the world. Frank has chaired its Board of Visitors since its inception. When the hospital system acquired St. Joseph Medical Center, Frank was asked to chair its new board. Under his leadership, the hospital is again profitable after facing years of significant debt. And, as a Member of the Board of Regents at the University of Maryland, he worked to ensure Maryland's flagship colleges maintain a stellar reputation.

I have always admired Frank's commitment to his faith. Frank lives out his faith and values each and every day and always stands by his principles, even when they are not politically popular. He is deeply pro-life and fighting for his beliefs may be one reason he ultimately lost his seat in the State Senate. Frank has raised a great family rooted in faith and service, and it has been a joy to watch Frank's kids—Frankie, John, David, and Bryan—share these values with their own children.

I know Frank is incredibly proud of his boys, now men, and his grandchildren. Some of my favorite memories with Frank occurred while driving up to Cornell together to watch Frankie play lacrosse and stopping for pizza, wings, and subs along the way. By the way, the Kelly family produced and continues to produce some of the best lacrosse players in the country. Frank's kids have all grown up to be successful in their own right, helping with the family business and living the "Kelly Way" of helping others, giving back to their community, and living their faith.

A huge part of Frank's life is his wife, Janet. Don't discount Janet! Like Frank, Janet is extremely smart and compassionate. Together from their basement, Frank and Janet grew their business into one of the region's top health insurance brokers and administrators with nearly 500 employees. Theirs is a great American story of hard work and determination, and it would never have happened without Janet. She is the force behind many of Frank's activities in the community and their family's tradition of philanthropy. She is the backbone of the family.

Frank and I still debate with each other almost every week. While we disagree often, we always respect each other's point of view. Frank is a constant reminder of what politics should be all about—listening, sharing ideas, and finding common ground. Politics is not an easy game. Sometimes people attack you. It has been a blessing to know that I always have a friend I can rely on, even when he doesn't always agree with me. Frank and I know we have each other's backs.

Frank, I have enjoyed sharing our mutual passions of sports, politics, the beach, and Shock Trauma. Thank you for being an adviser and, more importantly, a friend who I can trust not only on political issues but life issues. I have listened to you more than you probably know.

P.S.—BF, you know I could always beat you at bodysurfing!

Afterword

Always There for Me
By Cal Ripken Jr.

Frank and I hit it off right away when we met at the Super Bowl. I realized quickly that we had a lot in common—we talked about philanthropy, helping kids, and how to put the platforms from our earlier careers to good use. He asked me insightful questions about what I might get involved in after baseball. He had this fatherly feel to him, and as I talked, I could see that he was thinking about how he might be able to share his wisdom and experience to help me. He was interesting, and interested.

Reggie Jackson told me that he had the same reaction when he met Frank at the Hall of Fame. You start a casual conversation with him, and before you know it you find yourself leaning forward in curiosity and engaging in a deep discussion about your goals in life.

My Dad had been my go-to guy for advice and support. I could always rely on him; he could make me swell up with confidence by telling me that I did a good job. When cancer took my Dad, I felt a little lost, but I found a friend in Frank, who is cut from the same mold. He became the sounding board I was missing and gave me the guidance I needed. Frank gave me the same feelings of stability and confidence that I got from my Dad.

Frank was the key person in getting the Foundation's feet on the ground, from helping me hire the right people to setting it in the direction that it's going now. He was instrumental in the success of the annual fundraising Gala. Our first one, with Archie and Peyton Manning, was successful, but Frank had the vision that the Gala could be an annual event—a fundraising annuity that would continue to grow. We held our fourteenth Gala in 2018, and it has become one of the Baltimore events that many look forward to every year.

Just like my Dad, Frank knows that the little things go a long way, such as his 24-hour rule for returning texts and emails. He really wants everyone to respond to him in a few seconds, but sometimes I've waited until I knew I would see him in a few days. "You can't do that," he tells me, "people have to know that they've reached you." I laugh about it, and I've gotten better over the years, but he still reprimands me occasionally.

I admire his "can-do" attitude. Some people give you nothing but reasons why you can't do something, but Frank is always optimistic. At the same time, he has a calming effect. He doesn't just tell you what to do, he enables you. He can take a good idea from a brainstorming session, give you a roadmap and the confidence to get it done. He takes the fear out of moving forward on a concept like building 50 fields in 5 years.

The part of our Hall of Fame trip that I cherish the most was not at the Hall of Fame. It was the hours together in the car driving up and back. It reminded me of the times with my Dad driving around the country to minor league baseball games. Frank and I talked about the directions our lives were heading, and how to help more kids and more people. I love the little phrase he uses when he says goodbye: "It was great being with you." When I dropped him off at his house at the end of that weekend, and every time I say goodbye to Frank, I think, *Yes, it was great being with you, too.*

How many people can you trust like your Dad? How many people truly look out for you? In my life, Big Frank, you are one of the few. Thank you for always being there for me.